Christianity i[illegible] than Fundamentalism

A series of critical studies
examining the nature
of biblical authority

Kevin M. Hindle
M.A. Research
Sheffield University February 2003

Christianity is Larger than Fundamentalism

A series of critical studies
examining the nature
of biblical authority

DENNIS LINES

The Pentland Press
Edinburgh – Cambridge – Durham – USA

First published in 1995 by
The Pentland Press Ltd
1 Hutton Close,
South Church
Bishop Auckland
Durham

ISBN 1-85821-285-5

Typeset by Carnegie Publishing, 18 Maynard St, Preston
Printed and bound by Antony Rowe Ltd, Chippenham

To all those youngsters who have aided me in my disability and allowed me to drink from their well of youthful exuberance and sense of fun; those whose needs have given my life meaning; those through whom the face of Christ shines

Table of Contents

GLOSSARY OF THE PRINCIPAL TECHNICAL TERMS

apocalyptic	a corpus of material or a belief which portrays a catastrophic upheaval of the world order
eschatology	the study of the 'Last Days' and the end of the Age, involving the winding up of history
exegesis	the painstaking examination of the biblical text, as opposed to the devotional reading of the Bible
existential	the term relating to human existence and the teaching of the meaning of life which is derived from the study of human fulfilment; the doctrine of Existentialism is the philosophy of human existence
fundamentalist	a person who believes in the inerrancy or infallibility of the Bible as the sacred 'scriptures'; the teachings of fundamentalism may not necessarily include the belief that the Bible was divinely dictated by God, but it is the belief that the Bible was divinely 'inspired', with each author serving as a mere channel of God's control (some prefer the term 'Conservative Evangelical')
kerygma	the content of the preaching message of the early Christian community
legend	a story of a venerated person, having little likelihood of historical fact
milieu	the social environment or cultural setting
myth	a story that might have a core of historicity but which has been partially modified and utilised to propound a truth
nabi	a prophet in Israel, a charismatic figure, who speaks under the influence of God's spirit (*ruach*)
numinous	the indescribable, ineffable element in 'religious experience', from the Greek *numen* meaning deity
parousia	the first-century Christian belief in the physical return of Jesus to the earth—the word denotes the literal coming of one to another

psyche	the term has been used to describe the spirit, the soul or the life of man; I use it to describe the 'mind', not just the rational deductive faculty of human beings but also their imaginative dimensions
ruach	the spirit or breath of God, his very life force—the term became identified with the Greek *pneuma* in the New Testament
Sitz im Leben	the situation in life from which an idea or a belief stems; the historical and social stratum in which a literary form was developed
Synoptics	the first three Gospels—Matthew, Mark and Luke
yahweh	the name of God in the Old Testament

All quotations are from the NEB unless otherwise stated

PREFACE

This book is written primarily for those Christians tied to the Bible. I do not mean a biblical faith, in the sense of a trust in God, but a fundamentalist belief in the absolute authority of the Christian scriptures. Christians can be said to be fundamentalists if they contend that the Bible is 'inspired' by God, that it is his very 'Word' made known to us, and that its printed words serve as the authority by which each must serve God. Further, it is held by such Christians that the *authority* of the Bible is such because the writings are inerrant and the truths infallible. This book is an examination of this premise in the light of critical scholarship.

I will not pretend to have kept up with the most recent theological writings—a daunting task indeed—but I present the thoughts and critical insights of some of those theologians and exegetes of the last two centuries who have led the field in biblical studies; I refer to those who have contested the presupposition of an inerrant Bible. For those fundamentalists remaining in the staunch belief that such a presupposition ought not be questioned, this book is not intended, for I consider that nothing will move them! There are other Christians, however, who wish to become liberated from the beliefs of their upbringing; having been brought up under rigid dogmatic persuasions, they have begun to move away from the faith of their childhood and have searched for a new form of independent spirituality. Some have found it necessary to break away from their community in their search; others have found it difficult to cut themselves off and move on. Intellectually they believe it right to become free from the constraints of biblical fundamentalism, but family ties and a fear of stepping out into the unknown hold them back; those with enough courage to make the break often feel an irrational sense of guilt for having 'forsaken their first love'. In both cases, the wish to discard the faith of the forefathers does not necessarily arise from apathy but from a quest for meaning. This book is designed to give such *come of age* Christians the confidence to leave the past behind and explore new depths in their own spirituality.

I have been challenged on occasions by Evangelical Christians to accept the injunctions and imperatives of biblical teachings at face value, as though God had sent his 'manual' of conduct through the post. Naive and simplistic programmes have been pushed in front of me and biblical passages quoted as though I had never read them before or considered them seriously, or as though they comprise all that can be said on a particular religious topic. The motive is one of trying to persuade me to accept all that is written in the Bible without question. While I do not question the sincerity of such stalwarts, this is an erroneous form of proselytising and I find it patronising and irritating! None of us can know all the answers, and no scripture can speak definitively on every social or ethical question. Our task in this book is to rescue the essence of biblical faith from the dogmatism of fundamentalism; to bring out the spiritual depths of the biblical authors. It is not to communicate the pseudo-relevance of a book of antiquity to the contrived needs of the modern world—I leave that to the fundamentalists!

The book will begin with a thorough-going criticism of the position of the biblical fundamentalist. I will then attempt to describe, from the basis of critically established data, the mind and person of the most remarkable figure of religious history, Jesus of Nazareth. My purpose in finishing on a positive note is two-fold.

First, I wish to convert fundamentalists from their dogmatic-propositional faith to one which is more open-ended and comprehensive—a faith that involves a search for a spiritual meaning to life in a modern age of expanding knowledge and a pluralist interpretation of human experience. I have sometimes been asked: 'Why do you wish to convert fundamentalists?' The answer is clear: there is an inevitable arrogance and bigotry that accompanies the sectarian belief-system that claims to know all the answers to life's riddles and complexity—a stance which is anything but spiritual. Fundamentalists have frozen the process that began in the New Testament of liberating human beings from the shackles of religiosity; the process which discarded the obedience to the Law in favour of an exploration of a life lived under faith: *for fundamentalists, the message of the New Testament has become the legalism of the Old!*

Second, I wish to attract the *reflective* person who has rejected the message of the Jesus of history for misguided reasons of intellectual scepticism; the sort of person who is searching for a form of spirituality not grounded in either rationality or superstition. This book is ideally suited to this second type of reader, for it examines the nature and validity of the *numinous* or 'non-rational' element of spirituality.

Theological students commencing their first-year courses will find the book instructive in that it forms an introduction to some of the leading works of biblical scholars and exegetes; it also offers some insight into how fundamentalist beliefs, such as the second coming of Christ at the end of the world, affect the attitudes and practices of such rival groups as the Christadelphians, the Seventh-Day Adventists, the Plymouth Brethren, the Jehovah's Witnesses, and the highly controversial sect called the Children of God.

I wish to acknowledge my gratitude to the many good friends that have helped me in the proof-reading of draft manuscripts before arriving at the final text, particularly Deirdre Barber, Ron Colemann, Ian McHaffie, Ivan Harrison and Michael Green.

I am particularly grateful to Doctor Michael Goulder for his contribution. Those familiar with Michael will know of his keen, critical mind and lively sense of humour, and the part he has played in biblical scholarship in stimulating modern Christians to re-think their stance. Many will not agree wholly with his current position, including myself, but I am honoured that he agreed to write the Foreword.

Dennis Lines 13/9/94

FOREWORD

BY

MICHAEL GOULDER

For most Christians in Britain and America the central authority has been the Bible. From about 1860 other authorities arose, modern scientific knowledge and critical study of the Bible itself; so perhaps it was not *scripture* but *reason* which had the final say. This caused a split in the Church. The leaderships of most mainstream churches —Church of England, Presbyterian, Methodist, etc.— accepted the new science, and the problems raised about the Bible, and took a so-called *liberal* position: reason and scripture were both authoritative. But a strong minority in these churches, and a majority in other churches, especially in America, feared that this meant a watering down of the faith. Between 1895 and 1909 such people produced a series of statements stressing the *Fundamentals* of Christianity as they saw them, the first of these being the truth of the Bible. In the course of time they became known by the liberals as *Fundamentalists.*

They were certainly right to be nervous about the effects of liberalism. I was brought up to believe in a liberal Christianity which seemed to make not too many demands. God existed, of course, and we should lead a life of love as Jesus did, and go to church sometimes. So when I went to Cambridge I had a shock when I met David. He was the first person I had ever met who seemed to be totally dedicated to God. He got up at six in the morning to pray and to read the Bible; he ran prayer meetings and Bible Studies during the week; he was going to be a missionary, and he missioned me, if that is the word. I did not want to be a hypocrite, and he was so obviously genuine that I joined the Christian Union too. The central point of the CU's faith was the truth of the Bible.

I remained in the CU for six very uncomfortable months. Being a real Christian seemd to mean belonging; but then I kept realising that I could not, as an honest man, accept that the Bible was totally true. What I needed, but was fifty years too early for, was a copy of Dennis Lines' *Christianity is Larger than Fundamentalism.* I commend the book to anyone who may find themselves in my position. Dennis has been through the mill himself, and writes with sympathy. He has been a teacher so he writes clearly. He has read widely, so he writes as one informed. Not least he has a positive message. The fundies were not only wrong about the Bible; they were wrong about the Church as well. Liberalism, or, to give it a more straightforward label, honesty, does not rot the guts of religion. I have known half a dozen Christians in my life whom I would dare to call saints, and none of them has believed the Bible to be without error. This is Dennis's conclusion, and his own life is a testimony to the genuineness of his faith. He has survived a terrible accident, and has shown the most persevering courage in keeping up his teaching, his studies and his devotion. His book is a testimony not only to his thinking but to his faith.

Easter 1995

INTRODUCTION

Fundamentalism is on the rise. Religious fundamentalism is not only seen in Islam, it is to be found widely in the western world where Christianity still holds influence. Christian fundamentalism is rooted in the Bible, and many of the splinter groups that have emerged since the Reformation have adopted biblical teaching as their *authority* on life and as their major basis of faith. Some groups are classified as sects by sociologists of religion and others as denominations. Sects tend to be exclusive, authoritarian, and dissenting from the State, while denominations are less reactionary to the government and are democratic in style. Quakers (The Society of Friends) began as a sect but has become a denomination with the passing of time, and many other sects have become less exclusive as they have developed. Fundamentalists are largely from sects, but can also be found in denominations.[1]

Alan Richardson defines 'Fundamentalism' in the 1950 edition of Chambers' Encyclopaedia as "the theory of biblical inspiration that regards the written words of the Bible as divinely dictated".[2] Richardson's definition is based on a view of fundamentalism as a movement reacting to nineteenth-century biblical criticism, a movement that represented a hardening of the traditional pre-critical view that the Holy Spirit miraculously communicated the truths of revelation. Richardson had cause to modify this definition in later editions, in recognition of the fact that not all fundamentalists believe that the Bible was divinely dictated by God. He was correct in one detail however: he saw fundamentalism as a belief in a narrow view of biblical inspiration formed to counter the radical conclusions of biblical criticism.

Embodied in fundamentalism is the notion that each fundamentalist group has the 'Truth', despite the fact that no two fundamentalist sects have exactly the same doctrinal beliefs. All educational disciplines pursue truth, quite naturally, but it would take a very arrogant researcher to claim that he had found the truth regarding a certain matter in an absolute sense; only the bigot would say that he had discovered everything on a particular topic. Fundamentalists confuse the distinction between an 'incontrovertible fact' and an 'opinion'. A fact is an assertion backed up with sound empirical evidence, and an opinion is a judgement made without supporting evidence but from held presuppositions, presuppositions which are themselves in need of verification. This lack of distinction is nowhere more evident than in the doctrine of the 'inspiration of the Bible' held by most fundamentalists—as viewed in the narrow sense that God dictated the Bible. It is not difficult to see the reason why the fundamentalist holds to the doctrine of biblical inspiration so adamantly. There is an emotional investment made in a teaching that underpins a person's *authority*. To surrender the doctrine of the 'inspiration of the Bible' means running the personal risk of losing meaning for one's existence, even though it may ratify a community's marginalised existence in the larger world.

Fundamentalists claim that the Bible makes clear and *infallible* statements about God, the physical construction of the universe, the divine plan for mankind, the nature and well-being of man, future world destiny and the unfolding path of history from prophecy. Such knowledge is obtained through careful and prayerful study of the scriptures, since God would not leave the pious soul in ignorance of his will and the *true nature* of all things. At the opposite extreme, critical scholars regard the Bible as a collection of written documents representing *various views* of God, *human constructions* of the welfare and nature of man, and *theological interpretations* of the outworking of history. Truth is not absolute but relative. Bible knowledge is, for the critics, an accumulation of *different perspectives* by human beings in *differing social contexts* and *changing historical settings*; it is the product of opinion. We are to examine some of the major issues involved in the debate between the fundamentalist and the critical scholar regarding the authority of the Bible.

What are we to make of the Bible as we have it today? At the outset we have to examine ruthlessly the presupposition that the Bible is inerrant, and this may demand a dismantling of the fundamentalist view of the Bible to see whether its position as the authoritative 'voice of God' is as valid as fundamentalists claim.

We shall search in the Bible for a *spirituality* by a methodology based upon critically founded principles. As the reader follows through the argument, the method of thorough-going criticism might initially appear negative and destructive, with the effect that he or she might assume that no biblical teaching remains universally valid, verifiable, or even meaningful, yet nothing is further from my intention. It seems that most of my religious life I have felt the need to be sceptical to make my point. The avowed atheist, Bertrand Russell, reminds us that, "everyone knows that to read an author simply in order to refute him is not the way to understand him".[3] If we apply such a maxim to the Bible as we might to any other book of literature or philosophy, the fundamentalist would argue, we are not likely to come out of the exercise understanding very much of the mind of God; humble acceptance is what is required. This reasoning is confusing, however, for any reservation about critically studying the Bible which is based upon a superstitious fear of 'upsetting God' is naive, and any reservation one might have about finding new truths from a presupposition that all handed-down textual knowledge is infallible and should be accepted in faith and obedience *lock, stock and barrel* is infantile and lacking in intellectual integrity. Both reservations arise out of a belief that the 'Word of God' is synonymous with the written Bible. This premise is examined carefully in the light of biblical criticism. We shall touch upon the important question of whether or not universal and endurable truths can be found in the Bible for our times. My intention is not to shatter the faith of those who are insecure in their spiritual lives, but to rebuild such a faith on a firmer footing than the Bible of the fundamentalists. In brief, I am asking whether Christianity is equal to or not much larger than fundamentalism.

Even though secularism has eroded religious belief in the industrialised societies, Christian fundamentalist groups proliferate and appear to offer something in troubled times, even to those brought up within a critically evaluative culture. It seems that the sceptical ethos of the theological universities has made little impact upon the salvation-hungry masses. People need simple answers and the experts have sold them short! Where does this leave the searching soul, which neither feels content to live under the delusion of a world-view absolved from radical criticism, nor has the faintest idea as to what the scholars are talking about. As a basis for belief, the former is a charade and the latter is unintelligible.

So what is the need that fundamentalism fills? What is so appealing about rigidly dogmatic belief systems that philosophical prognostications and open-ended enquiry fail to satisfy? There is a dichotomy in the practice of modern-day religion for some. People who are not short of intelligence and who hold prestigious office in modern society can attach themselves in their religious lives to unquestioned dogmatic beliefs—a gullibility which in their professional capacities would be unthinkable. In much the same way that children hold on to fairy tales and myths long after their reasoning faculties tell them that such things cannot be, so many educated people amongst civil servants, scientists and academics become drawn into discussions at Bible study classes on such mythological topics as how the world was created in six days, the historical evidence for Noah's flood, and the imminence of Jesus' literal return to the earth. This would indicate that human beings operate on other levels than those which are rational and empirical. This is a particularly important point when considering the reasons why members of Christian fundamentalist sects and denominations become hostile towards the disciplines of biblical criticism.

All fundamentalists hold rigid propositional beliefs. Such beliefs, though varying from one group to another, are drawn from a particular view of the Bible that sees it as God's uncompromising Word to man. Trust in the Bible is so fervent that adherents appear to *worship* the Bible more than the God of which the book speaks; they practise a 'bibliolatry', that is to say they place the authority of biblical knowledge higher than any other body of knowledge, certainly any human body of knowledge. The passion for defending the Bible amounts to almost a worship of it as though it were God. There is room for numerous interpretations of biblical teaching, but there is none for any critical appraisal that might undermine the contention that the Bible stands as the very voice of God. It is held by Christian fundamentalists that the many books that constitute the Bible are indeed one unified whole. It has no errancy because the various writers were all *inspired* by God to write, in much the same way that Muslims believe the Koran was written by Mohammed under the dictation of Allah. There can be no error, therefore, arising from human limitations. In our world of shifting values and altering standards, where leaders of every kind are unsure of their basis of morality, it is not difficult to see the attraction of unquestionable codes and mores by which people should live. Furthermore, at a time when modern society has lost its way, with little hope on the horizon of the former religious kind, it is not unreasonable that some clutch hold of life-lines offering an escape from the turbulent contradictions of twentieth-century modernism.

Fundamentalists are largely unaware that what they parade as the 'Truth' is really a set of very subjective propositions. What authorises their allegiance to a particular body is not necessarily a divine directive but a subconscious wish to satisfy certain psychological needs. Within each of us there is a survival instinct prompting us to overcome particular personal inadequacies by cultivating a sense of belonging, and religious communities offer fellowships in rich variety. All such needs and inadequacies may not be conscious of course, and ulterior motives may regulate the behaviour of some—religion has been a notorious crutch and distraction from confronting the real world.

A distinguishing feature of most fundamentalists is that they tend to be obsessive in their faith, almost to the degree of fanaticism; strict adherence is endorsed because it strengthens the resolve to keep the commitment high. Leaders of fundamentalist sects and denominations, such as Christadelphians, Jehovah's Witnesses, Seventh-Day Adventists, Mormons, and Evangelical Christians, regard the members of the larger conventional churches as lethargic in witness and sentimental in worship. There is a double blindness in this derisive judgement of the larger churches: *the selection of a particular sect or denomination is in itself an indicator that certain psychological needs have been met, and the joining of a community sub-culture may have been the product of subtle sociological conditioning rather than the result of personal divine direction.*

Many fundamentalist sects will point to their charismatic founders experiencing traumatic events in their private lives, compelling them to search for truths not otherwise known to their religious contemporaries. Such a search involved, primarily, a reverent study of the scriptures. Naturally, psychological needs were met by such quests, and similar needs were met for the small groups of first converts following in the wake, caught up as they were by the persuasive influence of their respective founders. They often searched for an identity when life had lost meaning. It is not uncommon to find that inflexible dogma settled in quickly as the following grew. A new fixed identity emerged to give the community an established and static character. This was unlike that of the community's origins but was no less intense.

Fundamentalist sects have not sprung up in a vacuum but have come into being within a historical context. The context was one of a highly charismatic person leading a group after finding for himself a novel religious meaning to life. In some cases the founder's soul was troubled by a historical dilemma, in others a traumatic division of personal consciousness was experienced which led to a sense of guilt and a feeling of unworthiness. Salvation was found and the neurosis was healed. The guilt was vanquished by a dedication to complete a commission believed to have been 'revealed by God'. The zealous obedience to follow the divine calling calmed the restless *psyche*, and after personal esteem was attained, the founder's psychological needs were met. Fundamentalists are prone to surround the founder's life with a spiritual aura and mystery, but that mystery will rapidly disappear when followers examine critically the details of the founder's key stages of spiritual enlightenment. Where such details are available for scrutiny, it is soon discovered that there are natural processes at work rather than blinding flashes of revelation—the reading of books, the sharing of ideas with others, and the pondering of significant events. After a thorough examination of these factors, it is discovered that many ideas and insights were not as novel as the evangelising propaganda suggests, but were largely selected by natural cognitive processes from the founder's social environment.[4] It is important that successive followers remain detached from their founder's human quests, so as to preserve the mystery and divine sanction of it all. In reality the divine authorisation may be artificial, but it serves to satisfy the group psychological need nevertheless.

Closely allied to psychological factors are a number of sociological ones that govern a community's character and composition. Most small exclusive sects gain their converts from family members or close-knit friendship groups. It would appear that the influence and persuasiveness of family and friends have most effect upon individuals already tied to the religious sub-culture of the particular group, especially the young, where friendship bonds are most important and where emotional feeling-states are volatile and open to auto-suggestive conversion experiences. The search for individual meaning and self-identity gives way to communal identity, and the activities serve to keep the group uniform in outlook. This social conditioning is prevalent in most exclusive sects, and efforts are made to reinforce conformity and continued allegiance by attendance at religious conventions, youth clubs, camping holidays and social events, all under strict control and all monitored by the *big brother* standing over the shoulder! The aim is to keep the focus of interest confined and restricted. It may be a *fact* that a person has been called by God to a particular Christian church, but it may also be a *fact* that a person's leanings have been determined by the pull of those of the same subculture. The two *facts* are not mutually exclusive.

These empirical factors are not necessarily controversial or unspiritual; they just need to be recognised for what they are. Most of our social preferences are a complex mixture of emotional and social interests, which are no less spiritual for so being. A more pressing issue for analysis is the question of where the spiritual elements fit into the division of personality. It is not clear for psychologists and psychoanalysts where the border is to be drawn between our psycho-emotional needs and our spiritual ones, but for fundamentalists there is no confusion.[5] Fundamentalism supports a spiritual side to man's being, which is 'other than' human nature. It subscribes to an objective 'out-there' theology, where God has made clear to his mortal subjects 'down here' what his will is through the writings of the Christian scriptures. Is spirituality, then, something we cultivate from within ourselves, or is it something which God 'clothes' upon us? Is Christian spirituality only defined by what the fundamentalist sees as 'biblical teaching' or is it something else? This book is an attempt at answering such questions by evaluating the doctrinaire stance of fundamentalism, and by promoting the idea that *Christianity is larger than fundamentalism.*

Many Evangelicals are both fundamentalists and charismatics, in that they combine the doctrine of an inerrant Bible with an intuitive belief that God speaks to them through the Spirit in a very personal and practical way. Charismatics are to be found in the larger churches which are not specifically fundamentalist in ideology. For such Charismatic Christians, the Bible is not the only source of knowledge and truth about God. They look elsewhere for more tangible signs of God's revelation in everyday events. In some ways their position is not quite as detached from the real world as that of some fundamentalists, but there are problems similarly with this form of subjective revelation. Events that are of religious significance for some may be considered banal and mundane for others. No observer can interpret random and apparently meaningless events consistently without a model from which to work, and models cannot be adopted mechanically for all time and for every situation; they require modifying in the light of further understanding and experience. Having acknowledged that, is it not true that all experience is dependent upon the one called in to measure it? The whole enterprise is therefore very subjective. God might be persistently calling men and women through everyday events in modern times whether they are aware of it or not. Quakers believe this to be as valid a spiritual experience as a meditative reading of scripture, a euphoric celebration of the Eucharist or a directive given by the Holy Spirit. Conversely, God may not be in it at all and the whole matter a delusion.

The validity of subjective versus objective experience will be explored as we come to the meaning and implication of the *numinous* experience. This is no one-sided enquiry however; it is not a flight into absolute reason. There is the need to weigh up carefully whether empirical data can be regarded as the only basis of knowledge, since the critics cannot cease to be self-critical. They must apply their radical methods to some of their own conclusions too, particularly if their conclusions are based less upon fact and more upon opinion.

NOTES

1. B. Wilson, *Sects and Society*, London, 1961, examines three sects: the Elim Pentecostals, the Christian Scientists and the Christadelphians. In a later book, *Patterns of Sectarianism*, London, 1967, Wilson describes the difference between sects and denominations. Sects begin as dissenters protesting against conventional forms of Christianity and the State, following charismatic leaders. They are exclusive and practise excommunication for departing from the true faith. Their self-identity is that of an elect group, a remnant. There is no clergy; their preachers are of the lay-community. Denominations begin as sects, but in time become more democratic and conventional, losing much of their former anger as the context of their breaking away becomes changed. They become more tolerant and broad in the acceptance of variations of belief. They also have a professionally trained ministry, pages 23–25.
2. *Chambers' Encyclopaedia*, 'Fundamentalism', page 10. Richardson has completely dropped the 'divine dictation' theory as the basis of fundamentalist belief in the 1973 Revised Edition of Chambers' Encyclopaedia. The term 'fundamentalist' was coined in 1920 to designate those "doing battle royal for the Fundamentals". Also figuring in the name was *The Fundamentals*, a 12-volume collection of essays written in the period 1910–15 by 64 British and American scholars and preachers. Three million copies of these volumes and the founding of the World's Christian Fundamentals Association in 1919 gave sharp identity to fundamentalism as it moved into the 1920's. Leadership moved across the years from such men as A. T. Pierson, A. J. Gordon, and C. I. Scofield to A. C. Dixon and R. Torrey, W. J. Bryan, and J. G. Machen (*Grolier's Encyclopaedia*, 1993).
3. B. Russell, *Mysticism and Logic*, London, 1918, page 26.
4. A recent review of the founders of the Christadelphians—Dr John Thomas and Robert Roberts—has been undertaken by R. McHaffie, 'Finding Founders and Facing Facts', in *The Endeavour Magazine*, No 91, May 1994, Editor, R. Coleman, 34 Copse Hill, Purley, Surrey CR8 4LH.
5. Many similar processes of community origin, organisation and decline, have been identified in the newly developed Schools of Psychotherapy, see J. McLeod, *An Introduction to Counselling*, Buckingham, 1993, pages 134–135.

I

THE CONFLICTING PATHS OF SCIENCE AND RELIGION

Most Christian fundamentalist sects emerged during the last century in a world that was very different from the one we know. Bible knowledge and disputes over interpretation were of general interest to many, and sectarian rivalry was commonplace. Today, many of the religious differences that occupied such an inordinate amount of time seem to be irrelevant and largely out of place for the majority; clearly, the broadening of knowledge has accounted for much of this change. The obvious starting point, then, for dismantling the Bible of the fundamentalists will be a brief analysis of those significant stages in understanding that have pushed the Bible off its centre-stage position. It is no longer the absolute embodiment of knowledge. The expansion of science and technology has brought with it an unresolved conflict between empirical forms of knowledge and matters of faith. Early on, the two disciplines of theology and science produced head-on collisions, but in modern times systematic theologians have found a middle course which has partially eased the tension.

ASTRONOMY: AN EARLY SCIENCE OF THE COSMOS

It is hardly surprising that Galileo recanted his discovery of the sun being the centre of the universe. When faced with the prospect of the Inquisitor's torture rack, he had little choice:

> I, Galileo Galilei, son of the late Vincenzo Galilei, Florentine, aged seventy years, arraigned personally before this tribunal, and kneeling before you, most Eminent and Reverend Lord Cardinals, Inquisitors General . . . having before my eyes and touching with my hands, the holy Gospels—swear that I believe, do now believe, and by God's help will for the future believe, all that is held, preached, and taught by the Holy Catholic and Apostolic Roman Church . . . I must altogether abandon the false opinion that the sun is the centre of the world and immovable, and that the earth is not the centre of the world, and moves, and that I must not hold, defend, or teach in any way whatsoever, verbally or in writing, the said doctrine, and after it had been notified to me that the said doctrine was contrary to the Holy Scripture . . .
>
> Therefore, desiring to remove from the minds of your Eminencies, and of all faithful Christians, this strong suspicion, reasonably conceived against me, and with sincere heart and unfeigned faith I abjure, curse, and detest the aforesaid errors and heresies, and generally

> every other error and sect whatsoever contrary to the said Holy Church . . .
> I, Galileo Galilei, have abjured as above with my own hand.
>
> 12 April 1633[1]

The discovery of the central position of the sun was not entirely his own. Nicolaus Copernicus had begun considering the all too important question of observation being dependent upon the position at which the viewer might be standing at any given point in time. Copernicus' simple model of the sun as the centre of the orbiting planets was based upon geometrical principles and, since he died in the same year as the publication of *The Revolution of the Heavenly Orbs*, he was spared any reaction his book was to provoke.[2] This was not the case with Galileo. As he turned his telescope toward the heavens, he saw evidence that would prove the Ptolemaic system false, not by hypothesis but by observation.

Galileo avoided the route of martyrdom and was compelled to surrender his mind—and thereby his science—by the outrageous dictates of a religious authority that was extremely deceitful. He had been carefully watched since 1611, some twenty-two years before his trial—not that he was aware of it. He thought he could count on the support of the educated and liberal Pope Urban III, Maffeo Barberini, but was sadly mistaken. The trials were despicable to say the least, with all the usual shady practices that accompany such travesties of justice: forged documents, false allegations, prejudicial procedures, etc.. The account of Galileo's trial in Jacob Bronowski's abridged version is a pitiful read indeed.[3]

Galileo began life as a doctor and knew all too well what damage the rack could wield. We can imagine his frozen look when escorted towards the beastly implement, as one account of the time graphically illustrates:

> As the levers bent forward, the main force of my knees against the two planks burst asunder the sinews of my hams, and the lids of my knees were crushed. My eyes began to startle, my mouth to foam and froth, and my teeth to chatter like the doubling of a drummer's sticks. My lips were shivering, my groans were vehement, and blood sprang from my arms, broken sinews, hands and knees. Being loosed from these pinnacles of pain, I was hand-fast set on the floor, with the incessant imploration: 'Confess! Confess! [4]

With the prospect of the rack before him and under the influence of a vivid imagination, Galileo Galilei recanted. This is a most repugnant example of the courses of scientific research and religious authority meeting head-on, and where religion had to come out the loser! In this instance, the Papal authority won the battle but lost the cause.

Astronomy was an early science, as is evidenced by the Mayan calendars, the cuneiform tablets of the Fertile Crescent and early Greek thought. There was always the need for the ancients to measure the seasons. During later periods, when mariners (like Columbus) were discovering the New World, it served the purpose of navigating sailors across the vast oceans.

The times of Galileo were turbulent indeed. The Roman Church was mounting its Counter-Reformation and, in the light of this tension, Galileo made two mistakes that were to prove his downfall. The first was his decision to move from the freer atmosphere of Venice to his native town, Florence, and the second was to assume that the publication of his book, *Dialogue on the Great World Systems*, in support of the

Copernican thesis, would not initiate an almighty revolt. Since he was a mathematician, not a theologian this was hardly surprising. Although Galileo was permitted to publish his book, the Pope later overturned his decision.

The Church was not always against alternative forms of knowledge, however. It had successfully absorbed the teaching of some of the Greek thinkers of the past, such as Aristotle's philosophy assimilated in the twelfth and thirteenth centuries. Thomas Aquinas had written a synthesis of Christian revelation and intellectual bodies of knowledge (*Summae*). The Ptolemaic picture of the universe was taken for granted by Christian folk at the time. Claudius Ptolemy was a Greek philosopher working in Alexandria at about AD 150. He had devised a system that, while complex, was derived from a simple deduction which runs as follows: The perfect form is the circle, the moon obviously revolves around the earth, the sun and the planets must therefore do the same. For fourteen hundred years this model had suited Arabs and Christians, but the Renaissance brought a period of storm, and the Inquisition was authorised to exercise the strictest censorship over books and beliefs that might promulgate anti-Christian doctrine and teachings of heresy.

Galileo was forbidden to speak with Protestants and was put under house arrest—two orders in force till the day of his death. His contemporary, René Descartes, the founder of modern science, remained in Venice as a consequence. The controversy between science and religion simmered down for a while with the coming of a man who was as much a biblical scholar as a scientist, Sir Isaac Newton—born on Christmas Day in the year of Galileo's death. Newton took great interest in biblical chronology and the book of Daniel, and Newtonian astronomy provided a congenial climate for the religious apologetics of Natural Theology—as the new science was known. For a while, then, the dust of the conflicting courses of knowledge began to settle.

THE THEORY OF EVOLUTION

The second major upheaval took place in the mid-nineteenth century with Charles Darwin's theory of the origin of species—a thesis in conflict with the book of Genesis. In the seventeenth century, the earth had been knocked off its central place of importance, and now it was the turn of man himself to move aside; man's pre-eminence as 'lord of creation' was now under threat!

The book that upset the Victorian clerics was *The Origin of Species through Natural Selection*. It was the painstaking work of a naturalist whose previous intention had been to become a clergyman. Ironically, the course of his life was radically altered from that which he had planned. HMS Beagle was commissioned by the Admiralty to make a survey of the southern hemisphere in 1831, and the expedition was in need of a naturalist. Much against his father's wishes, Darwin took up the challenge to sail for five years.

Darwin's argument was progressive. From his observations he first began to doubt the immutability of species:

> When I was on board the Beagle I believed in the permanence of species, but as far as I can remember, vague doubts occasionally flitted across my mind . . . I did not

> become convinced that species were mutable until, I think, two or three years had elapsed.[5]

A number of facts struck him during the voyage that seemed at odds with the view that each species was the product of individual creation:

> Why did closely allied animals replace one another as one travelled southwards? Why did extinct fossil species show such a close structural relation to living animals? Above all, why, in the Galapagos islands did the finches and the giant tortoises show slight variation from island to island, so that the local inhabitants could tell from which island a tortoise had come? [6]

The more it appeared to him that species might share a common ancestor, the less plausible seemed the hypothesis of a separate creation for each particular species. The key to understanding his observations lay not in changes taking place in the adult organism but in the reproduction of heritable variations. By 1837 he had an answer that would account for the extinction of one species and the preservation of another: natural selection by the survival of the fittest. Nature was unstable, variable, not static, and "those forms that slightly favoured getting the upper hand and forming species" would survive.

The Victorian theological climate was not conducive to the acceptance of free scientific thought that might contest religious belief, and the publication of the *Origin of Species* was poorly received at first. William Paley wrote a comprehensive book in 1802, entitled *Natural Theology: or Evidence of the Existence and Attributes of the Deity*, that became the standard text for university graduates reading biology. Paley presented an accumulative argument as evidenced by a complex special creation. God was the Master-Designer. This suited the current apologetic of the Protestant Natural Theologians. Paley's prime example of design was the eye but Darwin had other theories to account for the eye's apparent design. At this time also David Hume, a Scottish philosopher, was driving the final coffin nails into the proposition that God was the Divine Clockmaker, and in the eighteen forties the German historical critics began a work on the Bible that would unsettle the rigid Victorian beliefs by questioning the validity of the Creation narratives as 'scientific' documents, *per se*.[7]

Then, in 1859, the *Origin of Species* was published and the swords were drawn. *Punch* magazine ridiculed the work, so that Darwinism, unkindly and inaccurately, became known as the 'monkey theory'. This, no doubt, prompted the celebrated retort of T. H. Huxley to Bishop Wilberforce. The Bishop had asked Huxley whether he would claim descent from an ape on his father's side or his mother's. His cynical reply was that he would rather have an ape for a grandfather than a man who misused his rhetorical gifts to obscure important scientific discussion through religious prejudice!

Fortunately, Darwin's life was blameless; he was not eligible for insult on irrelevant issues, such as sexual misconduct, as some were. Huxley's counter-attack was on moral grounds: it was immoral to believe without proof, "to sit down as a little child, before the fact!". Most other attacks of the period were over things that Darwin never in fact said, such as the idea that men were descendants of apes, as opposed to both having a common ancestor.

Much of this religious rivalry and controversy seems irrelevant to most people today, but the issues of the Bible versus Science were very contentious during the nineteenth century. In general, we have accommodated the theory of evolution as our normal way of thinking. In the political sphere, Marx and Engels adapted the biological evolutionary theory to the class-war system; this had an enormous influence upon the world. In biology, the Catholic theologian, Teilhard de Chardin, is one among many to have presented a comprehensive interpretation of man's origin and destiny by combining two forms of knowledge—in his case, Palaeontology and a mystic theological vision suitably blended into a unified coherent system. With the exception of the fundamentalists of the American Bible belt, most Christians today would not see any antithesis between the Genesis Creation narratives and the scientific theories of mankind's origins.

THE RISE OF CULTURE

An account of man's cultural and educational growth has been presented by Jacob Bronowski in *The Ascent of Man.* I think this study is biased towards an empirical-mathematical view of the development of cultural man at the expense of his aesthetic and imaginative dimensions; nevertheless, it is a fascinating thesis. Like most scientists, Bronowski seeks patterns throughout the early cultures he examines. His view is that we now have a more enlightened view of how man masters his environment than formerly:

> When I was a young man, we all thought that mastery came from man's domination of his physical environment. Now we have learned that real mastery comes from understanding and moulding the living environment.[8]

Not a very earth-shattering statement but let us move on to see how he applies this model to the example of the civilisation of ancient Jericho:

> Here wheat and water came together and, in that sense, here man began civilisation. Here, too, the bedouin came with their dark muffled faces out of the desert, looking jealously at the new way of life. That is why Joshua brought the tribes of Israel here on their way to the Promised Land—because wheat and water, they make civilisation: they make the promise of a land flowing with milk and honey. Wheat and water turned that barren hillside into the oldest city of the world.[9]

This makes sense, but it is not the way the story is narrated in the book of Joshua. We would not expect it to be, of course. The Old Testament relates the story within a theological framework of Yahweh bringing his people from the slavery of Egypt to the land promised to the seed of their patriarch, Abraham. Bronowski, on the other hand, has naturalist explanations based upon archaeological evidence.

Jericho is a microcosm of history. When Kathleen Kenyon excavated the city's ruins in the nineteen fifties, she discovered the ancient hollow tower which revealed layer upon layer of past civilisations. She estimated that by 6000 BC, Jericho contained within its walls three thousand people in an area of ten acres. Women ground the wheat with stones in a way characteristic of a settled community, while men moulded clay bricks. Archaeological research has moved on since Kenyon's work, yet her general point is still valid, namely, that Jericho holds a vast library of information of a settled community.

At some point the scientist parts company with the fundamentalist in his presuppositions of data analysis. Most fundamentalists accept the possibility of a miracle (a suspension of natural law) within their working hypothesis but few scientists could allow the *non-explicable* to influence their deductions.

Two questions, says Bronowski, intrigue the travellers who visit the ancient ruins: "Did Joshua finally destroy the city? Did the walls really come tumbling down?" The answer to the first question, he claims, has to be "yes, quite definitely". Joshua, he argues, led the tribes towards the Fertile Crescent, which ran up the Mediterranean coast and along the mountains of Anatolia down towards the Tigris and Euphrates. Jericho had the key that could unlock the passage to the mountains of Judaea. They had little choice but to conquer, and conquer they did, at about 1400 BC. Were the walls, however, felled by an almighty miracle of Yahweh? Archaeological evidence in support of the biblical text is wanting. There is no evidence that any single catastrophic disruption brought the walls down, there is only evidence that many minor turbulences frequently levelled the walls of civilisations over many periods of time (during the Bronze Age, the walls of Jericho were rebuilt sixteen times). At this stage, Bronowski gives his own assessment:

> This is earthquake country. There are tremors here still every day; there are four major quakes in a century . . . The Red Sea and the Dead Sea lie along a continuation of the Great Rift Valley of East Africa. Here two of the plates that carry the continents as they float on the denser mantle of the earth ride side by side. As they thrust past one another along this rift, the surface of the earth echoes to the shocks that well up from below. As a result, earthquakes have always erupted along the axis on which the Dead Sea lies. And in my view that is why the Bible is full of memories of natural miracles: some ancient flood, some running dry of the Red Sea, the Jordan running dry, and the walls of Jericho falling down.[10]

He clearly derides the possibility of a miraculous event here, as we might expect from a scientist. The question that remains for us to answer is whether we should accept the narrative as it stands—miracle and all—or whether we are permitted to accept the mere skeleton of history in this Old Testament story? Have the records been embroidered or modified to suit a specific theological outlook? Is this deliberate exaggeration to highlight the supernatural or can it be counted on as reliable history?

THE DEFENCE OF A BIBLICAL FUNDAMENTALIST

A more conservative rendering of the rise and demise of culture, and an example of how a fundamentalist might read the past differently, is that of Francis A. Shaeffer, in his book *How Should We Then Live: The Rise and Decline of Western Culture*. The book puts a greater emphasis upon the development of art and culture but it is an extremely straight-jacketed treatment throughout. Shaeffer's answer to his rhetorical question of "How should we then live?" is given in a completely biased and superficial manner: get back to the teachings of the Bible and all will turn out well! For example, when examining the period of the Middle Ages, Shaeffer says:

> The pristine Christianity set forth in the New Testament gradually became distorted. A humanistic element was added: Increasingly, the authority of the church took prece-

dence over the teaching of the Bible. And there was an ever-growing emphasis on salvation as resting on man's meriting the merit of Christ, instead of on Christ's work alone . . . Much of Christianity up to the sixteenth century was either reaction against or reaffirmation of these distortions of the original Christian, biblical teaching."[11]

Again, he writes:

> The Bible gives a unity to the universal and the particular. First, the Bible tells men and women true things about God. Therefore, they can know true things about God. One can know true things about God because God has revealed himself . . . God revealed his attributes to people, the attributes are not only true to people but true to God . . . , what he says is not just relatively true but absolutely true. As finite beings, people do not have exhaustive truth about God, but they can have truth about God . . . And the Bible speaks to men and women concerning meaning, morals, and values.
>
> Second, the Bible tells us true things about people and about nature. It does not give men and women exhaustive truth about the world and the cosmos, but it does give truth about them . . . , especially why things exist and why they have the form they have. Yet because the Bible does not give exhaustive truth about history and the cosmos, historians and scientists have a job to do, and their job is not meaningless.[12]

These assertions are left unqualified in his writing and I have no idea what is meant by a statement like "The Bible gives a unity to the universal and the particular". Shaeffer supports the view that Christianity is the mother of science owing to its "medieval insistence on the rationality of God". In the chapter, 'The Rise of Modern Science', Shaeffer argues that there is no contradiction between the discoveries of science and the Bible. However, he only pays tribute to Christian scientists, not to atheistic ones. In the following chapter, 'The Breakdown in Philosophy and Science', Shaeffer sees the departure from biblical Christianity to liberal theology and the exalting of 'reason' as the decline of Western thought. He discounts Darwinism on the grounds that it is based on statistical studies of pure chance and random events within given time. He briefly reviews the existentialist philosophers—Rousseau, Kant, Hegel and Kierkegaard—yet scorns them for having contributed most to the modern lack of optimism and rise of nihilism. In theology, Shaeffer denounces the following: Karl Barth for bringing existential methodology into theology; Albert Schweitzer for questioning the supernatural elements attributed to the historical Jesus; mystical theology for being "contentless religious experience"; Hindu philosophy for seeing God as a descriptive term for everything; Paul Tillich for promoting a pantheistic God having no propositional content; and finally, Friedrich Nietzsche for declaring that *God is dead!*

This summary dismissal of all those thinkers that have faced squarely the 'uncomfortable' evidence against a thorough-going biblicist faith appalls me! This one-sided analysis refuses to face the objections that researchers for truth have raised concerning conventional biblical claims. How can his overview have any credibility? Shaeffer skates over David Hume's objections to biblical faith. He examines none of the arguments of the atheist-philosophers (like Bertrand Russell) against biblical Christianity. It is a biased treatment indeed. Surely, Christians should not dodge the questions levelled against some of their own presuppositions by opponents. There is barely a word or comment of biblical criticism, as though it didn't exist, yet the critical studies of the Bible, both in Europe and across the Atlantic, have made an enormous contribution to the way the Bible should be understood. Instead, we have the monotonous and facile panacea that every decline of Western thought is attributable to a disregard of the plain teaching of the Bible.

Furthermore, I do not understand what notion of truth Shaeffer has in mind when he says: "the Bible tells us true things about people and about nature. It does not give men and women exhaustive truth about the world and the cosmos, but it does give truth about them". The comment is made without qualification that "because the Bible does not give exhaustive truth about history and the cosmos, historians and scientists have a job to do, and their job is not meaningless". These assertions are superficial, naive, and meaningless! He fails to specify what in-exhaustive truths about people and nature the Bible gives us. He does not put forward any of the propositional truths which he obviously holds, so that we might examine their validity. In one sentence he wishes us to turn back to the Bible—without qualification, without reasoning, without explanation—then, in another, he tells us that not all truth is given in biblical history and cosmology, "but it does", he continues, "give truth about them". Does he mean selective truth, interpreted truth, relative truth, or what? Is he thinking of objective historical events, values, morality, laws of physics, or what?

This glib appraisal of biblical directives for the maintenance of social and moral stability, as though they were value-neutral, is a superficial programme of unsubstantiated belief; it is prejudice. As soon as we select a single passage from the Bible, we bring to our comprehension, albeit unconsciously, a whole range of presuppositions as we make sense of what is read. Now this head-burying pseudo-theology will not do! We cannot move forward in our religious quest for truth by turning the clock back. We cannot take on board the biblical faith free of any interpretation as though biblical criticism never existed!

It grieves me that Shaeffer makes something of Nietzsche's reduction to insanity before his death.[13] Galileo, whom Shaeffer sees positively as having no disagreement with 'pure biblical teaching', went blind three years after his trial, as did John Milton in the year of his epic poem, *Paradise Lost*, yet I cannot imagine Shaeffer making a case that physical ailment is a sign of God's refusal to endorse a truth with these two venerated figures. This is a naive and immoral suggestion that the process of cause and effect is valid for determining truth from falsehood. It does not match experience.

THE BIBLICAL INSIGHT OF THE COSMOS COMPARED WITH MODERN UNDERSTANDING

The cosmology the Bible supports is hardly recognisable to the modern mind; in fact, the biblical world-view is wholly irreconcilable with modern physics and astronomy. Our universe is very different to that of biblical times. If we play the fundamentalist's advocate for a moment—with the presupposition that biblical teaching forms a coherent unity—and bring together the various texts that infer or present a Hebrew cosmology, what do we find?

The later references in the Old Testament presuppose a view of the world that is a three-tiered structure. The biblical writings do not describe the cosmos systematically; such pictures are revealed quite incidentally. Yet it is clear how the continuing drama of man within a spirit-world is to be conceived. There is an implied tension between two dominant poles: Yahweh is enthroned above the earth with his celestial messengers in heaven, and beneath man's stage is the underworld—a place of torment, occupied by spirits and monsters standing as adversaries to Yahweh. The Earth is hardly the place of natural everyday events, but is the arena upon which rival spirit-forces contend: God and his angels versus Satan and his demons. Miracles are everyday events and interventions from both worlds deny man any complete control of his own life. History does not follow an independent course but is moving predictably towards a catastrophic end, commonly referred to as the 'Day of Yahweh'!

The Old Testament speaks in parts of Sheol, describing it as a form of cave where the spirits of the deceased exist communally and from where they can be brought up to taunt mankind. They have a conscious existence, though a painful one. The texts are contradictory as to whether or not the *shades* (as the spirits are known) have any cognitive form of knowledge. The body that lies in the grave has its replica in Sheol, and Sheol is the place of complete isolation from God. It is most probable, according to H. H. Rowley, that the idea of Sheol is inherited from the remote past of Israel's neighbouring peoples.[14]

The Divine Court sits in heaven, and Satan travels to and fro in the earth to weigh up as evidence the unjust plights of men. Angels are Yahweh's vice-regents; they occasionally enter the earth to carry messages from Yahweh to men and women. Even lying spirits have their place in the heavenly assembly. Later on in Israelite belief, the Devil takes on a lordship role over evil spirits, rather than an adversarial one to Yahweh (largely due to Persian influence).[15] Isolated passages speak of Yahweh sitting above the circle of the earth (Isaiah 40:22 RSV), which some Christian fundamentalists use as an example of biblical inerrancy, but this is not the general picture (the text of Isaiah refers to the primitive belief of the firmament as a dome-like dish rather than an astronomical globe). Paul, in one place, speaks of the third heaven, thus reflecting the current view of the day that heaven consisted of a plurality of departments, presumably spherical, or hemispherical shells, as suggested by C. K. Barrett.[16]

This three-tiered structure is not novel to the cultures of the ancient world (particularly the Jewish Apocalyptic world) but it is unintelligible to the modern mind. Consequently, it is regarded as obsolete by most thinking people. For R. Bultmann, this view of the world is a mythical one, and he encouraged the enlightened Christian to strip the *kerygma* (Christian message) of its mythical clothing and discard everything that will not conform with current knowledge: "Copernicus and the discoveries of atomic theory forced us to abandon this world view. Romanticism led us to discover the value of the human subject more than previous philosophies would allow and nationalism opened our realisation of the place of history and the traditions of peoples."[17]

The climax of the end-event comes as we pass into the New Testament with the return of Christ to his Church (the *Parousia*). After a decisive selection at the Great Assize, those of Christ's Church who are found to be worthy would enjoy the bliss of eternal Paradise, while the rest would be damned. This basic scheme, that was expected to take place in the first few decades, must be regarded as inaccurate in the light of historical developments since the first century. This divine-interventionist programme describing the winding-up of history is obsolete for many today, apart from fundamentalists who wish to preserve an authoritative status for those beliefs recorded in the Christian scriptures. Christians must simply face the fact that Paul, the greatest witness of the New Testament, was in error when anticipating the second coming within his own life time and that of the first-generation Christians. Whatever history might unfold tomorrow, the *Parousia* did not take place as the early Christians had supposed or as writers of the New Testament had forecasted!

NOTES

1. J. Bronowski, *The Ascent of Man*, London, 1973, pages 216–7.
2. Bronowski is rather misleading on Copernicus. J. Burke, *The Day the Universe Changed*, says the following:

> On the 1 May 1514 Copernicus, the name by which Kopernig is better known today, circulated a manuscript called 'The Little Commentary' which questioned the entire Aristotelian system and suggested a sun-centred system with a moving earth. The fully developed heliocentric argument was not published until Copernicus died, in 1543 . . . For twenty years before Copernicus' theory was published it was discussed all over Europe. Ironically, the earliest attacks came from the Protestants . . . The Roman Church, sitting in Council at Trento only two years after Copernicus' work was published by the astronomer's pupil Johannes Rheticus, a professor at Luther's university, accepted the text without reaction. It was unconcerned with the apparently revolutionary nature of Copernicus' thought. [Quotations are then given from Gemma Frisius, Giovanni Pontano and an early medieval scholar John of Jandun to the effect that Copernicus' work was thought of as being only theoretical (like the 'epicycles' of the Ptolemaic system)]. Copernicus had satisfied everybody's demand that the hypotheses be as simple as possible and that they would 'save the appearance', or account for what heavenly phenomena appear to be, as exactly as possible. A fictional orbiting earth would do so. The scheme was taken up without demur and used to reform the calendar in 1582. pages 134f.

   I am indebted to Ron Coleman for directing me to this quotation
3. J. Bronowski, op. cit., chapter 6. See Codex 1181, stored with crucial documents in the Vatican, for the papal suspicion of Galileo's activities.
4. The account of William Lithlow who survived the rack in 1620, cited by J. Bronowski, op. cit., page 216.
5. C. Darwin, *The Origin of Species by Means of Natural Selection,* Middlesex, 1968, page 26.
6. Ibid., page 27.
7. D. Hume, *Dialogues on Natural Religion*, posthumously published in 1777.
8. J. Bronowski, op. cit., page 69.
9. Ibid., page 69.
10. Ibid., page 72.
11. F. A. Shaeffer, *How Should We Then Live: The Rise and Decline of Western Culture,* New Jersey, 1976, page 32.
12. Ibid., page 86.
13. Ibid., page 180.
14. H. H. Rowley, *The Faith of Israel,* London, 1956, page 159.
15. H. Ringgren, *Israelite Religion,* ET., London, 1974, page 315.
16. C. K. Barrett, *The Second Epistle to the Corinthians,* Oxford, 1973, page 310. In the first heaven, the birds fly, the sun is found in the second, and God resides in the third. The book of Enoch knows of a third, fourth and fifth, and so on to a tenth heaven.
17. R. Bultmann's influential essay on the 'primitive cosmology' of the Hebrews is found in *Kerygma and Myth,* ET., London, 1964, pages 3f. G. B. Caird, *The Language and Imagery of the Bible,* London, 1980, offers the following criticism: "Bultmann's thesis contained two enormous and unargued assumptions: that the mythical creature he called 'modern man' would be more

comfortable among the abstractions of existential philosophy than with the picture language of the Bible; and that biblical man took that picture language as flat statement of fact." (page 193) I accept the first criticism, but, regarding the second, it is probable that beneath the picture language of the Bible there is more of a concrete concept than an abstract one which the metaphor attempts to describe. Many examples of biblical cosmology are given incidentally to the main purport of the message, and the exegete's first method must be to take the words at their face value, unless it is inferred or specified in the text that the language is theoretical, poetical or figurative.

2

A CRITIQUE OF THE FUNDAMENTALIST'S VIEW OF THE BIBLE

THE BIBLE AND CRITICAL STUDY

Let us now turn to the historical and theological objections presented by exegetes to a fundamentalist's understanding of the Bible. When examining the structure of the Bible, the first point to make is that it is not one book but a collection of many writings of quite varied forms; the Bible has historical and fictitious prose narratives, proverbs and ethical codes, personal correspondence, lyrical and dramatic poetry, and prophetic and liturgical literature. In fact, most kinds of literary composition are found in the twenty-seven books that comprise the Bible. It is a collection of volumes spanning a considerable period of time (at least 1000 years), and it was the product of dissimilar and very varied cultures. Its origins can be explained in some instances as the provision of religious and philosophical answers to questions of human existence (aetiology). In others, the general purpose of the writing is not always obvious, apart from the wish to record something believed to be important. We should expect to find, therefore, some theological diversity in biblical ideology, message and content. Consequently, it will be argued that such a recognition validates the Bible as a rich and authentic record of *varied* religious experience. There is no getting away from the fact that there is a plurality of religious insights in the Bible. This diversity is not merely a question of emphasis, for there is evidence that some biblical writings contradict others in historical data, moral imperatives, value-systems, pictures of God, Christology (the study of the nature of Christ) and the forecasting of future events.

Some fundamentalists[1] argue that a unity of thought exists throughout the whole Bible (examined in chapter 4), and that this unity proves that the Bible is inerrant. The fundamentalists believe that God has revealed a consistent plan that can be seen from Genesis to Revelation. If biblical scholarship has established anything at all in the last one hundred and fifty years, it has demonstrated quite unequivocally that this viewpoint cannot be verified by biblical criticism and unbiased exegesis, but remains a presupposition for those who simply wish it to be. In support of such a narrow doctrine, fundamentalists spuriously select a few texts from their literary and cultural contexts and harmonise or weave them together in an ingenious manner, so as to form a cohesive and consistent doctrine. The doctrine is then presented as an unquestionable edict by virtue of being contained in God's Word. The belief in a unified Bible is thereby reinforced by a number of proof texts taken from scripture, and it becomes the authority by which the community stands. It is not the purpose of this study to refute systematically the idea of a unity of teaching in scripture by examining every passage used in its support, but to consider what grounds there are for using the Bible this way and for claiming that it is inerrant.

The Bible as literature has been subjected to the same scrutiny of critical scholarship as most other historical documents. The results of such research have illuminated our understanding of the various transitions through which the books of the Bible have passed in order to arrive at their present forms.

To approach the Bible as one might a modern book would give a distorted impression of the Bible's long history of coming into being. The various books of both the Old and the New Testament have been arranged by canonical schools at certain periods of historical conflict, and the placing of each book in its current order was conducted to suit thematic interests and historical continuity. With the literature purporting to be 'history', the criterion for placing one book before another has been determined largely by chronological content, not by respective date of composition or completion; consequently, we would get a clearer picture of religious development by reading the books in their order of being written, where this is ascertainable.

The science of Biblical Criticism serves as a tool in helping the scholar to achieve a more comprehensive understanding of the Bible.[2] Form Critical methods enable the exegete to obtain a clear insight into the development of biblical thought by tracing the antecedent literary forms behind the final texts as we have them today.

Form Critics and Source Critics have upset the fundamentalists by unearthing evidence to show that the various books of the Old Testament came into being by the process of an ingenious interweaving of various literary sources, sources in the form of books themselves that belonged to different schools or factions within the Judaistic faith. The most radical scholars have identified four such sources in the books of the Pentateuch. This discipline has also identified the earliest Psalm-like sources within the historical books of the Old Testament, sources which have been so skilfully interwoven that the completed text obscures its composite source material from all who are not experts in textual analysis.[3]

Another discipline to have revealed the human hand behind 'inspired' scripture is Redaction Criticism. The exponents of this science, while in no way unanimous in their conclusions, have demonstrated that some of the books of the Bible have gone through editing stages where amendments to the text have been made in order to satisfy the beliefs of the particular group bearing the tradition. These amendments are highly significant for those monopolising the tradition and serve (a) to correct obvious inaccuracies of historical data, (b) to represent later theologies as being in the mind of earlier writers, and (c) to reflect orthodox teaching in passages that are unclear or incongruous. It is a fascinating study indeed to identify the *earthy-red passions* of humanity in the earliest traditions from the more 'modernised' character of the completed biblical form. In fact, the earliest books proper were written as late as the eighth-century BC (Amos and Hosea); there is evidence that a core of the book of Deuteronomy was written during Josiah's reform in the seventh-century BC, and the final forms of the books of Genesis, Exodus, Leviticus, Numbers and Deuteronomy—purporting to have been written by Moses in the thirteenth-century BC—were likely to have been compiled in their completed form as late as the sixth-century BC, or even later.[4] This was done by groups of zealous Jews wishing to consolidate their beliefs by re-shaping and codifying the early traditions into exclusive forms of dogma.

What are the theological objections, then, that have served as landmarks in under-cutting the presupposition that the Bible is unified and that it is a coherent record of God's Word, inerrant and infallible?

THE DIVERSITY OF OLD TESTAMENT THOUGHT

The book of Genesis is not the earliest literature known to us. There is evidence that the early chapters contain legends and myths which have their origin in earlier 'heroic' epics[5] of a different culture from that of Hebrew—the culture producing most of the Old Testament. These earlier epics are often only traceable through root words, motifs or ideas, but have been thoroughly worked over and rewritten from their original source material to present an entirely different and, in some cases, quite contrary theology of the way the Hebrews saw the working of Yahweh with his people (as in *Enuma Elish*, the Semitic Creation story). A critical study of the narratives of mankind's origins in Genesis will reveal not one creation story but two. These two records are complete in themselves and have been placed side by side without any interweaving (Gen. 1:1–2:4 and 2:5–25). The narratives are not contradictory (apart from the detail of when vegetation was created), neither are they supplementary, but are quite different in theological point and emphasis.

The episode of Noah and the flood has its antecedents in the Akkadian cuneiform epics of *Gilgamesh* and *Utnapishtim*, but the biblical narratives have been thoroughly worked over.

The unfolding patriarchal narratives of Abraham to Joseph are written up with great economy of style and are not bare history but theological history. This is not to say that they may not contain a kernel of objective history. The notion of 'objective history' began in the nineteenth century; it cannot be read into these texts. The study of comparative religious literature and archaeological material has opened up our understanding of the broader context of biblical history. Thus, early sagas are a back-projected writing[6] reflecting the religious insight of the prophetic faith: Corporate sin brings about corporate calamity; God calls and man is invited to respond; God's justice is pronounced, though not in absence of his mercy.

Some of the Psalms and Prophets preserve the age-old battle of Yahweh with the great sea-monsters in order to bring about the Creation, yet this idea has been noticeably suppressed in the Genesis Creation myths.[7] If the source material for 'objective history' is wanting in these early chapters of Genesis, it is implausible that any use of these texts can supply authentic data of mankind's origins to rival the evolutionary and anthropological ones (not that such theories tell the whole story). *The Bible's inerrancy cannot be substantiated, therefore, if inerrancy is understood to be the recording of bare historical facts of the way the world began and the beginnings of mankind. It cannot be a reliable report of what took place—the when, the where and the why—if the narratives have been composed from antecedent non-biblical sources.*

We are not justified in believing that God's Word is essentially that which the text of the Bible declares is God's Word by the regular phrase, "Thus saith the Lord".

The laws said to have been given by God to Moses, according to the book of Exodus, cannot claim originality as being revealed in an exclusive sense to Moses from the Mount. The Law did not simply fall down from heaven, for the whole of the Sinai precepts (the directives of the 'second tablet') go back to pre-Israelite semi-nomadic tribes, and have numerous similar counterparts in the Near East. The law of the goring ox in Exodus 21:29, is very close to the Babylonian law of the city, Eshnunna—a code which antedates Moses by some 500 years, yet is copied almost verbatim in the Book of the Covenant.[8] Clearly, the scribes of Yahwistic faith have incorporated such well attested precepts and seen them as being quite consistent with the requirements of Yahweh. In this sense, biblical tales, ideas and teachings are not necessarily unique. From this brief analysis, *it is clear that we are not to understand the process of revelation as something that was original to the Hebrews, for what was novel was the way that such universal sagas and teachings of the ancient world were taken over and used as a means of developing those peculiar religious insights lying behind the Yahwistic faith of Israel.*

THE DIVERSITY OF NEW TESTAMENT THOUGHT

Critical scholarship has established that the reason why the four Gospels differ from each other in questions of content, chronology and Christology, is that the theological interests of each of the evangelists and the communities their respective Gospels served were not the same. The altered theological situation, or place in the stream of life (*Sitz im Leben*), of each of the evangelists is a better explanation to account for narrative divergence than the fanciful notion that four independent eye-witnesses have recorded the same events and words from different perspectives. Many Christian fundamentalists account for the divergence by resorting to the method of harmonisation. They use the analogy of four witnesses describing a road accident from different positions; the marginal contradictions are therefore owing to changed emphases. This does not fit the facts of textual analysis.

The juggling of events in order to create a precise chronology of the life of Jesus is an impossible task; the narratives are fraught with contradictions and inconsistencies. The difficulty is such that any attempt to arrive at a mere sketch of the historical Jesus is considered to be virtually impossible by most leading theologians in the field, given the evidence as we have it today. Most leading researchers have abandoned the quest of the historical Jesus since Schweitzer's monumental work.[9] We can have confidence that some of the words of Jesus and his role as the herald of the kingdom are authentic,[10] but to arrive at a uniform picture of the historical Jesus, and a consistent Christology, on the basis of the Gospels alone is impossible. There is no way that the Johannine Person of Jesus and the Christology of the Fourth Gospel can be matched with the Synoptic portrayals, for the composition of each Gospel was determined by theological processes not by historical ones—a human element indeed! There is evidence that the Gospels reflect a move from an oral tradition to a written one,[11] and there is also evidence that at least two of the Gospel writers made use of previously written sources. They clearly have engaged in editorial borrowing and rewriting of material handed down to them.[12] There is linguistic evidence to suggest that some of the Gospel material, particularly in the Fourth

Gospel, has been edited and amended to bring it in line with the orthodox teaching of the church it served.[13]

It is accepted that Luke's second volume, The Acts of the Apostles, represents not so much a factual account as an idealised picture of the early Church (*Ecclesia*), written at a remove from the events. Yet, even in Acts there is evidence of a conflict between the Jerusalem community and the Greek churches of the Diaspora (i.e., the scattered Jewish community throughout the Roman world).[14] The conflict was not fully suppressed, in spite of Luke's wish to paper over the cracks, and the friction between Paul and Peter (and probably James)—so pointedly illustrated in Galatians and II Corinthians—is similarly not obscured from the record.[15]

There are theological contradictions of thought between Paul's writing and James' Epistle over the relationship of faith to works, even though some commentaries underplay the differences with philological reasoning (Romans 4 & James 2:14–26, both of which use Abraham as their model).

In short, the earliest historical witnesses appear to confirm the fact that the early Church embraced, not so much a unified message as a diversified one (not so much a *kerygma* but *kerygmata*). It had room not for one specific Christology but for many. The work of James Dunn has identified how sketchy were these unifying strands of belief in the early Christian period. Dunn has revealed the broad diversities in Christian thought and practise in the New Testament documents. One conclusion Dunn drew, after analysing the Judaising constraints upon the newly developing Christian community, was that "one of the earliest heresies was conservatism!". Again, when examining Paul's opponents in the heresy of the Judaizers and comparing them with those of the Hellenistic Gnostics (in early form), he says:

> The insistence on a strict conformity to a single authority and tradition [Jerusalem] he evidently regarded as more dangerous than the radical openness of diverse conformity.[16]

The structured ecclesiastical organisation that lies behind the Pastoral Epistles (I & II Timothy and Titus), with their terms of 'office' and strict ruling regarding 'apostasy from the Faith', hardly reflects the flexible charismatic style of the new liberal church at Corinth. Although Küng brings our attention to the fact that the secular meaning of 'office' was not intended by Paul but rather 'ministry'—carrying with it the idea of service—we, nevertheless, have a more organised and institutionalised community in this period as compared with that of I Corinthians. The Pastoral Epistles find a closer parallel in the early Patristic period with the writings of Ignatius and *The Didache.*[17] Clearly the seed of a divided twentieth-century Christendom was already evident in the early Church, begging the questions to which an 'inspired' Bible gives no clear answers. Which community was the early Church? The flexible one of Paul's founding or the staid one of Jerusalem? Which presentation of the message was in accord with the mind of the Church's founder? The *kerygma* of liberal Hellenistic Christianity or the *kerygma* of the orthodox Jewish-based Christianity?

DIVERGENT VALUES IN THE BIBLE

The value-systems embodied in the Bible are clearly disparate. Since the times of Marcion, defenders of the Faith have struggled to preserve the integrity of some of the Old Testament projections of God's requirements compared with those of the New. In our own times, some scholars of the Bible, influenced by biology and geology, have attempted to obscure the difficulty by applying the 'evolutionary' model. The idea of revelation as something static is qualified with terms such as 'development', 'progressive' and 'fulfilment'. Unfolding biblical history—and the value-systems carried along with each changing epoch—is a movement of successive events as though snap-shots were taken as the writer has apprehended what, in his experience, was the will of God. Consequently, the fundamentalists argue, we should not be embarrassed by such a revolting biblical event as that of Samuel's order to Saul, because the morality represented a transitional phase of what was to come:

> Go now and fall upon the Amalekites and destroy them, and put their property under ban. Spare no one; put them all to death, men and women, children and babes in arms, herds and flocks, camels and asses.
>
> I Sam. 15:3

Absurd moral judgements have sometimes been presented by fundamentalists in order to try to justify the crude conception that the prophet's wish was in line with the will of God. When the Psalmist writes, "I hate them with undying hatred" (Ps. 139:21–22), it should be boldly acknowledged that this is a far remove from the Gospel precept of "Love your enemies". The scandal of Jehu treacherously massacring the entire royal family in Jezreel (I Kings 19–20), even though incited by Elisha on the grounds of their idolatry, is challenged, quite rightly, with bitter condemnation (the "blood shed in Jezreel") a century later by Hosea (1:4). Modified moral perspectives illustrate all too clearly how religious attitudes change with new conceptions of the character of God—nothing is fixed! Since the earlier conceptions are retained in scripture like photographs, and are not necessarily altered by the pen of later redactors or successive 'inspired' writers in transmission (except in a few instances), we need a method of interpreting cruder insights of primitive times that does not depend upon harmonising such diverse pictures in order to preserve the belief in biblical inerrancy. *Whatever 'inspiration' was, it had certainly not influenced the New Testament writers in correcting or commenting upon the cruder conceptions of some of God's purported actions of earlier times, or his expectations of moral conduct.*

DIVERSIFIED PRESENTATIONS OF GOD

The God of the Old Testament is known by different titles, and the terms of address are both singular and plural in form. Some fundamentalist Bible students devise grand schemes around these significant titles and names of God, but the accounting for these varied forms probably lies in early combinations of different source traditions.

It is sometimes suggested that a few early passages in the Old Testament (Gen 3:8–9; 6:6; 8:21) present God in anthropomorphic terms (with human characteristics), while later Israelite faith projected him as transcendent, holy and monotheistic, but this explanation is too neat and is tied to the presupposition that revelations are granted to 'men of God' in a progressive and developmental sense. The view of 'progressive revelation' offers an escape route for fundamentalists who feel obliged to give an account of biblical diversity within an inspired and inerrant book which they claim is a unity—we shall examine this in due course. I think the textual evidence points to many concepts of God belonging to Yahwistic faith. Yahweh is presented as walking in the garden (Gen. 3:8), going down to explore what the citizens of Babel were doing (Gen. 11:5), shaping Adam's body from dust and Eve's from a rib (Gen. 2:7, 22). Yahweh pleads like a paternal parent: "I have taken especial pains to warn you . . ." [by sending out his prophets] (Jer. 35:14f.), but at times he regrets some of his actions (Gen. 6:6, I Sam. 15:10). *These concepts of God are plagued with philosophical problems if taken in any other way than poetically.* Hebrew idiom tends more to the concrete than to the abstract. In spite of this, there are many places where the context suggests that a literalistic interpretation is inappropriate and that the author has used poetic forms of writing and metaphors. Thus, the essence of meaning lies in the content of the message rather than the means by which the message is given.[18]

When we come to the study of Christology, the task of establishing a consistent clarity of thought is not straightforward.

DIVERSE CHRISTOLOGIES

Christology is the study of the nature of Christ, his human and divine attributes, and the combination of the two essences in the same person of Jesus. When Christians adopt a certain Christology, they do so on the basis of preferred New Testament passages which stand out for them as primary texts. From such authoritative biblical statements they explore the philosophical implications of those selected passages. Alternatively, they may base a Christological judgement upon philosophical reasoning that is felt to be conclusive, paying relatively little regard to scriptural formulae. The starting point for Christians will inevitably be the particular tradition or persuasion under which they have been brought up, or which has influenced them. It is beyond the scope of this study to examine the basis of philosophical presuppositions, definitions of terminology and the variety of interpretations leading up to and beyond the great Councils which fixed early pronouncements into creeds—a historical solution that stifled further enquiry and produced definitions of heresy! Our task here is to point out the rich diversity in the way the earliest witnesses grappled with and understood the nature of Jesus as 'the Lord'.

As a primitive source, the early speeches in Acts contain a preaching message (*kerygma*) reflecting the thinking of the early Jerusalem community.[19] There can be little doubt that some early references to Jesus are adoptionist in character:

'A man singled out by God and made known to you by miracles, portents, and signs . . .' [leading on to] 'But God raised him to life again . . . God has made this Jesus . . . both Lord and Messiah.'

Acts 2:22–36

That is to say that Jesus, born a man, became divine through the process of resurrection from the dead. The rabbi from Nazareth becomes the Son of God at the resurrection, after his messianic work of atonement on the cross has become complete (Rom. 1:4). The unknown author of the Hebrews speaks of Jesus in human terms in an attempt to identify his church's persecutions with those of its pioneer. The opening verses describe a high Christology but from 1:5 the citation is adoptionist in character,[20] though not in the same way as the speeches in early Acts. The earliest Gospel sources of Mark and the hypothetical 'Q' (the questionable source believed to lie behind the common material of Matthew and Luke) know of no birth narrative, and Matthew and Luke appear to have constructed their birth narratives from interests in Old Testament typologies and predictive fulfilments rather than sound historical evidence. Most early material in the Gospels preserves a human aspect of Jesus: he gets angry; he becomes hungry; he is not privy to all knowledge; he denies he is good; he tires; he becomes thirsty; he suffers; he weeps; he bleeds; he dies. They hold in tension with this a divine status not normally ascribed to a prophet or itinerant rabbi, not only implicitly but explicitly: he raises the dead and is himself raised from the dead; he performs miracles; he knows the mind of God; he forecasts future events; he is the herald of the kingdom; he heals the sick; and he exorcises the demons. He is the 'Son of God', the 'Son of Man', the 'Son of David', 'the Prophet', and 'the Messiah'. These titles suggest an exalted status belonging to a figure who is much more than a distinguished rabbi.

Jesus is not only addressed by the above titles—with all the theological significance they encompass—he was, in the later Gospel tradition, the "Word become flesh" ('Word' from the Greek *Logos*), and this takes us into a very different form of tradition.

It has been held previously by scholars that, while the Synoptic Gospels present us with valuable authentic sources for finding the Jesus of history, the Fourth Gospel, by contrast, presents a theological portrayal of Christ and a meditation on the coming of Jesus in the light of the resurrection. This thesis—while convenient in accounting for the contradictions in historical data, chronology and literary style—is rendered obsolete by modern-day scholarship for the following reasons:

a) it has been shown that the Synoptic Gospels also contain theological reflection in the light of the resurrection.[21]

b) the Fourth Gospel equally contains some authentic historical source material not found in the Synoptics.[22]

c) the date of the Fourth Gospel has been argued by one theologian to be as early as the Synoptics—a theory discounted by almost everyone.[23]

d) since the archaeological discovery of the Qumran scrolls, it has become evident that the style and language (principally, the dualistic thought) of the Fourth Gospel have similarities with the Judaean sect at Qumran. There is, therefore, no longer the need to ascribe the Gospel to a later period of Gnostic influence outside Palestine.[24]

Taking into consideration that no firm conclusions have been reached regarding Gospel origins, there inevitably remains the problem that there is a substantial difference between the Christ as presented in the Fourth Gospel compared to the Jesus of the Synoptics. It is a problem that cannot be ignored or resolved by harmonising the details without doing injury to the sources. In the Fourth Gospel, the Son is not the herald of the kingdom but is in Himself, in his very Person, the centre of revelation. The *Logos* (Word), as an essence—being with God and yet as God—descends from heaven and becomes flesh (*sarx*), reveals the Father to those fore-ordained as God's sons, suffers on the cross, and is risen to where he was before, in order to prepare living places for believers to be reunited with him. There is an inseparable bond between the Son and the Father, a bond that is offered to the believer. The Son comes from the Father and returns to him again. His authority, as disclosed in the 'I am' pronouncements, bears some relationship to those found in the Gnostic papyri of Nag Hammadi. This illustrates not only how syncretistic Jewish and Christian religion had become by this time, but to what extent a wedge had been driven between history and theological reflection—a theological development that led at least one New Testament scholar, E. Käsemann, to doubt whether we really have a human being to deal with here at all. A team of radical theologians in Birmingham wrote a book in 1977 called *The Myth of God Incarnate*, in which the authors were in no doubt that the divinity of Jesus was an invention of the Church.[25] There is a much stronger element of predestination and determinism in the Fourth Gospel than in the Synoptics, particularly with regard to the selection of God's sons, and this poses some moral difficulties in accepting the teaching at face value. In general, there is not a hint of adoptionism in the Fourth Gospel, but a divine figure comes to the fore through and through.

Here are the two extremes of Christology, from the adoptionist picture of a man becoming God to the presentation of a pre-existent and divine being. Between the two is a series of other Christological constructions, some paying greater respect to his humanity, others to his divinity.[26] *The idea of a unified biblical teaching on the nature of Christ is, therefore, a misnomer; it simply does not exist.*

Nowhere in the New Testament is there any systematic attempt at reconciling the two philosophically separate and distinctive natures within the same individual. That is a task left to the early Church Fathers to wrestle with at a much later time.

ESCHATOLOGY AND THE PREDICTING OF FUTURE EVENTS

Eschatology is a Greek derived term (*eschaton* meaning last) used in theology to denote the teaching regarding the 'end of the world', the main substance of which is found in the book of Revelation. Some of the content of Revelation (The Apocalypse) has led some of the more radical scholars to conclude that the book is sub-Christian, at least in part. Martin Luther believed that. "Christ is neither taught in it nor recognised". Nevertheless, this final book of the New Testament canon is not regarded as such by fundamentalist Christians and there can be no other book that has preoccupied the minds of so many Christian sects on the fringe as this one. Few other books have engaged the ingenuity of such escapist theologies, or produced more bizarre and eccentric forecasts of future world events, as the Revelation of John. Piecing together the jig-saw puzzle of continuing historical epochs is a highly subjective exercise carried out by pseudo-exegetes (I use the term to deride Bible students that are not prepared to match their expositions with critical studies). The varied predictions centre on this era closing down through catastrophic drama and the ushering in of the final age of bliss, when all shall be well for the saints and all ill for the damned! Spurious textual combinations are selected to form highly dubious interpretations—sometimes referred to by fundamentalists as the 'signs of the times'—which are based upon the assumption that the book which closes the New Testament is designed to give an authentic prediction of political events about to unfold in the world at large. The presupposition is that Revelation is an agenda of political history rather than a series of figurative pictures, and that the visions were always intended to forecast events beyond the first-century Roman *milieu.*

Most fundamentalist expositors of the book of Revelation have been forced to revise their predictions, somewhat ashamedly, as world events move in directions not matching their forecasts—the Children of God predicted that Christ would return in 1993. This revision and re-application of biblical prophecy took place in the early period too, indeed in the book of Revelation itself. The author faced an unresolved problem in the tradition; there was a contradiction regarding the time of the Judgement in the earliest witnesses. In the parable of the Sheep and the Goats, judgement coincides with the coming (*Parousia*) of the 'Son of Man' in glory (Mat. 25:31–46), but with the parable of The Rich man and Lazarus (Luke 16:22) and the saying of Jesus from the cross— "I tell you this: today you shall be with me in Paradise" (Luke 23:43)—there is a suggestion of an immediate entry into 'Abraham's bosom' (or 'Paradise') at the point of death. The latter implies an assessment of the individual's life instantly following his or her death, yet before resurrection, while the former implies an immediate glorification for those selected at the second coming. The writer of the Apocalypse gets round this problem by postulating a two-fold judgement scene and a second resurrection, separated by a millennial reign of Christ (Rev. 20:1–10).

Determination of the date of Revelation is based primarily on features of the book's visionary content. Opinions vary from the days of Nero's reign (when the temple in Jerusalem was still standing) to the closing years of Domitian (AD 81–96). The content also gives us some clues as to who could never have been the author; the tradition of John, son of Zebedee, being the author has no solid foundation. These questions however are of secondary importance as compared with the question of what the book is about.

The central question has to be: how are we to interpret the book's picture language? Can any part of the figurative imagery have a literal meaning for events beyond the first century? One notable commentator, G. B. Caird, has tied the book quite feasibly to the events of the first century exclusively. He has further suggested that much of the imagery might be lost to us today, even though it may have had an obvious and potent meaning for those early readers of the author's church.[27]

The book is an 'Apocalypse', and as such contains the recognisable features of other Jewish Apocalypses: an encouragement to resist pagan ideas; a certainty that God's elect who presently suffer will eventually be vindicated; a concept of the historical crises having their equivalents in heavenly conflicts, and that these symbols describe the age-long cosmic struggle between light and darkness. The key to interpreting the book of Revelation lies in recognising the imminence both of the coming crisis of Christian martyrdom and of the *Parousia.* The span of visions covers the limited time from the writer's situation to the rapidly approaching second coming of Christ. Caird says:

> We cannot, however, do justice to his very plain opening statement: 'The Apocalypse of Jesus Christ, given him by God, to show his servant what is bound to happen soon' (1:1), by saying that he foresaw a long series of events covering centuries, which could be described as imminent because they were to *begin* shortly. Whatever earthly realities correspond to John's symbols, he expected them to be accomplished quickly *in their entirety.*[28]

Augustine drew attention, not only to the moral problems within the book itself, but to the difficulties of visualising concretely some of the imagery belonging to the events surrounding the millennial reign of Christ. For example, speaking of the 'Book of life', he says:

> If this book be materially considered, who can reckon its size or length, or the time it would take to read a book in which the whole life of every man is recorded? Shall there be present as many angels as men, and shall each man hear his life recited by the angel assigned to him? In that case there will not be one book containing all the lives, but a separate book for every life. But our passage requires us to think of one only.[29]

In spite of such criticisms, fundamentalist expositors never cease to interpret the number of the Beast, 666, as the Papacy or other rivals of their sect (13:18), the Jehovah's Witnesses still interpret the 144000 saints quite literally (7:4), Christadelphians see the millennial reign as being exactly a thousand years (20; 4f.), and others see the Heavenly Jerusalem as more than just a figure of the new age (21:1f.).

The book of Revelation is not the only literature purporting to forecast the final age. These other visionary glimpses of the end of all things are not identical with the visions in Revelation, unless we distort the text to an unacceptable degree. Those Evangelical expositors who combine the visions of Revelation with other eschatological passages of the Old Testament, such as the visions in Daniel and the references to Israel's return from exile in Ezekiel 37–39, stretch the interpretations even further beyond credulity, holding again to the presupposition that these very varied books provide a unity of prophetic doctrine. It is widely recognised that the Apocalypse depends heavily upon motifs and imagery taken from the Old Testament, but *when interpreting the book we must set the visions within the context of the events of John's church rather than replace them in an artificial setting of later political events on a broader scale.* The writer uses Old Testament symbols and language in developing his theme, and to make sense of the writing, we are required to see the way in which the author has utilised the motifs, the figures of Jewish apocalyptic writing, and the imagery of the ancient world, for his more immediate purpose.[30]

In apocalyptic literature, above all other, we see that fundamentalists rarely examine their presuppositions in the light of biblical criticism. It is in this highly speculative field that the dubious practice of subjective passage-twisting to fit elaborately constructed schemes is prevalent—a method that obscures each biblical author's intention to make some poignant comment on that stream of life in which he lived.

NOTES

1. J. Barr, *Fundamentalism*, London, 1977. James Barr has given an exhaustive criticism of the fundamentalist stance in his comprehensive book on the subject, but more from a philosophical and sociological perspective than a biblical one. He draws a distinction between 'Fundamentalists' and 'Conservative Biblical Scholars', a necessary distinction to draw, but in what follows I define what I mean by a Fundamentalist biblical standpoint.
2. It is often assumed that biblical criticism began in the liberal atmosphere of the 'Age of Reason', that its principle aim was that of highlighting the defects, inconsistencies and contradictions found in the Bible, but nothing could be further from the truth. Biblical Criticism was active in the first four centuries, after which it stagnated throughout the Middle Ages: Origen of Caesarea wrote a most comprehensive and thoroughly critical edition of the text of the Old Testament in the third century; Dionysius of Alexandria reviews the authorship question of Revelation through a comparison with the Fourth Gospel, and much of his reasoning still stands today.

   When John Wycliffe made the Bible accessible to the uninstructed laity with his English translation, he not only fanned the flames of the reformation spirit but set in motion a chaotic surge for private and individualistic interpretations that dispensed with some of the tradition and critical analysis which the Church had preserved from the first to the fourth century. With the arrival of critical scholarship in the eighteenth and nineteenth centuries (coinciding with the classical studies of the Renaissance), there was a threat to fundamentalist biblical faith.

   'Lower Criticism' aimed at restoring the original text from the variant manuscripts that survived the course of transmission.

   'Higher Criticism' discussed questions of date, authorship, document comparison and conflation, textual divergence and thematic contradiction, etc..

   'Form Criticism' is the study of textual forms and 'Source Criticism' applies a scientific methodology for extracting the differing source material lying behind the final text. This science is not indulgent guess work, and it is certainly not carried through with personal preference or caprice, but seeks to employ the strictest methods of observation, analysis, hypothesis and verification; it is a scientific discipline that applies its principles to itself. For C. H. Dodd, "Its methods may in future be improved, its presuppositions revised, but it stands firm as a self-justifying part of the reasonable search for knowledge, and its abandonment would be a 'flight from reason'.", *The Bible To-Day*, Revised, 1960, page 25.
3. G. von Rad, *Old Testament Theology*, Volume I, London, 1975, gives a comprehensive study of early Old Testament sources: Jahwistic and Elohistic sources being the earliest source material. The Priestly source came next followed by the Deuteronomistic source from the times of the monarchy. M. Buber, in his informative little book entitled *The Prophetic Faith*, New York, 1949, presents an insight into the development of historical tradition from early source material.

   A chronology of the writings of the Old Testament based upon the researches of biblical criticism runs thus:

Century BC		Writings
13th	Exodus from Egypt	
12th	Settlement in Palestine	Oral traditions (laws, legends, poems) preserved in later writings
11th	Wars with Canaanites	
10th	Foundation of monarchy (David 1000 BC)	Court chronicles begin (incorporated in later books)
9th	Early laws and traditions:	Judaean collection ['J'] and Ephraimite collection ['E'] (later incorporated in Genesis-to-Joshua)
8th	Fall of Samaria, 721	Amos, Hosea, Micah, Isaiah

7th	Josiah's Reformation, 621	Deuteronomy, Jeremiah, Zephaniah, Nahum
6th	Fall of Jerusalem, 586	Habakkuk, Judges, Samuel, Kings, Ezekiel, II Isaiah, Haggai, Zechariah
5th		'Priestly' laws and narratives of Genesis-to-Joshua ['P'], Malachi, Job
4th		Compilation of Genesis-to-Joshua [out of 'J', 'E', 'P' and Deuteronomy]
3rd		Chronicles, Ecclesiastes
2nd		Book of Psalms completed (out of earlier poems), Ecclesiasticus, Daniel.
1st		Book of Wisdom.

4. P. R. Ackroyd, *Exile and Restoration*, London, 1976, pages 62–102. "The date of origin of the completed work is not difficult to discover . . . 561 BC marks a terminus a quo . . . 520 bc or thereabouts must be the latest date." (page 64). See also M. Noth, *The History of Israel*, London, 1965, pages 335–356 (particularly page 342) "The whole of the Chronicler's history was compiled—about 300 bc—with the purpose of providing the unique legitimacy of the Jerusalem tradition historically, as opposed to the Samaritan cultus." (page 356)
5. A. Heidel, *The Babylonian Genesis*, London, 1942. A copy of the comparative texts is given with a commentary. See also G. von Rad, op. cit., pages 136–153.
6. G. von Rad, op. cit., pages 165–174. From an old Credo in Deut 26:5— "A wandering Aramean who went down into Egypt and there became a great nation"—a historical-theological framework is composed, page 176. G. B. Caird, *The Language and Imagery of the Bible*, London, 1980, pages 93–94.
7. H. Ringgren, *Israelite Religion*, London, 1974, pages 104f..
8. W. Lambert, *Inspiration and Revelation*, 1990, pages 6–7. The texts run thus:

> If the ox was accustomed to gore and the authorities have brought the matter to the attention of its owner, but he has not kept it under control, and then it gores a man and causes his death, the owner of the ox shall pay two thirds of a mina of silver.
>
> The second law on the goring ox of Eshnunna
>
> But if the ox was wont to push with his horn in time past, and it hath been testified to his owner, and he hath not kept him in, but that he hath killed a man or woman; the ox shall be stoned, and his owner shall also be put to death.
>
> The second law in the Book of the Covenant, Exod. 21:29.
>
> "Although the penalty be different, the situation pictured is so similarly phrased as to amount to identity, if allowance is made for the different languages in which the two laws are found. Coincidence must be ruled out and since the Babylonian law is much earlier than that of Moses, it is difficult to argue that the Mosaic law came directly from God." (pages 6–7)

9. A. Schweitzer, *The Quest of the Historical Jesus*, London, 1936. H. K McArthur, *In Search of the Historical Jesus*, London, 1969. G. Bornkamm, *Jesus of Nazareth*, London, 1973. Bornkamm is less radical and denies the impossibility of establishing genuine historical data; nevertheless, he thinks that arriving at an accurate chronology of Jesus' life is not possible. Less radical too is Vincent Taylor in *The Life and Ministry of Jesus*, London, 1955.
10. J. Jeremias, *The Parables of Jesus*, London, 1972, says: "Comparison reveals a definite personal style, a singular clarity and simplicity, a matchless mastery of construction. The conclusion is inevitable that we are dealing with particularly trustworthy tradition. We stand right before Jesus when reading his parables." (page 12) T. W. Manson, in *The Sayings of Jesus*, London, 1975, says: "The ultimate source of all genuine matter in the teaching is the spoken word of Jesus Himself." (page 11)
11. R. Bultmann, *The History of the Synoptic Tradition*, 1931; M. Dibelius, *From Tradition to Gospel*, London, 1971.

12. B. H. Streeter, *The Four Gospels: a Study of Origins*, London, 1936.
13. R. E. Brown, *The Gospel According to John*, London, 1971. Brown gives a demonstration of this discipline in his commentary, see pages xxxii–xxxix, where he posits five stages of editing to reach the final form.
14. The point is contested by A. H. McNeil in *An Introduction to the Study of the New Testament*, London, 1953, pages 92f., and has been since the days of J. B. Lightfoot, but the fundamental point is still maintained by G. Bornkamm in *Paul*, London, 1975, pages 32f., as it is in the conclusion of James Dunn's study (note 16). The summarial sentences of Acts 2:42–47, 4:32 and 5:42, describing the harmony of the Jerusalem community, hardly reflect the tensions outlined later in the book of Acts, however suppressed such details have been.
15. M. Dibelius, *Studies in the Acts of the Apostles*, London, 1973, pages 93–101. Many studies point out the historical contradictions (as in C. S. C. Williams, *The Acts of the Apostles*, London, 1964, pages 22f.). This one begins from an examination of the literary style of Acts, see particularly page 100.
16. J. D. G. Dunn, *Unity and Diversity in the New Testament*, London, 1977 pages 266 and 306.
17. Ibid., pages 114f. H. Küng, *To Be a Christian*, London, 1977, page 486: Pluriform Church, pages 478–509; practical suggestions, page 526. On the linguistic problems of 'deacons', see G. B. Caird, op. cit., pages 81–82.
18. H. H. Rowley, *The Faith of Israel*, London, 1956, 'The Nature of God', pages 48f.. G. B. Caird, *The Language and Imagery of the Bible*, London, 1980, 'Anthropomorphism' Ch. 10, pages 172f..
19. C. H. Dodd, *The Apostolic Preaching*, London, 1944, pages 20f., and J. A. T. Robinson, 'The Most Primitive Christology of all', in *Twelve New Testament Studies*, 1962. Dodd argues that such a speech as this represents the preaching of the Church in its formative years, as M. Dibelius held, it was a typical sermon of AD 90: "These speeches contain at least incompatible Christologies . . . It is by virtue of the Resurrection that Jesus is Lord and Christ", Robinson, op. cit., pages 139–153. In other words, before the resurrection, Jesus was neither the Christ (Messiah) nor the 'Lord'—this is the inference behind the passage.
20. J. D. G. Dunn, op. cit., pages 259f..
21. A. H. McNeil, op. cit., pages 8f..
22. C. H. Dodd, *Historical Tradition in the Fourth Gospel*, London, 1963.
23. J. A. T. Robinson in *Redating the New Testament*, London, 1976, and *The Priority of John*, London, 1985. The Rylands *papyrus 457* from Egypt is a fragment containing part of John 18, which pushes the date of the Fourth Gospel into the first century at least.
24. The Dead Sea Scrolls: G. Vermes, *The Dead Sea Scrolls in English*, Middlesex, 1973. R. Bultmann, *The Gospel of John*, Oxford, 1971. Bultmann argues from the Mandaean writings that a Gnostic Redeemer Myth lies behind his two-source theory of John, but most English scholars discount this on the basis that the Mandaean writings are too late for the theory to hold. C. H. Dodd, *The Interpretation of the Fourth Gospel*, London, 1953, argued that the Mandaean writings provide evidence of the cultural *milieu* of the Gospel, along with other influences upon this evangelist; he therefore discounts any direct Johannine dependence on Gnostic sources.
25. J. Hick, ed., *The Myth of God Incarnate*, London, 1977. The team of theologians being John Hick, Michael Goulder, Don Cupitt, Maurice Wyles, and Frances Young, et al. J. D. G. Dunn, op. cit., pages 298f..
26. For a thorough exegesis of the Christology of the New Testament material, see O. Cullmann, *The Christology of the New Testament*, London, 1959, in which he concludes that, even though they are mutually influential, the Christological formulations of the New Testament are incapable of synthesis, pages 315f.. For a fuller discussion on the development of Christological doctrine, see J. N. D. Kelly, *Early Christian Doctrines*, London, 1959.
27. G. B. Caird, *The Revelation of St John the Divine*, London, 1966.
28. Ibid., page 12.
29. Augustine, *The City Of God*, book 20, Ch. 14.
30. The subject of eschatology and mythology is discussed more fully in my second book, due to be published in 1996, *Fundamentals without Fundamentalism*.

3

ERRORS OF DETAIL IN GOSPEL NARRATIVES

The preaching message of Jesus is not quite the same as the *kerygmatic* faith of the early Church. Critical scholars see the difference but fundamentalists in general do not. Within the New Testament period the *later beliefs* of the Christian communities *had influenced and shaped the presentation of the historical Jesus* and not the other way around. It is true that the Faith of the Church emerged from the teaching of Jesus, but the written forms of Jesus' proclamation have had superimposed upon them the living faith of a number of Christian communities. There was growth, there was development, there was reflection, and there was a tendency to recall the past from what was experienced in the present. The records of the ministry of Jesus, therefore, speak as much about the faith of the communities as about the historical Jesus.

The Greek world was in need of salvation and the message of Jesus had a great appeal in the first century. Christianity had expanded rapidly by filling a vacuum of religious dissatisfaction and pessimism brought about by doctrines of fate. Within a very short period of time, Christian churches could be found worshipping Jesus throughout Asia Minor and Palestine, but their respective beliefs and practices were not wholly identical with each other. The simple message which the preachers had proclaimed was the *kerygma*, but once the churches had been formed they required something more to keep the faith alive.[1] They needed teaching (*didache*) in order to defend their beliefs against the arguments of rival religious groups, exhortation to keep them from falling into immoral ways, and ethical guidance to resolve their internal disputes. The faith of the early churches was not static for having to survive in a changing world. Some ideas were absorbed from the religious environment as a way of expressing a truth (the *Logos* doctrine), while others came dangerously close to heresy (Nicolaitan teaching). The place and importance of Jewish observance and circumcision for the Greeks nearly split the Church in two. Before the canon arrested the process of change and the movement towards syncretism, there was no literary discipline to decide which writings should be accepted as authoritative.

There was not one Christian centre where development took place then, but a number—Ephesus, Antioch and Jerusalem, etc.—and the communities had no central organisation in which to regulate belief and practice in the early period (Jerusalem was losing its hold by the sixties AD). The believers at different centres worked out their salvation in contest with the cults and ideologies around at the time. Consequently, the traditions evolved with marginal differences as Christians at each of the centres strove to preserve the faith against varied religious opposition—a Jewish influence in one town, and a Hellenistic one in another. In view of the differing situations of each of the Christian centres, and in view of the fact that much of the Jesus tradition developed far away from Judaea and Galilee (the location of its origin), there were likely to be variations in their literary traditions, variations which may have been contradictory. It is my belief that contradictions and inconsistencies are evident in the Gospel records. The fundamentalist will deny this of course, but the likelihood of differing traditions producing conflicting records will soon become apparent after we have begun to answer some pertinent questions of historical interest about the Gospels:

1. *Why were there four Gospels* preserved in the Church's canon—three which are similar in structure though different in emphasis, with a fourth that is very different in style, structure and emphasis? *Are there contradictory details* of the ministry of Jesus as presented by the evangelists which are *impossible to harmonise?*

2. Are there *significant alterations* made to various sayings, parables, events and chronological details from their 'original forms', as exegetes suggest, which cannot be explained away by transmission from Oral Tradition to written form, or from the translation of Hebrew or Aramaic to Greek?

3. *Is the 'Jesus story' historically plausible? Why did the Jewish people not see the nature and significance of Jesus' historical mission* when, according to the Synoptic Gospels, his miracles were so public? Why indeed, according to Mark, were the demons only permitted to understand his Messianic mission?

4. *Does the 'Jesus story' fit the facts of what is known? Why did the authorities feel compelled to execute him* when they were quite at liberty to let him go and label him as a fanatical and misguided charlatan?

The Gospels were some of the latest New Testament documents to be written, and were likely to have represented the variant theologies of the particular early Christian centres. Before the Gospels were written, many of the conflicts and early disputes would have been reflected in the Oral Tradition. When the evangelists composed the Gospels they made use of the recollections of the Oral Tradition—sayings, parables, paradigms, tales, legends—such as it had become written down on papyri and parchments, much of which had already become combined in lengthy source documents (the passion narrative).[2] Although the Gospels are similar in structure, in that they present a uniform ministry of Jesus, they are dissimilar in other respects, in that they preserve material and reflect the particular views of the centres they each represented—a fact which is not immediately obvious to the lay reader. As such there are bound to be contradictions and historical anomalies in the documents, as we should expect.

The import of the fourth question is heightened with the realisation that it was not only the Jewish people at large that failed to grasp the purpose of his mission but the disciples too. The Synoptic Gospels suggest that Jesus himself was also ignorant about some aspects of God's plan of salvation. Naturally, this is an argument in favour of the historical trustworthiness of narrative details, in that not all the traditions were influenced by the faith of the earliest communities. At some point, however, we have to face a number of historical anomalies in the Gospel accounts as they stand in the New Testament. This chapter addresses these issues. Fundamentalists are happy to wrestle with some of the historical anomalies of the Jesus story, but they are less prepared to acknowledge that details in the Gospel narratives may be contradictory as a result of being composed more from a motive of propaganda than preservation of historical data. This is because the fundamentalist believes that the *scriptures* should not be questioned or tampered with, that they are God's 'inspired' Word, that they are inerrant, and that they serve as our *authority*!

There are two methods of studying the Gospels open to the Bible reader:

i) harmonisation of detail;

ii) comparison and contrasting of detail.

The Gospels lend themselves to a study of comparisons, since they are supposed to be four independent witnesses which each purport to record the ministry of Jesus. Although the opening introduction of Luke states the author's purpose as that of writing an 'orderly account' from those who were eye-witnesses, a careful exegesis of Luke set alongside Mark shows that the former is dependent upon the later, and that Luke's work was not as original as the opening verses imply. Some of the textual contradictions are in danger of being glossed over if we adopt as a working rule of exegesis the method of harmonising the Gospels (a method as old as the second century[3]). If, alternatively, we choose to contrast, compare and set side by side the divergent sources—highlighting the alterations and deliberate changes[4] of later reflection—then, we shall see a very different picture emerging. Since the fundamentalist will be reluctant to apply the second working method in favour of the first, let us not assume the presupposition that harmonising is invalid, but move forward slowly to examine it by considering with an open mind the evidence that contradictions and alteration for propaganda purposes exist in the Gospel records.[5]

CONTRADICTION, MODIFICATION AND ALTERATION

The assertion being made, then, which forms the basis of this chapter, is that there are contradictions of detail that cannot be accounted for other than by accepting that the original sources had been modified in the light of the Church's post-Easter faith. This is not novel to those studying New Testament theology, but it is radical for fundamentalists who read the Bible with an unquestioning acceptance that what is being read is an account of events as they actually happened. Of the numerous instances that could be taken as examples, I have selected those which I think are impossible to defend or which are not open to metaphorical interpretation.

A Statement at the Cross

At the foot of the cross the Roman centurion is reported by Mark to have said: "Truly this man was the Son of God" (Mark 15:39 RSV—earlier RSV translations render 'a son of God').[6] Luke's version of the same pronouncement has the soldier declaring: "Certainly this man was innocent!" (Luke 23:47 RSV). We must face the contradiction; we cannot assume that the centurion made both statements, for it would have been improbable for a declaration to be made twice, one drawing attention to his status as 'the Son of God', the other exonerating him of guilt. The prose-narrative style of the Gospels covering the crucifixion is economical in words and to the point, and it is questionable whether many in the Church would have witnessed the cross. We have little choice, then, but to accept that through transmission the one record of what the centurion *actually said* must have been mis-reported, and must therefore be inaccurate! Again, we might argue that one record had been altered consciously and quite deliberately. Suppose, argues the exegete, Luke modified his source because he realised that a Roman centurion would never have declared Jesus *historically* to be the Son of God; that would have been too incredible for his readers to accept. If he was at liberty to make such a change and represent the declaration in a more acceptable form for his audience, then surely Luke was guilty of representing *false information*? Conversely, suppose Mark wished to emphasise—with all the literary skill he felt legitimate—that Jesus was unequivocally the 'Son of God' (Mark 1:1—see note 6), to present the confession as the substance of his message, his *kerygma* (even having the demons make such pronouncements, Mark 5:7), could not Mark's rendering also have been a literary invention? Can we not propose equally that Mark had modified the statement to illustrate to his readers in Rome that *even the Roman centurion* was convinced that Jesus was the 'Son of God' after witnessing the crucifixion?[7]

Whatever the case, we cannot avoid the conclusion that, while both statements may represent a theological truth, one of the declarations (if not both) cannot be a verbatim report of what was actually said, in the sense of an objective record of words spoken.

The Parable of the Lamp

Let us take a further example, the little parable of the Lamp recorded in the three Synoptic Gospels and the Gospel of Thomas (Mark 4:21; Matt. 5:15; Luke 8:16 & Thom. 33b):

> Do you bring in the lamp to put it under the meal-tub, or under the bed? Surely it is brought to be set on the lamp-stand.
>
> Mark 4:21

In the different contexts in which each writer has placed this little parable, there is a different meaning given to it: Mark and Thomas relate the parable to the Gospel, Matthew to the disciples, and Luke to the inner light.[8] The parable is not substantially different in form, apart from one detail found in a variant manuscript of Luke. We are to imagine a peasant's clay oil lamp placed on the ledge of a small windowless house, one having no chimney. Extinguishing the flame without a cover would produce an offensive smoke and an unpleasant smell, as well as the risk of fire should it be put under the mattress. Generally, the lamp would be left aflame throughout the night so as to give a faint light to the occupants. The bushel-measure was used to cover the lamp to contain the offensive smoke when blown out. The point is clear. The purpose of the lamp is to illuminate the room, not to stand under cover. The modified version in a variant manuscript of Luke replaces "under the bed" with "putteth it in a cellar". The change was made by someone unfamiliar with a peasant's sleeping arrangements, whereby a man will retire with his whole family on a floor-mat. A Palestinian peasant's house would not have had a cellar like the homes of Luke's Hellenistic readers. Hence, this scribe felt at liberty to alter the saying in order to suit a different non-Palestinian audience, thereby, not rendering the saying as it was first handed down.

Given that each evangelist has supplied a meaning to the parable by placing it in a different context, we might ask what was the original context and purpose of the parable when first voiced by the historical Jesus? To take refuge in the explanation that Jesus may have spoken the parable on many occasions and for quite different purposes, is to avoid facing the problem that alterations have occurred to a fair proportion of preserved sayings in the Gospels.

Parable Alterations for Christian Propaganda

The question we wish to explore now is whether the parables as originally uttered by Jesus have been consciously modified to further the purposes of Christian proclamation and propaganda. There are good linguistic grounds for accepting that the key to each of the three following parables were later post-easter applications. The Sower (Mark 4:13–20), The Tares amongst the Wheat, and the Seine Net (Matt. 13:37–43; 49–50) are each given an allegorical interpretation. There is more of an over-emphasis on the point of separation than Jesus would have intended, and the words in the allegorical passages are clearly not original.[9]

Some early forms of parables that have a private individual as the subject, such as the host in The Great Supper in Luke 14:16 (Gospel of Thomas 64), have the subject changed in later forms to a king (Matt. 22:2). This is a clear modification in the light of the post-easter faith. The deliberate change was licensed by a faith which proclaimed the exalted status of Christ as King. The motive for interpreting some of the parables as allegories was to secure the belief that the Christian programme of the *kerygma* was previously in the mind of Jesus.

There is a subtle difference in Mark's parable of The Wicked Husbandmen (Mark 12:1–11; Matt. 21:33–44; Luke 20:9–18; Thomas 65) as compared to the renderings of Luke and Matthew. It seems plausible to suggest that the earliest form of the parable was allegorised by the evangelists to fit the known *facts* of later Christian understanding. Mark describes the son being slain *inside the vineyard*, and the corpse being flung over the wall, without even the dignity of a grave! There is no recall of the passion of Jesus here. Not so, Matthew and Luke; they both present the son as being *first cast out of the vineyard*, and then killed on the outside—a clear reference to the passion, where Jesus is slain outside the city of Jerusalem (John 19:17; Heb. 13:12f.).[10]

There appears to be a crude conflation of subjects in Matthew's parable of the Last Judgement (25:31–46). From the original figure of a Palestinian shepherd, Matthew inserts the Messianic titles of the 'Son of Man' and 'the King' when outlining the post-easter programme of the *Parousia* and Final Judgement, and by doing so destroys the literary unity of the shepherd figure.

Chronological Contradictions

There are obvious contradictions in the chronological details of the ministry of Jesus. These are clearly evident when we contrast the accounts objectively. The method of conflating the material and harmonising the events in order to *make them fit* should be avoided. Mark and Luke have minor differences in the itinerary and in the order of events, yet each reads coherently. The Fourth Gospel is equally coherent, but has a considerable difference in chronology and emphasis compared with the Synoptics. A simple chart may suffice to show the marked differences in the sequence of events, subjects and emphases:

		Synoptics	John
1.	Beginning of Ministry	After the arrest of John the Baptist (Mark 1:14)	During John's ministry (John 1-4)
2.	Length of Ministry	One Passover, one year (Mark 14:1)	3 Passovers, explicitly (John 2:13; 6:4; 12:1)
3.	Locale of ministry	Chiefly Galilee and the north except for the final week	Back and forth between Judaea and Galilee
4.	End of ministry	Last Supper was Passover (Mark 14)	Last Supper before Passover (John 13:1; 18:28)
5.	Focus of Ministry	Kingdom of God	Eternal life as present, result of a response to Jesus
6.	Controversies	Interpretation of the Law	Attitude towards Jesus
7.	Messianic Question	Messiah's identity—not disclosed explicitly	Public Messianic claim from John 1 onwards
8.	Manner of Teaching	Parables, brief aphorisms	Allegories, extended discourses
9.	Temple Cleansing	At end of ministry, possible cause of arrest (Mark 11:15f.)	At beginning of ministry (John 2:13f.), Raising of Lazarus causes the arrest
10.	Role of Jesus	Proclaimer of the Kingdom	The Son sent by the Father

The differences must be blatantly obvious to every discerning reader, and critical exegetes have shown unequivocally how the evangelists have used literary connections to join up the events and stories, which suggests that the itineraries cannot be accepted as being historical with any confidence. Generalised summaries are used to join episodes or pericopes, which are peculiar to each individual evangelist and which can be understood as their own personal style. For example, Mark's Gospel has a number of linking summaries: that of the Galilean ministry (1:14–15); the teaching with authority at Capernaum (1:21–22); the tour of Galilean Synagogues (1:39); events by the sea (2:13); retirement to the hill country (3:7–19); a collection of parables (4:33–34); the mission of the Twelve (6:7, 12–13) and the return of the Twelve (6:30). Mark usually joins each section with the word 'And'; Matthew uses 'Now' and 'Then'; Luke uses all three along with 'Afterwards' and 'In those days'. This suggests that topics and themes dictate the framework of the ministry rather than a factual account of itinerary and events. I am not suggesting that the whole construction of the ministry is invention, for, as some English critics have pointed out, there is a general framework discernible in the Gospels that has some basis of historicity.[11]

Prediction: *Vaticinia ex eventu*

The few examples of Gospel narrative differences presented above illustrate how the reporting in the early period was dubious compared to what we would expect of a modern historian. The evangelists were not interested in the precise details of what Jesus actually said and did. Their aims were evangelism and instruction, and we should not expect to see the methods of modern scholarship exercised in the writing of such religious documents as the Gospels. Other examples of imprecise reporting are a collection of sayings that purport to forecast the future. We begin with Luke's rendering of the advice given by Jesus to the disciples:

> When you are brought before the synagogues and state authorities, do not begin worrying about how you will conduct your defence or what you will say. For when the time comes the Holy Spirit will instruct you what to say.
>
> Luke 12:11–12, see also Mark 13:9–13

We know that the first Christians faced trials in the Jewish synagogues (principally, from the book of Acts, 17:1–9, and the anti-polemic use of 'the Jews' in the Fourth Gospel). The question that presents itself is this: Did the historical Jesus predict this situation and offer the advice beforehand, or has the evangelist (or his source) put this prediction into the mouth of Jesus from a later perspective? The fundamentalist may feel happier to opt for the first, but how is he or she then to account for the disillusionment of the disciples after the crucifixion (Mark 14:50; 16:10–11, 14) when Jesus so frequently predicted his own downfall and resurrection under the title of the 'Son of Man'?

> And he began to teach them that the Son of man must suffer many things, and be rejected by the elders and the chief priests and the scribes, and be killed, and after three days rise again. And he said this plainly.
>
> Mark 8:31–32 RSV (9:9–13, 30–31; 10:32–34, 45; 12:11; 14:21, 27–28 and parallels)[12]

Matthew has placed the parable of the Lost Sheep in an artificial context of Church conduct (18:12–14). It clearly illustrates that he understood the parable quite differently from Luke (15:3–7), whose context appears more fitting. It is hard to imagine that Jesus had in his mind the Church of later development when he spoke such parables. The whole body of teaching material found in Matthew 18 reads more like a manual of ecclesiastical conduct ('brother':15; 'congregation':17—'church' in RSV) than a verbatim record of Jesus' words.

The altered promise of Jesus as recorded by Matthew after the confession of Peter: "You are Peter, the Rock; and on this rock I will build my church . . ." (Matt. 16:19), is, indisputably, an expansion of the more original saying preserved in Mark 8:29. The Matthean version was influenced by the faith of the post-easter community. I cannot find any evidence to support the view that the historical Jesus had in his mind the notion of the Church of later development as the natural outgrowth of his small band of followers that accompanied him throughout the ministry.

We cannot prove anything dogmatically from the above examples of prophetic forecasts, however, because the conclusions depend so much upon our own presuppositions: Mark's saying at Caesarea Philippi may be abridged, and the parallel saying in Matthew may be original—Jesus could have been granted foreknowledge of a projected future programme by some divine telepathy, but it does not seem plausible. The view of Jesus being omniscient is also in contradiction to what Jesus himself had spoken of his own partial ignorance regarding the future (Mark 13:32). Further, other historical anomalies are left without resolve, such as the disciples being taken by surprise at his death and Jesus' purpose for riding into Jerusalem.

A more plausible explanation is to regard the 'Son of Man' predictions of the Passion and other isolated forecasts found in the Gospels as *vaticinia ex eventu*—prophecies constructed on the basis of their fulfilment, formulated later and in the light of the events. This technical term is used for a literary genre that occurs frequently in the Old Testament and in ancient literature generally. Whenever Jesus is reported to have predicted his Passion, it is normally presented in the Synoptic Gospels with the enigmatic title of the 'Son of Man' (the exceptions being Matt. 16:4; 21; 21:33f.). Two early 'Son of Man' pronouncements are clearly not predictions but Christological declarations of the role of Jesus to forgive sins and be sovereign of the Sabbath—they can be substituted with the personal pronoun 'I' without any alteration of sense (Mark 2:10; 28). The other 'Son of Man' sayings, in the main, are predictions which appear artificial—Jesus speaks in the third person, as though referring to another (Mark 9:31, Matt. 10:23). The whole Gospel context, however, makes it quite clear to whom the evangelist believes the title refers. The 'Son of Man' title was evidently popular in the early community, and the evangelists appear to have had few reservations in placing the title within sayings which did not include it, or in changing others that had 'I' for their subject, and vice versa. What we cannot be sure about is the primary form of the saying and what represents the verbatim word of Jesus. The earlier view of scholars was that the 'I' pronouncements represent the primitive Palestinian Tradition, with the 'Son of Man' titles being interpolations, but more recent criticism has challenged this.[13]

The 'Son of Man' pronouncements are aids to the proclamation; they are part of the *kerygma*. They are not prophecies or predictions in the strict sense. We cannot know historically whether or not Jesus was aware that his suffering and death were a necessary culmination of his ministry with only the prediction sayings to go on, since they are evidently *vaticinia ex eventu*.[14]

Regarding the post-Easter faith in the *Parousia*, there can be little doubt that the historical Jesus believed that the consummation of the world would come in his own lifetime.[15] In addition, he certainly did not want to prepare for the coming of God's kingdom by founding a special community of the future, as distinct from Israel, with its own creed, cult, constitution and ministries, etc..[16] It is quite clear that he expected the kingdom of God to arrive within his own time (Mark 14:59–63; Luke 24:26). Schweitzer contended that Jesus thought the kingdom would come just before the missionary tour spoken of in Matt. 10:23 had ended. The post-easter faith had to account for the delay of the *Parousia*, and the faith of the community was adjusted to present the delay as being within the divine plan and within the mind of the historical Jesus.

The following is a rule of critical exegesis: *If sayings or events are obscure and difficult to understand, or if they bear no connection to contemporary Judaism or Christian propaganda, or if they are uninfluenced by the post-easter faith or tied to a Messianic title, then they are more likely to be attributable to the historical Jesus.* Having said that, the distinction between the 'historical Jesus' and the 'Christ of faith' is not always clear.

Using this rule of exegesis, we find more authentic material describing the humanity of Jesus in the first Gospel than in those coming later, i.e., before too much reflection had taken place. Mark reports the views of some who regarded Jesus as mentally disturbed (3:21), yet the insult is passed over in silence by Matthew and Luke. We find Matthew tones down the miraculous features from the early primitive forms in Mark. We find Luke idealising the twelve from the earliest records of their ignorance—in one instance, Jesus' denouncement of Peter found in Mark is removed completely (Luke 9:21–22/Mark 8:53). There is a saying of the virtue of remaining a eunuch preserved in Matthew which, though reflecting the eastern stigma of the unmarried status, may well be a self-justification for Jesus' own lifestyle—he had no family for which to provide (Matt. 19:12). It would be a gross error, however, to suggest that a general rule of exegesis *always holds true* for every saying of Jesus; the authentic corpus of Jesus' teaching must include simple pronouncements as well as obscure ones, ones of conformity as well as ones of a radical stance.[17]

I am not advocating in all that has been said above, that we should be suspicious of everything written of Jesus in the Gospels. I am saying that the material needs thinking about and should not be accepted as objective happening simply because it appears to be written that way. There are important lessons of exegesis for the fundamentalist to consider here, but there are lessons for the historical critics too. The critics should not cease to be self-critical, for much is discarded by some of them on very weak grounds indeed. Behind the New Testament documents there was a very real and remarkable person that walked and taught in Galilee during the first century. The task of finding this figure we reserve till later.

NOTES

1. The classic study on the difference between the *kerygma* and the *didache* of the early Church is C. H. Dodd's, *The Apostolic Preaching and its Developments,* London, 1951 (see pages 7–35).
2. M. Dibelius, *From Tradition to Gospel,* London, 1971, pages 1–8.
3. The method of harmonising the four Gospels began as early as 170 AD with Tatian's *Diatessaron,* and later on with Origen's *Commentary on John, Book X*; Augustine's, *The Harmonisation of the Gospels,* was written in the fourth century.
4. The terms 'alterations' and 'modifications' are loaded words. Such terms carry the assumption that the Gospel writers have *altered source material with a deliberate motive of deluding the reader and disguising the 'truth'.* I do not use these terms in such a pejorative sense, however. We know that the evangelists were quite liberal and unrestrained in their writing when, for instance, they adapted Old Testament proof-texts and re-applied some of the prophetic texts to further their aims. We also know by consulting a simple synopsis chart that the evangelists have preserved different versions of the same saying which cannot be accounted for by translation from Aramaic to Greek to English. We can only conclude, therefore, that the urgent requirement of the early Christians to present the *kerygma* to the Greek world justified the evangelists in freely adapting their sources as they felt necessary to further their most pressing needs, even though such exercises would inevitably lead to contradictions in the final narratives.

5. J. Jeremias, *The Parables of Jesus*, London 1972, page 120.
6. The preference for the title to be rendered 'The Son of God' as opposed to 'a son of God' is made on thematic grounds, for both translations from the Greek are possible. What is important is what meaning Mark wished to convey by this declaration. If the centurion is merely recognising that Jesus was a *remarkable man* by his facing of death, indeed a 'son of a god', then this hardly carries much evangelistic weight. If, however, his intention was to portray the centurion as a prototype and forerunner of the countless multitudes of heathens who would be converted by the message of the crucified, then *The divine Son-ship* is revealed precisely through his death. The opening confession 'the Son of God' in Mark 1:1 may not be original (it is not in all early manuscripts and it is difficult to imagine why a scribe would wish to delete it), but the theme of the demons recognising his divine status comes early in this Gospel. At Caesarea Philippi the confession of Jesus' status comes from Peter. In Mark 15:38 the significance of Jesus' death for the Jewish world is portrayed in the tearing of the temple curtain. How significant for Mark therefore is the confession of the centurion in the next verse for the Gentile world? See D. E. Nineham, *The Gospel of Mark,* London, 1968, pages 430–431. M. Dibelius, *From Tradition to Gospel,* London, 1971, says: "He recognises in Jesus the Son of God (not, shall we say a son of the gods)—and that this is a miracle since it lies outside historical and human 'possibility'." (page 195)
7. M. Dibelius, op. cit., page 194–195. Dibelius thinks that in the Lucan version there is the recognition of the 'psychological miracle'. It is seen "in numerous martyrologies, viz. the executioner convinced by the martyr. Mark is dealing with a greater miracle, the conversion of an unbeliever by the dying Saviour". (page 195)
8. F. D. Sparks, *A Synopsis of the Gospels*, London, 1970, page 84.
9. J. Jeremias op. cit., pages 77f.; 224f. The allegory is not consistent: the seed in Mark 4:14 = 'word', and in 4:16 the seed = people.
10. Ibid., pages 70f..
11. For a more conservative English view, see C. H. Dodd's criticism, 'The Framework of the Gospel Narrative', in H. K. McArthur's, *In Search of the Historical Jesus,* London, 1970, Ch. 11. Examples like these could go on *ad infinitum*, and the interested reader is advised to contrast the variant versions of sayings, events and parables of the Gospels in the Revised Version, where the language is more direct, so that the point can be fully carried (the task is made simple by consulting a Gospel Synopsis chart, where the gospels are set out side by side—H. F. D. Sparks, *A Synopsis of the Gospels,* or K. Aland, *Synopsis of the Four Gospels*).
12. The classic study is H. E. Todt's, *The Son of Man in the Synoptic Tradition*, London, 1965. See also F. H. Borsch, *The Son of Man in Myth and History*, London, 1967.
13. H. Borsch, *The Christian and Gnostic Son of Man*, London, 1970. A recent criticism of the earliest traditions of the 'Son of Man' sayings has focused on Jeremias' recognition that the Synoptics have eleven identical 'Son of Man' sayings of which the parallel versions have not the title of the 'Son of Man'. Alternatively, some versions have the subject 'I' rather than 'Son of Man', and others vice versa:

1.	And every man who speaks *a word against the Son of Man will be forgiven, but he who* blasphemes against the Holy Spirit will not be forgiven. Luke 12:10	All sins will be forgiven the sons of men and whatever blasphemies they utter, but whoever blasphemes against the Holy Spirit never has forgiveness. Mark 3:28f.
2.	For as Jonah became a sign to the men of Nineveh, *so will the Son of Man* be to this generation. Luke 11:29f./Matt. 16:4	Why does this generation seek a sign? *No sign* shall be given to this generation. Mark 8:12
3.	Everyone who acknowledges me before men, *the Son of Man will* also acknowledge before the angels of God. Luke 12:8	Everyone who acknowledges me before men, I also will acknowledge before my Father who is in heaven. Matt. 10:32

4. And he began to teach them that the Son of Man must suffer many things, and be rejected . . . Mark 8:31/Luke 9:22	From that time Jesus began to show his disciples that he must go to Jerusalem and suffer many things . . . Matt. 16:20f.
5. Who do men say that *the Son of Man is*? Matt. 16:13	Who do men say that *I am*? Mark 8:24/Luke 9:18
6. Blessed are you when men hate you, and when they exclude you and revile you, and cast out your name as evil, on account of the Son of Man. Luke 6:22	Blessed are you when men revile you and persecute you and utter all kinds of evil against you falsely on my account. Matt. 5:11
7. For the *Son of Man* also came not to be served but to serve, and to give his life as a ransom for many. Luke 22:27d	. . . but *I am* among you as one who serves. Mark 10:45/Matt 20:28
8. Truly, I say to you, in the new world, when the *Son of Man* shall sit on his glorious throne, you who have followed me will also sit on twelve thrones judging the twelve tribes of Israel. Matt. 19:28	You are those who have continued with me in my trials; as my Father appointed a kingdom *for me*, so do I appoint for you that you may eat and drink at my table in *my* kingdom, and sit on thrones judging the twelve tribes of Israel. Luke 22:28–30

Discussion of the earliest forms of the 'Son of Man' logia is given in F. H. Borsch, op. cit., pages 15–28. The 'Son of Man' logia are found in Q, a very primitive though still hypothetical source. We have no *a priori* grounds, therefore, in assuming that the Marcan logion always represents the prime source. In saying 1, for example, the Lucan form has obvious parallelism—a known feature of Jesus' sayings—which is not there in the Marcan form. There are parallel sayings found in other parts of the New Testament, which similarly do not have the title of the 'Son of Man', indicating again how freely the evangelists have adopted and applied the title to logia which would not have had it (the *Parousia* of the 'Son of Man' coming in glory in Mark 13:26/Matt. 24:30 compared with Rev. 1:7 and John 19:37).

14. R. Bultmann, 'The Primitive Christian Kerygma and the Historical Jesus', in H. K. McArthur's, *In Search of the Historical Jesus*, pages 161–162; H. Küng, *On Being a Christian*, London, 1977, pages 320; 389; 398.
15. H. Küng op. cit., page 216.
16. Ibid., page 284.
17. The grounds for judging the primacy of a given logion of Jesus are governed by its complyance with the following: (a) it being shorter; (b) it appearing 'harder'; (c) having more 'source' witness; (d) having come from a more reliable 'source'; and (e) being more reflective of Aramaic vocabulary and/or grammatical patterns.

4

UNITY OF THOUGHT IN THE BIBLE

After showing a friend an early draft of chapter 2, 'A Critique of the Fundamentalist's view of the Bible', he asked me to carry out a different task that was far less controversial. He wanted me to look for a unity of thought in the Bible that would contrast with my radical thesis of a diversified Bible. When I set to work on his suggestion, there were unified themes that came readily to mind, but they did not run consistently throughout the Bible. For each one, I could think of notable exceptions to the rule. The task was not becoming very straightforward. I was not too sure that the Bible could be proved to be a unified book. C. H. Dodd had this to say of the Bible:

> The Bible is a unity of diverse writings which together are set forth by the Church as a revelation of God in history.[1]

Naturally, the Bible can be said to be a 'unity' if all that is meant by unity is that it forms one single volume of many constituent books, but fundamentalists see a greater form of unity than that of diverse books brought together under one comprehensive title of the Bible. The case is made by fundamentalists that the unity of the writings verifies the fact that the words composed under God's 'inspiration' are genuine pronouncements by him in written form. Fundamentalists search for evidence in support of the belief that the Bible has a thematic unity of nature and purpose by virtue of it being 'God's Word'. Since God is held to be the overriding author of his Word, it seems reasonable to suppose that we should find *similar thinking*, if not *identical ideas*, preserved in the various books of the Bible. Further, if the Bible has one presiding author, then we could expect to detect a characteristic style, just as is found in many novels of a particular author of fiction, even though such an expectation might subject God to human categories of thought. Although Dodd uses the terms 'unity' and 'diverse' to ascribe a cohesive wholeness to the Bible, those terms surely must have an opposing sense, for they carry more than a trace of contradictory meaning. So, I ask: How can a 'unity' exist in a collection of 'diverse' writings? I am in agreement with Dodd when he speaks of a unity of "consistent narrative", that "gives a kind of 'cavalcade' of human life through many centuries, beginning in the cloudy realms of myths and legends, and emerging into straightforward history",[2] but that hardly tells us much about unity.

In the Old Testament, a case can be made for arguing that the covenant of Yahweh with Israel underlies much early Hebrew religion, though not in every book, of course, and it is more a case of an implicit theme than an explicit citation. The covenant is taken up in the Christian era of revelation as the New *Testament*, to describe the quality of relationship of the chosen community with God, but the ritual seals to the covenants of both Testaments have no unified practice but a number of varied forms and different legislative requirements.

It can be claimed with less certainty that 'God's plan'—made evident through his promises—forms a substantial unifying strand of Old Testament theological thought. There is the question of unfulfilled predictions, and the various biblical promises (e.g. Gen. 3:15, 8:21–22, 12:1–3; II Sam. 7:1–16, etc.) are open to multiple interpretations. It is not easy to see the relevance of Old Testament 'promises' to the New Testament revelation when so few of them are taken up specifically in the New Testament.

The cultic demands of ritual and sacrifice reveal no consistent pattern. The sources illustrate a tension between the priestly documents (Leviticus and the 'P' source of Genesis) and some of the prophets (Amos 5:25 and Jeremiah 7:22–23), to such a degree that one wonders whether the early faith of Yahweh ever prescribed sacrifice and cultic offerings at all.

To highlight Israel as being consistently the people of God in the Old Testament is nothing more than stating the obvious. The Bible is a *historical revelation*, and a revelation through and for Israel, just as the life of Jesus, his death and resurrection, and the practices and issues of the Church are the subject of the New. We would expect to find such a restricted focus by authors upon their own people. The authors' primary interests are likely to have been their own nation or church, and the controlling factors of the canon would naturally have left preserved the writings which best suited the interests of propaganda. There are three exceptions to this restricted focus, however: first, the book of Jonah suggests that the people of Nineveh found favour with God; second, there are some pronouncements of the prophets which hint at an extension of God's mission to all nations; third, the Gospel message of the New Testament similarly extends the boundaries of God's favour well beyond the Jewish race.

The stereotype pattern of the book of Judges—Israel going astray, the people repenting, God sending a deliverer and fortune resulting—is a literary device that illustrates a particular theological interpretation of history. The pattern does not follow consistently throughout the Bible but breaks down in the period of the exile. This, in turn, prompts a new religious outlook and interpretation of God's historical intervention with his people.

Terms such as *development* and *fulfilment* are used by fundamentalists to get round the problems of diversity and contradiction, but they are strange qualifications of the idea of unity. Unity must take on board the idea of that which is of the same nature, character or substance, not that which is similar, transitional or developmental. I think it is more fitting to use a term like 'continuity' when grouping similar topics and interests throughout the Bible, for there is clearly a continuous theme of the community of God occupying both Testaments—Paul describes the Church as the 'Israel of God'.[3]

In the early source material of the Gospels, Jesus' existential message of the call to the kingdom can clearly be demonstrated to be different in form and content to the messages (*kerygmata*) of the early Christian communities.

The varieties of primitive confessional formulae about Jesus have taken on different theological outlooks. There is little unity other than that of their subject, the 'Lord Jesus Christ' of the post-easter faith (or as Küng prefers, *the post-paschal faith*).

The concepts of ministry found in Paul's Hellenistic churches differ from those of the Jerusalem community, represented by James and Peter.

There is no decreed or unified pattern of worship found in the New Testament. Jesus prescribed no formal sacrament, as far as the sources disclose, and the meanings given to the sacraments of Baptism and the Lord's Supper serve different purposes for different writers: an eschatological purpose in some cases and a liturgical one in others. Neither is there any uniformity of religious experience found in the New Testament, apart from the means by which the experience came to the recipient, i.e. the Spirit.

There are many Christologies found in the New Testament and each is peculiar to its author. The varied presentations are, in the main, incompatible with each other. The Christological outlooks may differ marginally with some biblical authors, but with others the differences are considerable. For example Matthew's Christology may differ little from Mark's, but there is a considerable difference in Christology between Colossians (1:15–20) and I John (4:2–3), between Philippians (2:5–8) and Luke (2:6–7) and between Ephesians (2:4–7) and Hebrews (1:9; 4:15). The overall range of New Testament Christologies is considered by scholars to be completely inconsistent, philosophically lacking in reason, and wholly beyond systematic harmony and syncretism.[4]

It is misleading therefore to speak of a New Testament teaching as though uniform thinking and identity of expression existed in the minds of its various authors. On the contrary, it is more fitting to speak of the teachings' of the books of the New Testament, because each author has his own particular style, purpose, bias and emphasis as he commits himself to writing. Predispositions and personal slants are obvious in some books yet only discernible with close study in others. In some cases, it may not always be clear what that slant may be, and what might have prompted a given piece of writing in the first place (such as the Gospel of Mark, where a primary motive or singular clear-cut theological perspective is not easy to identify). As far as the Gospels are concerned, what stands out clearly is the very different and non-uniform style of each of the four evangelists when compared with each other; in no way do the four Gospels form a single cohesive whole. J. Dunn's statement on the lack of unity in the New Testament seems to me quite apposite:

> Christians will simply have to accept the fact of different expressions and interpretations of 'the kerygma' and live with them—accepting the necessity and the validity of the different expressions, and not being upset over them or grieving over them as 'sinful divisions' or 'heretical schisms'.[5]

A discerning reader of the Bible may well ask: 'Can we recognise the Yahweh of the Old Testament from what we understand of him as the Father of Jesus in the New?' This is a vexed question in the light of the development of moral consciousness, and the question is quite legitimate when set against some traditional projections of Yahweh in the Old Testament. When fundamentalists attempt to harmonise the various pictures of God in the Old and New Testaments, there is a tendency to lose some of the distinctive religious and cultural edges of the different portrayals. When we contrast some of the earliest cruder conceptions of God with the modern humanistic outlook of the world, we similarly come up against moral difficulties. The error lies in pushing for universal unity of presentation and understanding when a richer picture can be seen by using the method of comparison and contrast. I wonder, then, which of the following assertions is most accurate? Does the Bible reveal *something* of God, or *many things* of God, or a *pluralistic presentation of God?*

These questions are not merely of technical, philosophical or academic interest; they have enormous practical consequences for the divided Church and for individual Christian conduct and discipleship. Dunn's exhaustive study on New Testament unity and diversity presents an accurate assessment of multiple confessions:

> We have surely seen enough to recognise the justice of E. Käsemann's famous claim: 'the New Testament canon does not, as such, constitute the foundation of the unity of the Church. On the contrary, as such . . . it provides the basis for the multiplicity of the confessions.' This conclusion has not been sufficiently reckoned with in the twentieth-century ecumenical movement, and its possible corollaries for modern denominational diversity need to be thought through with much greater care and thoroughness.[6]

There is only one element of biblical teaching that can be presented as a consistent theme; it is the idea of God bringing order from chaos. In Genesis 1–2 the Creation is the result of God's word over chaos. The perfect order of Paradise is ruined by the disobedience of man and woman, and chaos returns. There are further falls of man—Cain slays his brother, the flood in Noah's day and the story of the tower of Babel are God's pronouncement on the wickedness of man. Genesis 12 to Revelation 22 can be viewed as the programme of salvation and the restoration of order from chaos. This scheme, however, is not obvious throughout the whole Bible; it is only an outline that is apparent in a few biblical passages. The scheme could therefore be an artificial construction of a final redactor whose aim was to re-write the traditions emphasising his own point of view. So, in attempting to satisfy my friend by finding an overall unity in the Bible, I must confess to have failed.

Considering that the Bible has little unity of thought but rather that its pages provide substantial evidence of a rich deposit of multifarious themes and ideas, it is questionable whether one can legitimately base the authorisation for a lifestyle upon something appearing as uncertain and unclear as an inerrant and infallible Bible, if inerrancy and infallibility are the natural corollary of the Bible being a unity. Fundamentalists cling on to this belief, since it has become the authorisation of their lifestyles, but why is this, and what is the basis for such a stand? In closing the first part, we shall explore the fundamentalist's need for an *authority*, initially through the doctrine of 'the inspiration of the Bible', and finally through the belief that *revelations* from God can be found within 'inspired' biblical writings.

NOTES

1. C. H. Dodd, *The Bible Today*, London, 1946, page 14.
2. Ibid., page 2.
3. This cannot be understated. The Church clearly saw herself as the continuation of the *community* of God, but with a difference; the community of God was conceived in some mystical

sense as existing 'in Christ'. This continuing identity was variously expressed as the 'Israel of God' (Gal. 6:16), the 'People for God's own possession' (I Peter 2:9), 'Kings and Priests to God' (Rev. 1:6) and the 'Righteous Remnant' (Is. 10:22–23, Rom. 9:27–28), C. H. Dodd, op. cit., page 70.

4. J. D. G. Dunn, *Unity and Diversity in the New Testament*, pages 29–32, 121–123, 148–149, 171–173, 199–202, 226–231. Dunn's comment is apt:

> The fact is that *there is no one single christology in first-century Christianity but a diversity of christologies.* There is no single Christology to which we can point and say, 'That is the view of Christ which the churches of the first century recognised as orthodox', page 226 [Dunn's italics].

5. Ibid., page 32.
6. Ibid., page 122.

5

THE PROCESS OF BIBLICAL 'INSPIRATION'

We shall now examine the biblical basis for the fundamentalist belief in the doctrine of the 'inspiration' of the Bible. Although most Christians consent to the belief that the Bible is inspired by God, it is the fundamentalist that draws far-reaching consequences from the belief. We begin by posing a series of questions, the first of which is rhetorical and which only the fundamentalist is required to answer:

a) Why don't all Christian sects and denominations professing a belief in an inerrant Bible arrive at the same doctrinal basis of faith?—*Is God the author of confusion?*

The problem is startlingly obvious to critical scholars but appears never to dissuade the members of fundamentalist sects and denominations from continuing in their exclusive walks of faith. D. Cupitt's assessment of them seems to me to be accurate:

> All those neo-conservative Christians who are so numerous today appear to identify 'being a sound Christian' with 'assenting to all the right propositions'. Having a strong faith is equated with scoring the maximum on a doctrinal check-list—and this on the part of people who sincerely believe that their own religion is biblical![1]

b) Why does the Bible contain inaccuracies if it is held to be inerrant? Though a few New Testament passages might suggest scripture is inspired, are we to infer from these that the Bible is indeed inerrant—having no mistakes at all? The mistakes that are perceived to be there—having been determined by critical research and conflicting empirical evidence—are they to be regarded as being not really there in actual fact, but serving as examples of personal errors on the part of scholars who are deluded in not having taken 'God's Word' with sufficient piety and reverence?

We have previously explored some contradictions and inaccuracies in the Gospel records, with the result that it cannot be maintained that the Bible is wholly unified; there clearly are textual, numerological, cosmological, factual and historical errors in both the New and the Old Testament, which cannot be explained away by the argument that the authors have made use of metaphor and idiom. Surely such 'mistakes' cannot be wholly imagination on the part of scholars having no respect or reverence for God's Word? In my experience, I have not found many critical scholars show an absence of respect for the Bible; I have found quite the opposite in fact. Readers must judge for themselves.

Let us ask two further groups of questions on the doctrine of biblical inerrancy, which are of a psychological nature, and which will be impossible to answer definitively. We ask the questions in order to expose the nature of the problem that arises when fundamentalists claim biblical infallibility:

c) What was the precise mechanism whereby God communicated his thoughts through the minds of human beings? Where are the distinctive boundaries to be drawn? What was God's part, what was man's? Where was the freedom of the human mind if God took over? Were the inspired writers of Holy Writ mindless automatons? Were their cognitive and psychic processes manipulated in some telepathic way such that they became driven to compose words and sentences from concepts which were alien and meaningless to their normal experience and cognitive processes?

d) Through what medium does God's 'inspiration' work? Did God speak audibly through the Hebrew tongue to Moses, polished Greek to Luke and John, and Aramaic to Jesus? Did he cause men and women to have dream-visions or put them under trance-states and override completely their mental faculties? Did he send angelic spiritual beings to 'men of God' with messages that were expressed orally, or by intuition, or in written script? Might he have programmed men and women thus to arrive at ideas which they perceived to be their own but which, in actual fact, were not really their own but the result of his omnipotent and deterministic control?

THE 'INSPIRATION' OF GOD

'Inspiration' is understood, historically, as the condition described by Küng as one in which "the spirit seizes a person in ecstasy and where individuality appears to be extinguished under the divine frenzy". The idea of inspiration in secular usage has the meaning of a person being energised, uplifted, or enthused, to apprehend something otherwise beyond normal cognisance, and the term is commonly applied within art, poetry and science. Yet, fundamentalists reserve the word for a unique description of the divine influence upon the human subject when composing biblical verse. In wishing to emphasise the *dissolution of human individuality*, fundamentalists utilise the term to describe the authoritative character of a biblical author in the maintenance of the Bible's inerrancy and infallibility. For fundamentalists, the qualification of a writing being 'inspired' by God is to see it in some way as being consistent and unified. I have tried to show that such a belief contradicts the facts. Fundamentalists would probably regard the whole phenomenon of God's communication with man as a mystery beyond human comprehension, which I think is avoiding the problem. For myself, this will not do, for the more one becomes immersed in the biblical world, and the more one is able to grasp the historical situation within which each writer of the Bible lived, the more the human factors of divine communion become apparent and the mystery becomes intelligible. However, we are jumping the gun! What does 'inspiration' mean in relation to *scripture*?

'Inspiration' and *Scripture*

Both the New and the Old Testament are regarded by Christians as sacred *scripture* unequivocally, and irrespective of what translations are used. They are believed to be God-given documents for our salvation and enlightenment, but there is the need to qualify what is meant by seeing the Bible as something given by God. The Bible for the fundamentalist, carries with it its own claim of authority, to be 'God's Word', simply because it is 'inspired' by God (*God-breathed*) and, therefore, by implication, inerrant and infallible. It carries a double stamp of infallibility in cases where one authority authenticates another. For example, when Jesus—who speaks in God's name—cites David by quoting a Psalm (Mark 12:35), he is declaring, by inference, that David wrote the Psalm. When Paul—as Christ's apostle—uses the figure of Adam in support of his thesis (Rom. 5:12f.), he is disclosing this figure, by inference, to be the historical person who fathered the human race. Who are we, argue the fundamentalists, to question such monumental figures as Jesus and Paul? So, runs the argument, David wrote the Psalm and Adam must have been a historical person. This type of reasoning, however, takes us round in circles; we cannot verify one possibility with another unverified possibility. We cannot prove that David wrote a particular Psalm or that Adam was a historical person by adducing the beliefs—or the *recorded beliefs*—of those of a later age. We come back to the word that carries these beliefs along, the word 'inspiration'. What does 'inspiration' mean, then? What are the implications of applying the word to give authoritative status to the *scriptures* as the 'Word of God'?

The word 'inspired' is extremely rare in the New Testament and its meaning is not clear. It occurs in II Timothy 3:16, and this text forms the basis for fundamentalists to claim that *all scripture* is 'inspired' by God, but to argue the case—whether or not the assertion is true—from this verse is a misapplication of the passage. The context of the word is that of holding on to what the reader has been instructed. Paul says to Timothy:

> . . . Remember that from early childhood you have been familiar with the sacred writings which have power to make you wise and lead you to salvation through faith in Christ Jesus. *Every inspired scripture* has its use for teaching the truth and refuting error
>
> A transliteration of the passage reads thus: Every scripture God-breathed and profitable for teaching, for reproof, for correction, for instruction . . .
>
> II Tim. 3:16

The expression "God-breathed" (*theopneustos*), or "inspired scripture", is not defined in the sentence or the whole passage. *'All scripture'* (AV) can be a correct translation but it is not likely to be what was intended. Even if the sense is stretched to include the whole Bible, it remains difficult to know at the time of Paul's writing which books constituted *scripture*. The quotation carries the assumption of the authoritative status of *scripture* without qualification, but it does not verify the case, it merely states it. The point of the statement is to establish the *scriptures'* efficacy in declaring truth and prescribing acceptable Christian conduct; it is not to authenticate its God-given character. That is assumed. Considering that no 'inspired' *scriptures* were selected to form the body of the New Testament at this time, and considering that no Jewish canon of the Old Testament was fixed till well after this letter was written (at the earliest, the Synod of Jamnia in AD 90), I wonder precisely what books were viewed as *scripture*. Can we know what Paul regarded definitively as *scripture* so as to be able to verify a given piece of writing as an infallible expression of the mind of God? Let us expand the question of what we can know of *scripture* from what is known of the New Testament canon.

Scripture and the New Testament Canon

The early Christians saw in the Old Testament an *authority* that gave shape to their new Christ-centred existence. They studied diligently the Septuagint Old Testament (Greek version), as the character of the Church became Hellenistic, but, whether Hebrew or Greek, the Old Testament stood as the authoritative *scripture* for Christians, just as it had for all the divided factions within Judaism.

The writings of the New Testament were collected together within a much shorter period of time compared to the Old. Some were not broadly accepted as authoritative *scripture* at the beginning, but after a lively period of debate the canon of 'Holy Writ' became settled.[2]

The canon of *scripture* arose from the need to reinforce and consolidate the Church's faith. It arose to counteract a movement in which Christianity was losing its distinctive identity by being absorbed within the syncretistic religions of the Graeco-Roman world. The battle that brought about a fixed collection of Christian writings was not prompted by the trials of the martyrs under tyrannical rulers like Domitian, but by a much more subtle and insidious enemy: *the theological compromising of the early kerygma.* Church Fathers, such as Irenaeus, fought hard and long to preserve the 'true doctrine' against teachings of rival groups (in his case, the Gnostics) whose beliefs were not wildly astray from orthodox Christian teaching. This fanatical drive to secure the 'one true Faith' is still with us today. It is erroneous indeed, for it is based upon four false premises:

(a) *that the Church of the early period was wholly united in its beliefs.*

(b) *that 'orthodox' Christian teaching is easy to ascertain from the early sources.*

(c) *that the Church was uniform and distinctive at the close of the first century.*

(d) *and that the Church's early authority figures were clearly evident and universally accepted by all the first-century Christian centres.*

The decision about who was acknowledged as the pillar of the 'true Faith' and who as the heretic, or, conversely, what teaching was held as orthodox and what heresy, depends largely upon what side of the fence the judge may be sitting. Secondly, the very motive of attempting to establish a unity of belief by fixing the canon suggests to us that such a unity never existed at all in the earliest Christian period. What is clear from a study of the Patristic period is that the early Christian theologians were not so bound by biblical authority as the sole arbiter for true faith as I think some fundamentalists are today. It also seems to me that an unprejudiced reading of the letters of Paul hardly suggests that the author regarded his own writing as infallible to the degree that he regarded the Old Testament as infallible. In retrospect, we see that the written word of the Bible has become the sacred authority of scripture, yet all the books of the New Testament cannot be of equal spiritual worth. J. Dunn believes that a greater spiritual depth can be found in a few of Luther's writings than in some late New Testament documents—a view based on the spiritual substance of the writings' content.[3] The infallible nature of *scripture* is the inference drawn from writings' claim to have been 'inspired' by God. If an author who was widely accepted as being in tune with the *mind of God* should write a book—such as Solomon in the

Old Testament, Paul in the New—then that book would automatically have been accepted as *scripture*, but not all religious books are written by clearly known authors. Some books had pseudonymous or anonymous authors, and others were fictitious. In such cases, different criteria had to be used when settling the canon. It appears that time had to be an essential factor for religious literature to be classified by those having the say as having been 'inspired' by God. Whatever the quality of its content, without the passing of time to lose its *mundane* character and add to its sense of *mystique*, a book or a letter or a Gospel cannot be credited with authoritative status as being binding upon the way we live, as *scripture*, as 'Holy Writ' or as the 'Word of God'. Another essential factor is power, where he who shouts loudest wins! Those holding the power, exercise for themselves the right to determine what ought to be selected within the canon of the New Testament, what is to serve as an *authority*, and what is to be rejected. I am obviously not thinking of exploitative 'power' here, as seen in political monopolies, but religious leaders of the past have been guilty of wielding the most insidious and coercive forms of power when engineering what they want or what they believe to be in the cause of truth. The 'written' *word* was not the only *word* listened to in the early Christian period. There were some like Papias who would not trust the *written word* that later became *scripture,* but preferred instead to listen to the *spoken word* of those that had been in the company of the first disciples:

> For I did not suppose that information from books would help me so much as the word of a living and surviving voice.[4]

The idea of *scripture* being a broadly recognised datum to serve as an *authority* is unsound, therefore. We cannot be absolutely certain what *scripture* was for Paul, apart from some books which constituted what we now recognise to be the Old Testament. To argue that *scripture* is the evidence that God has 'inspired' the Bible, as fundamentalists do, will not get us very far. It is mounting one uncertainty upon another.

THE PSYCHOLOGICAL IMPLICATIONS OF 'INSPIRED' WRITING

J. W. Burgon, in a sermon preached at Oxford in 1860, has this to say of the authorship and origin of the Bible:

> The Bible is none other than the voice of Him that sitteth upon the Throne! Every book of it, every chapter of it, every verse of it, every word of it, every letter of it, is the direct utterance of the Most High![5]

This is a declaration that the writings of the biblical scriptures are in sum the very 'Word of God', not in part, but in full, not by degree, but in entirety. It is a rhetorical affirmation of the divine origin of *all scripture* by virtue of the Bible being 'inspired' by God. There is a natural and inescapable corollary to this belief in verbal inspiration. It is the contention that the text of the Bible must in every part be inerrant, with the revealed truths being infallible. Yet, the moment we claim the Bible is inerrant and infallible, we come against obstacles. We set the Bible up for the sceptic to fire his cynicism at it, and quite justifiably, as C. H. Spurgeon has said: "Defend the Bible? I would as soon defend a lion." [6]

Burgon's statement does not say explicitly that the Bible was verbally inspired by God, though it is difficult to avoid drawing the conclusion that he implied it. Added to which, not all fundamentalists would subscribe to the view that the *scriptures* were dictated in any mechanical sense. The Koran was supposed to have been preserved in heaven and dictated sentence by sentence as Allah's direct word to man, infallibly, but the Bible does not make any such claim of 'verbal inspiration'. This belief of inerrancy—classically known as 'verbal inspiration'—can find little support from internal biblical or extra-biblical evidence. There is an unmistakable difference in the form and style of the Hebrew and Greek *scriptures* of the various books of the Bible, and there is no evidence that the Bible has been miraculously preserved from scribal and textual errors in the course of transmission.

W. Lambert has written on the subject of 'inspiration',[7] and in a letter I have received from him, he has defined 'inspiration' as:

> The effect of God's Spirit on particular humans so that their thoughts and actions are raised above their natural level toward God. One can understand this very easily because the same happens in human society with outstanding leaders, e.g., such a person draws out of people more than they would of their own selves ever achieve . . .

I present Lambert's view because it represents a way out of the dilemma of authorisation. His position is not one of mainstream fundamentalism but could well be described as a compromise position. When he compares 'inspiration' of God to the effect of a highly influential human leader, we immediately lose the point of the uniqueness of divine 'inspiration' as compared with that of human inspiration; the assertion becomes an article of faith that is beyond verification.

Another text often used in this debate is II Peter 1:20–21:

> No one can interpret any prophecy of Scripture by himself. For it was not through any human whim that men prophesied of old; men they were, but, impelled by the Holy Spirit, they spoke the words of God.
>
> A transliteration of the passage reads thus: This firstly knowing, that every prophecy of scripture of [its] own solution not becomes; for not by will of man was borne prophecy at any time, but by Spirit Holy being borne spoke from God men.
>
> (Other ancient authorities read "moved by the Holy Spirit holy men of God spoke")

I will pass over the question of the authorship of II Peter. The context of the above appears to be that of rooting out heresy and false prophets—in the form of false predictors and impostors. The referent of the passage appears to be the question of avoiding individualistic interpretations of prophecies that are God-given. The term 'impelled' (*pheromenoi*) is variously rendered by fundamentalists as 'God-driven' or 'God-moved'—expressions describing the subject being carried away by *divine frenzy*, out of personal control in the sense of Küng's *extinguishing of individuality*. It is a language that portrays the absolute overruling character of God to signify his endorsement of written statements of revelation—there is no error or human opinion. This position cannot be maintained if we mean by it that the whole Bible is unified, inerrant and infallible, as we have seen. What I am saying is that the assertion of the writer of II Peter 1:20–21 is incapable of verification, and is evidently wrong if taken to mean that all writings of prophecy must always be right because they are recorded in the Bible.

A more precise question, however, might move us forward. *When we believe the Bible to be God's inspired Word, what should we expect to find in a book of such claim?* In other words: *should we expect the Bible to be inerrant and to contain infallible truths?* The fundamentalist might answer: 'The Bible will contain all that appertains to the truth'. Yet, what is meant is unclear. There is a self-contradiction: if we search in the Bible for truth in one sense, and then expect to find it there in another, we have argued in a circle! The question also postulates an agreed understanding of *God's inspired Word*, which cannot be assumed. We could equally ask the same question by omitting the word *inspired.*

Now, let us move on and explore the idea that the work of an 'inspired' writer implies a valid and incontrovertible truth of God being communicated to man. This view holds that any alternative use of an inspired thought to mean little more than an intuition, premonition or inkling, carries no absolute status to serve as an *authority* (we speak more generally of people being inspired than ideas or writing being inspired, but if a person being inspired chooses to write under such a condition, then his writing may be said to be inspired). When we claim that the written records of the revelation of God are 'inspired' words, we are saying in effect that in some way or other God has influenced the writing of the Bible (and, by inference, perhaps, monitored the process of its preservation), but is it reasonable to conclude from this premise that it proves or implies biblical inerrancy? Influence does not equate with ideas infallibly transmitted from one to another. We have to ask in what way God may influence a person. I may influence my students to master a new skill of literacy, but that doesn't mean that the final skill skill produced is of my own making. I may influence my students to think more abstractly or reason more objectively, but that doesn't mean that they will think as I do. I may influence the birth of a new insight by either an incidental or purposeful comment, but that doesn't mean that the insight has come from me. We cannot prove biblical inerrancy, therefore, from the contention that God has influenced or 'inspired' the Bible's authors, unless we *a priori* establish with greater precision what we mean by 'inspiration'. We are required to explain the way the divine influence should be understood, rather than accept the doctrine of biblical inerrancy at face value. Further, it would be useful if we could avoid any generalisations by keeping clear in our minds *what truth* is understood as having been 'inspired' by God. For example, which of the following might be understood to be a divinely 'inspired' writing expressing an infallible truth:

a) an *intellectual apprehension* of what God is like: whether he has an essence or personality; whether he is one or many?

b) an *understanding of a metaphysical unknown*, such as the following: the nature of man; life beyond death; the Devil; heaven and the underworld?

c) a *conception of how history might unfold:* whether there is a plan that can be predicted with any certainty, or whether history is determined?

d) an *awareness of universal conduct* expected by God from man: what precise moral choice must the individual make in every situation?

e) a *belief in whether or not God might intervene* in individual or national history, and if so, how might we imagine such an intervention, given that it does not violate freedom of will and ascribe human caprice to God?

When fundamentalists claim that the Bible gives us authoritative pronouncements on all or some of these teachings, they do so under the comprehensive belief that all such pronouncements are 'inspired' by God. They may segregate some moral imperatives as having a relative or situational relevance, but they rarely suggest that others of the list are optional or conditional beliefs.

It would be pretentious for me to claim that the writing of this book was 'inspired' in the sense that fundamentalists believe the Bible to be inspired, no matter how many hours were put into the reading, drafting, re-drafting of each successive manuscript put forward for publication. It also seems to me that some parts of *scripture*, such as the historical books of the Old Testament, bear little evidence of 'inspiration', just a painstaking effort to write accounts from extant source material, similar in fact to the diligent endeavours of the modern historian. We are driven to pose two radical questions, therefore, that fundamentalists are loath to ask: *Are some parts of scripture more inspired than others? Are some parts of scripture not inspired at all?*

Even if the fundamentalist might concede part of the mystery element and accept that the human recipient has a part to play in the complex process of a communication of God, that it is not all a one-sided phenomenon, there still remains some confusion over what he or she might expect to find in a book that is believed to be *wholly* 'inspired' by God. If the divine Spirit pervaded the thinking of those who wrote the Bible, this ought to be recognised in the content of the proclaimed message, I suggest, rather than by any self-disclosure that the writing was a record of something genuinely spoken by God. A more legitimate method of enquiry, then, is to lay aside completely the presupposition of an 'inspired'—and thereby, inerrant and infallible—Bible and look into the spiritual heart of the biblical faith. We shall follow this line of enquiry in subsequent chapters, but before doing so, let us give some thought as to whether the *authority* of the Bible is that it contains records of genuine *revelation* from God.

NOTES

1. D. Cupitt, *Taking Leave of God*, London, 1980, page 125.
2. F. D. Moule presents an analysis of the problems centring on the New Testament canon in *The Birth of the New Testament*, London, 1966, Chapter 10, 'Collecting and Sifting the Documents'. After discussing the disciplinary and theological motives and principles behind the long process of the New Testament canon's coming into being, Moule concludes: "All the time, moreover, it is viewed, so far as possible, as a human process." He makes this bold assertion, however, with a somewhat weakening qualification: "That it is also the tale of a divine overruling of the gropings and mistakes of men is here assumed without further discussion." (page 209) Summarising the evidence of chapter 10, we find the following stages leading up to and confirming the 'canon' of scripture:
   a) The twelve eye-witnesses of the scope of the *kerygma* provide the first stage of authorisation—from the beginning to the resurrection (Acts 1:23f.).
   b) Reasoning based upon the 'argument from Scripture'—meaning, naturally, the Old Testament (mainly the Septuagint version): "There is no known official pronouncement embodying a Jewish 'canon' of scripture until near the end of the New Testament period [although there is evidence of long debate before this]. The Synod of Jamnia [Jabne] in AD 90 is usually claimed as the occasion of this pronouncement." (page 188)

c) Pre-Gospel sources (tracts we might imagine) in circulation in the various churches. Then, the four Gospels—probably Mark first (prior to AD 70), followed by the other two Synoptics, Matthew and Luke.

d) Marcion, at about AD 140, composed his heretical revision of the Gospels, in which he may have worked from the four Gospels collected as part of the canon. The earliest extant manuscripts—the *Chester Beatty papyri* and the *Synaitic Syriac*—take us back to AD 250, or earlier, for the four existing together. But the Gospel of Peter (AD 150) and Tatian's famous *Diatessaron*—the conflation of the four into a single Gospel (similarly, at about AD 150)—suggest an early date of collection.

e) The Pauline corpus was collected at about AD 180, as evidenced by the fact that the letters were cited by the martyrs of Scilli or Scillium.

f) Of the Johannine corpus, we know very little.

g) Ultimately, II Peter, Jude, I, II John and Hebrews were confirmed as being part of the canon, along with the other books of the New Testament already accepted in Athanasius' 39th Paschal letter of AD 367 and the Council of Laodicea.

All in all, it was a very contentious period of controversy and strife regarding the selection of authoritative documents to bolster and consolidate the 'orthodox' Faith against heresy. Some documents were known in the earliest period but have subsequently been lost (a letter from Laodicea, Col. 4:16, for example). Apart from the disputes over the authorship of books like Ephesians, Colossians, Matthew, John, Hebrews, II Peter and Revelation, fictitious authorship was known to exist (page 190); this leads to uncertainty regarding the tradition of some of the book's ascribed authors. There is evidence, also, that the rigorous standards of criticism that were evident after AD 150, may not have been exercised in the earlier period (K. Aland, page 192).

3. J. D. G. Dunn, *Unity and Diversity in the New Testament,* London, 1977, page 386, writes:

> . . . nor would I want to say that the New Testament writings are canonical because they were more inspired than other and later Christian writings. Almost every Christian who wrote in an authoritative way during the first two centuries of Christianity claimed the same sort of inspiration for their writing as Paul had for his. And I would want to insist that in not a few compositions Martin Luther and Charles Wesley, for example, were as, if not more inspired, than the author of II Peter.

4. Eusebius, *Ecclesiastical History*, Volume I:I, Ch. 39, Loeb Classical Library, translated by Kirsopp Lake, London, 1949, pages 291–293: Papias' statement applies to the 'Oracles of the Lord', and is often cited to illustrate the divided views on authority in pre-Gospel times.
5. J. W. Burgon, *Inspiration and Interpretation*, reprinted 1905, page 86. The text of his sermon was II Timothy 3:16. Burgon's quotation is a popular one, which is cited and discussed by J. I. Packer, *'Fundamentalism' and the Word of God*, reprinted 1958, pages 9–14, 178–180. W. Lambert, *Inspiration and Revelation*, reprinted 1990, also quotes this statement in his treatment on biblical revelation, page 4.
6. Cited by J. I. Packer, op. cit., in the Foreword.
7. W. Lambert, *Inspiration and Revelation*, reprinted 1990, Edinburgh.

6

THE AUTHORITY OF BIBLICAL REVELATION

Having myself been spiritually brought up within a fundamentalist sect, I was expected to believe the following without question: that the Genesis Creation story was a factual and scientific account; that Adam and Eve were real people; that the Fall was historical; that Moses parted the Red Sea and received tablets of stone from God; that God brought down the walls of Jericho using Joshua as his general; that Elijah ascended to heaven; that an angel stopped the mouths of lions for Daniel; that Jesus withered a fig tree and caused a fish to be caught with a coin in its mouth for his tax; and that raised bodies once roamed around Jerusalem. All must have happened because the 'inspired' Word of God has recorded them as historical events. I do not dispute the reality of all that might be regarded as *miraculous* or *supernatural*, but I do feel obliged to question such episodes as objective 'history', just as I question the belief that the end of the world may still come owing to the fact that the first believers were of that persuasion. When I became a Christian, I was expected to accept this whole package of beliefs because they were *revealed* in a book which had become my *authority*.

THE RECORD OF A REVELATION FROM GOD

Regularly used religious terms without precision of thought can lead to misunderstanding. When wishing to preserve biblical authority, there is confusion amongst fundamentalists over the similar notions of the 'inspiration of God' and the 'revelation of God'. A short article by W. Lambert, *Inspiration and Revelation,*[1] examines many of the issues that surround these two quite distinct ideas. Although the article is brief, it is informative. Let us consider for the moment the question of God *revealing something to man* by looking at a passage often quoted in this context, the opening verse of the Letter to the Hebrews:

> In many and various ways God spoke of old to our fathers by the prophets; but in these last days he has spoken to us by a Son . . .
>
> Heb. 1:1 RSV

The first part of this statement is an overview of the Old Testament period of revelation, but the "various ways" are not to be understood as being synonymous with the written books of the Old Testament. It is also certain that "the prophets" refers not only to those 'men of God' known as the classical prophets, but to all those who "of old" received revelations from God. The revelation coming through the medium of writing is one amongst many "various ways" that God uses to reveal something to man. Less than one third of the Old Testament is prefaced with the formula, 'Thus saith the Lord', or an equivalent phrase; even these sections are best understood as records of those words, rather than the utterances written up verbatim.

Forms of biblical revelation other than written words include the following:

a) the evidence of the 'heavens'—what we call the universe.

b) dreams and visions granted to 'men of God'.

c) visitations of angels, often in disguise.

d) the mysterious use of Urim and Thummim by the Levitical priesthood.

e) significant events of Israelite history—by far the most common form of revelation.

We are told that this broad range of God's revelation closed with the words of God's Son. It would be very misleading, however, to equate the phrase, ". . . he has spoken to us by a Son" with '. . . he has spoken to us through the New Testament'. Not only was the New Testament canon far from complete at the time of writing, but there is no evidence that Jesus committed any of his teaching to the written word. We are justified, therefore, in concluding that the New Testament is the *record* of the message "spoken to us by a Son", not a verbatim record *per se*, just as we are justified in concluding that the Old Testament is the *record* of the revelation of God, not the revelation itself. God reveals himself through a more comprehensive range of media than the written Bible. Each biblical author should not be understood as having interpreted the revelation in an unbiased sense. So the revelation of God is to be seen as being much more than the Bible, not as being identical with it. The words will inevitably have elements of human judgement.

'OFFENDING PASSAGES' IN THE BIBLE

Separating the idea of 'God's revelation' from the written word of the Bible, as Lambert does, is not nearly so contentious for fundamentalists as questioning the claim that God has 'inspired' an inerrant Bible. Also, there are many respected biblical scholars who hold the presupposition that the Bible is an *authority* on 'the truth' without substantiating in what way a book can record such 'truths' infallibly.[2] They qualify what they understand by a written work having authoritative status, by resorting to the belief that it has been 'inspired' by God. Yet, there is often no attempt to verify the proposition of the Bible being the Word of God in the light of some of the material found in it that describes the deeds of the 'worthies of old' as despicable and which have been authorised by a God believed to be holy and moral. Lambert refers to this material as *offending passages*. We may take as examples the following: the butchering action of the Levite who dismembered his concubine's body and sent the pieces throughout the clans of Israel to summon their support for vengeance (Judges 19–20); or the impulsive vow of Jephthah to sacrifice his daughter as a "whole-offering" (Judges 11:29–31); or Elisha's cursing of a group of children and their subsequent slaughter by a bear (II Kings 2:23–24); or Saul's merciless slaughter of the Amalekites, including the women, children and babes in arms, for an act their forefathers had committed in a previous generation (I Sam. 15), to mention just a few. It takes little discernment to see that these deeds hardly reflect the Spirit of Christ, yet they are preserved in the 'inspired' scriptures of God's Word. If what is meant by 'inspiration' is little more than excelled *human motivation and intuition* to perceive something brilliant or ingenious, then there is no problem, for inaccuracy and fallibility are permissible. If on the other hand, 'inspiration' infers that a divine mind has *revealed* unconditional and eternal truths—whether in deeds or attitudes—that are not contingent upon cultural beliefs of people at certain periods of time, there is indeed a major problem!

We cannot get round the problem by suggesting that *offensive passages* serve as moral examples of how not to behave. In some instances the behaviour of biblical heroes and heroines is condoned, or even applauded, and in others their behaviour is simply ignored, or passed by with little to no comment. There is no indication in the text of divine disapproval! God not only sanctions some of the deeds, he orders them!

We cannot close our eyes to the problems that some of the imprecatory Psalms present to a morally educated person seeking consistency. Psalm 137, for example, was written by a poet in captivity and contains a commendable spiritual attitude of allegiance to Jerusalem, the city of God: "If I forget you, O Jerusalem, let my right hand wither away!" Yet, the Psalm closes by venting uncompromising hostility and vengeance on the wives and children of the enemy: "Happy the man who repays you for all that you did to us! Happy is he who shall seize your children and dash them against the rock!" We are justified in being suspicious of a poet speaking under divine 'inspiration' when uttering sentiments such as these. The first pledge is indeed noble and virtuous, but the final pronouncement, from the Christian perspective, is clearly 'un-inspired'—except, possibly, in the view of those who support sectarian violence! The dilemma is not removed by acknowledging that this sentiment requesting God to act destructively is a *human address to him*, as opposed to being a *revelation from him*, because the Psalm is still preserved in scripture as part of God's 'inspired' Word. As such, the *offending passage* is part of God's *overall revelation.* I am not certain where Lambert stands on this point. He seems to be arguing that the Bible *contains* a partial revelation of God, which, of course, sets us up as arbiters for determining what is *revelation* and what is not, yet he states clearly in his article that he is against any subjective and all too human decision on what parts of the Bible may be judged to be 'inspired' by God.[3] Lambert believes that the whole Bible is 'inspired' by God and is thereby authoritative. He certainly would not say that *only some parts* of the Bible are 'inspired', as he would say that only some parts of the Bible are God's *revelation.* I am at a loss to see how the same biblical material illustrates the difference. The separation of the two notions—written records which are 'inspired' by God from written records which contain divine *revelations*—seems to me to be a red herring in our quest for an *authority*, since we have no easy way of accommodating *offensive passages* with those that are noble passages in a wholly 'inspired' book.

The acknowledgement that incongruent thoughts and ideas exist side by side in biblical writings is not new. Marcion in the second century recognised and circumvented the problem by editing out those bloodthirsty aspects of the Hebrew tribal god that were inconsistent with the loving Heavenly Father of Jesus. His book, *Contradictions*, was produced to fulfil the need for a uniform Bible, but fundamentalists would not agree with Marcion's solution! [4]

THE HUMAN FRAILTY AND REVELATION

A reasonable solution might be to argue that what the Bible reflects is the people's perceptions of God's Word for that time—a conditional or relative truth, not an absolute one—or to believe that God has no choice but to work through early man's frail perceptions and misconceptions, since dialogue between two unlike *minds,* such as that of the human and the divine, is not imaginable. However, this time-conditioned relative picture is not the general belief of fundamentalists when prescribing an *authority* for the Bible. Where I disagree with Lambert's reasoning is over the implications he draws from an 'inspired' Bible. He believes that God needs to "approximate" his communication to men according to their ability to understand, much in the way that parents simplify information for their children's level of comprehension, but this does not get round the problem, if I understand him correctly. He writes: "In inspiration God communicates some measure of divine perspective to the human recipients" (in the sense of what they are able to receive). My reply is to say, 'let readers judge for themselves what "divine perspective" is taught in the *offending passages* cited above, that are given under inspiration.' The sense in which Lambert appears to understand 'inspiration' is of a value-neutral force operating upon human authors. This is not, however, the way that fundamentalists generally view the doctrine of inspiration. They understand God's Spirit to have moral content (*Holy* Spirit) and to be an active medium of communication, which is anything but a value-neutral force!

Naturally, this analysis exaggerates those 'immoral' parts of the Bible from the later perspective of modern-day morality. Indeed, much Old Testament teaching is exceedingly rich in moral and spiritual content—even for our own day—but, for the purpose of examining the fundamentalist's position, we are required to amplify these incongruous passages. The clash is explained away by some fundamentalists with the solution that the New Testament has superseded the Old, but this evades the problem by failing to acknowledge that the incongruent feature is still there, and in a book that is believed to be *wholly* 'inspired'! To have recourse to the argument that the New Testament supersedes the Old is no answer, for the 'New Covenant' only serves to illuminate the deficiencies of the Old by putting the problem into greater relief. If 'inspiration' is supposed to monitor the preservation of some of those narratives that portray the glory of an unchanging God, but do so as one who *behaves* in an obscene, intolerant and barbaric manner, then it is not a question of mediating the essence of God in terms that are meaningful and comprehensible; it is a case of preserving one picture of God that is diabolical and which the New Testament authors have not felt the need to qualify in the closing books of the Bible. We acknowledge that it is impossible for God to speak with man in a 'direct' manner, but why has 'inspiration' not worked upon some authors to have corrected *all* false presentations of God as time moved on in biblical history or made some later writers express their rejection of them? There are no new footings, just a building erected on foundations, most of which are magnificent but some of which are distasteful.

Of those fundamentalists that see the problem, there are some who believe the solution lies in the notion of *progressive revelation* to account for man's growing awareness of what constitutes the will of God (Lambert's position). In both Testaments a case can be made for suggesting that a *progressive revelation* of God has taken place from the earlier books to the later. This will be considered in due course (chapter 11). In this discussion, we are interested in the nature of truth, and it is broadly recognised that truth is relative, but what sort of truth are we thinking about when we claim that biblical truth is relative?[5] When Lambert comes to the problem of scriptural inaccuracies, he argues for 'the relativity of our knowledge', in which he has a choice of two meanings: he could say that *God has revealed something of his nature and purpose but only to the degree which human beings at the time were able to receive owing to their limited faculties*; alternatively, he could say that *God's revelation is always pure and complete at the point of being given, but, owing to human frailty and restricted comprehension, man is not able to receive or interpret it as such outside his cultural concepts*. The first option puts the emphasis on God's management of revelation, the second on human inadequacy during reception. In a later letter he clearly prefers the first, and says: "God adjusted his message to the possibilities of each situation." However, he qualifies the statement with, "either answer is not really dependent on evidence, but on supposition", which indicates that the statement remains an opinion. Without answering such an *a priori* question more clearly, the discussion cannot proceed; his position is an unverified article of faith! Lambert's criterion of divine *revelation* centres upon the nation of Israel. When answering my letter asking him to be more specific, he replied:

> You still, like others, have not grasped the significance of the relativity of our knowledge. We are not looking at things from God's viewpoint, but with only a glimmer of His knowledge and spirituality . . .
>
> So, the question about the Old Testament is this: does it actually show a society in which the revelation of God had raised people higher than the level of others around them who lacked this revelation? From my study of the ancient world I am convinced that the Israelites were on a higher moral and spiritual plane generally speaking than others . . .

Lambert is well qualified to contrast Israelite faith with that of her neighbours, but his definition—which recognises the pre-eminence of Israel's religious status over that of her contemporaries—while fitting the facts, as he says in his letter, hardly establishes any unique or distinctive character in God's influence upon human beings that is measurable, quantifiable, or verifiable, from the benefit of hindsight. Some nation may be designated as the most advanced religious culture, but that does not necessarily prove that God has been the influencing factor.

THE HUMAN FACTOR IN BIBLICAL REVELATION

One way round the problem of God appearing to condone some of the distasteful deeds preserved in scripture, is to argue that while the seer or prophet may have thought such a message or act was God's will—even by proclaiming it as such with 'Thus saith the Lord'—we are not compelled to agree with the writer's opinion that it was God's will, only that he believed it so. The position of D. Cupitt is radical for the fundamentalist:

> Until the Enlightenment it seemed reasonable to believe that one's religion had to be revealed by God. It was 'objective' divine truth. Usually people were not so crude as to suppose that the thing revealed was a set of propositions. The intellectualist or realist heresy is rather modern . . . It is clear by now that revelation-beliefs are mythological. They are picturesque enforcers of the authority of the scriptures. Every religion claims that its scriptures and its paths to salvation have come down from heaven, but what really happened is that the books were written and the path was worked out by human beings.[6]

Although I have some sympathy with this view, I recognise that it is no less an opinion if stated without verification. Such an assessment conceives the process of bridging the divine and the human mind to be wholly "worked out by human beings", and as such denies the communication of any God-given content. Consequently, Cupitt's position, like that of Lambert's, is an article of faith. We have reached an impasse! Perhaps there is a middle path between the views of Lambert and Cupitt in our search for an *authority* which recognises the bridging of the *mind* of God with human apprehension.

It seems inconceivable to me that God would by-pass the human mind when revealing something to man, as J. Hick has recognised:

> God's self-revealing actions are accordingly always so mediated through the events composing our temporal experience that men can only become aware of the divine presence by interpreting and responding to these events in a way which we call religious faith. For if God were to disclose himself to us in the coercive manner in which our physical environment obtrudes itself, we should be dwarfed to nothingness by the infinite power thus irresistibly breaking open the privacy of our souls. Further we should be spiritually blinded by God's perfect holiness and paralysed by his infinite energy.[7]

God can only *reveal* himself "through the events composing our temporal experience". This makes sense to me but it is not the way that the Bible records divine activity. The Bible claims that God did act "in the coercive manner", and therein lies a major philosophical difficulty and a problem for modern-day religious *authority*.

The movement of individuals and nations throughout biblical history has been accounted for by sociologists of religion by natural forces exclusively, but I think with such treatment there is a missing ingredient that escapes empirical observation. The writings of the Bible have been interpreted and understood by specialists, quite coherently, as the product of natural and sociological factors alone, disregarding completely all forms of *God-given* and *supernatural* elements and influence.[8] For my part, I do not think this interpretation in purely naturalistic terms tells the whole story; I think there is a *mysterious* component without which the Bible would not be what it is. I am not reverting to a God-of-the-gaps theology, but I am recognising that there are imponderable quirks of history recorded in the Bible, which are unanswerable for me by natural interpretations. Why, for example, did the nation of Israel survive its series of national calamities and leave us such a rich legacy of religious insight? It was largely because of the prophetic visions of seers giving a particular view of history from their own *personal encounters* with Yahweh—theophanies, so called. Cannot such theophanies be real and legitimate experiences emanating from a divine being? The prophets carried Israel through crisis after crisis, from a single-minded conviction that they spoke the very words of God—'Thus saith the Lord.' The New Testament carries on in the same vein. With a sensitive and imaginative reading of the Bible, there appears to be a *hidden factor* combined with the natural factors that go to make up history. This *supernatural factor* cannot be explained away or edited out of the writings without leaving them flat and meaningless. It can be seen and yet not seen. The indescribable cannot all be the product of illusion or imaginative invention, for it exists as a coherent and indivisible whole. Something *hidden* is going on through the triumphs and calamities of the people of God, even when the records of those experiences can be shown to be the product of a human hand rather than a divine. We are left with the dilemma of *feeling that there is something there* without being able to 'prove' it by empirical means. We are left also with the phenomenon of *religious experience*, for, even when we today attempt to expose the mechanisms of the prophetic consciousness with our methods of psychological analysis, the validity of the nature of the experience may still elude our analysis.

THE CRITICAL APPROACH IS INESCAPABLE

One remedy used by fundamentalists is to place all the emphasis upon *obedience* rather than morality, that is to stress that 'inspired' writings record men of God who may not always have acted morally but have certainly *responded obediently*. God ordered, men jumped! When fundamentalists follow this lead, however, the results (supposing the instruction is clear and unambiguous) can sometimes be disastrous and beyond repair if not balanced with moral reasoning. Were some of the Nazi party truly obeying God in the Jewish Holocaust? Are Jehovah's Witnesses truly following God's wishes in denying a youngster a blood transfusion? Are Christadelphians carrying out God's wishes when they disfellowship a believer for marrying out of the faith? It has to be unwise to commit oneself slavishly to biblical imperatives and the legislative commandments of 'Holy Writ' in an age that demands a rational justification for much of what we do. The modern context calls for a careful weighing-up of gain and loss in the decisions we take, and an application of biblical principles implies a spirituality that calls for reasoning. To place a blinkered trust in pre-selected biblical passages, simply upon the grounds that the book is believed to be an *authority* on divine requirements of human conduct—inerrant and infallible, having been 'inspired' by God—without being able to verify that fact, is philosophically quite absurd.

Christian fundamentalists make an enormous emotional and spiritual investment in the doctrine of biblical inspiration. The questioning of a person's beliefs is unsettling, particularly when the whole bedrock of those beliefs is undermined. This is because the basis of personal existence is under threat. If belief were just a question of accepting a number of fanciful ideas and theoretical propositions, there would be no problem, but religious belief draws upon people's deepest feelings and emotions, and provides for them a whole basis for spiritual existence—an *authority*. What is clear is that we have reached a point of no return since the advent of biblical criticism. In religious circles there is a prevailing call by many conservative Christians to return to those former times of spiritual security, but I think we have little choice but to go forward. The believer, like the lover, has no absolute certainty, he must always trust. In Roman Catholicism, Vatican II achieved the most remarkable revolution of thought, but the pace of intellectual growth has slowed down since that bold revival. There is no return, infers Küng, commenting upon the sterility of Church leaders "who have not introduced people to critical freedom but always preached to them with the emphasis on unity, prayer and obedience".[9] His controversial book, *On Being a Christian*, emphasises the need to have an "open-mindedness for what is modern, extra-Christian, non-Christian, human, and for relentless criticism of our own positions, for dissociation from all ecclesiastical traditionalism, from dogmatism and biblicism".[10] It is not a question of believing unquestioningly in research, in theological scholarship or in the results of scholarship, for such can never be infallible. It is only the message elucidated by the research that provides any reason for faith. No turning back, then, for there is no place for refusing to face truths that are concealed by prejudices, and there are considerable dangers in being theological ostriches, as Küng recognises:

> Naiveté in matters of faith is not evil but at least dangerous. Naive faith can miss the true Jesus and lead us with the best intentions to false conclusions in theory and practice. Naive faith can lead the individual or a community to become blind, authoritarian, self-righteous, superstitious. Both at the beginning and also today faith should be an intelligent, justifiable faith. But intelligent, justifiable faith today presupposes—directly and indirectly—historical research, at least in its general results.[11]

A non-self-critical faith "can miss the real Jesus". This is the risk of fundamentalism. The search for the *real Jesus* we shall postpone till the closing chapters of the book. If this more liberal outlook on scripture does not suit the fundamentalists, it is incumbent upon them to establish criteria for determining what is truly the Word of God as distinct from what is presupposed to be the Word of God. Literary criticism helps us to see what the Bible is as opposed to what we might wish it to be. It is of little wonder, then, that biblical criticism is shunned by most leaders of fundamentalist groups, and it is hardly surprising that this form of study is not actively pursued by members of the fundamentalist communities either. How sad this suppression of critical knowledge is.

In view of the ambiguity surrounding the doctrine of the 'inspiration' of God for vouchsafing the Bible as an authoritative voice for people of the modern world, there is no place for dogmatism. In view of the uncertainty of establishing a *genuine revelation* of God without a criterion other than that of its written record being in the Bible, we have no basis for fulfilling the fundamentalist's need for an *authority*.

So we can make the following statements about the Bible:

- It is a *continuous record of human aspirations* to grasp 'God's ways' in vague terms, but it is not a clear manual of what to do.
- It is *consistent in historical outworking*, but it is not really a unified catalogue of instruction, custom, liturgy or practice.
- It is *rich in diversity* of religious views, beliefs, judgements and opinions, but it is not a document of single-minded unified propositions, teaching, conduct and morality.
- It has *diversified predictions and conflicting hopes, dreams and visions*, but it has no clear-cut unilateral metaphysical constructions and speculations. It could never be described as being consistent in analysis of individual psychology and philosophy.

What, then, are we to put in the place of a misguided belief in an inerrant Bible that can give the Christian a more dependable authority for life? We offer an answer in what follows, after broadening out the discussion of what we can know of the human psyche and its capabilities for receiving visions and messages from another world.

NOTES

1. W. Lambert, *Inspiration and Revelation*, reprinted 1990, Edinburgh.
2. Ibid., page 3. Lambert's reasoning runs thus:

   In the chapter, 'The Character of Inspiration', Professor Lambert refutes the premise that an inspired book must be 'uniform'. I agree with him that the Bible is not uniform and much of this study attempts to substantiate this fact. Lambert accepts the proposition that all the Bible is inspired, including those parts of the Bible which are contradictory to the Spirit of Christ. He has established, quite convincingly, that all the Bible is not to be understood as being equivalent to the revelation of God, but can it not equally be argued that those *offending passages,* as he calls them, suggest that only parts of the Bible have been inspired rather than the Bible as a whole?

   The question that inevitably forces itself upon me is in what sense should 'inspiration' be understood? Of course, God could have chosen to preserve only those parts of scripture that have presented him in a *favourable* light—and who are we to question God's wisdom—and cause to be lost those more objectionable parts, but the fact is that these objectionable texts are preserved *alongside* those which are commendable. What purpose does their retention serve if God does not make clear in later scriptures that earlier presentations of him were inaccurate and offensive? The fact remains that virtually none of the *offending passages* are explained away, modified, or reinterpreted by later biblical writers (the overall picture is altered, in the sense that the New Testament supersedes the Old, but the specific pictures are not) when they were forward to reinterpret Messianic texts in the light of Christian understanding. It is as though the problem we see was never seen by later biblical writers; there is a total absence of comment. Take for example, the narrative of the Levite and the concubine (Judges 19–20), with the ensuing slaughter of the clans of Benjamin by Israel. These barbaric deeds—characteristic of the books of Joshua and Judges—are all, we are told, at the Lord's instruction. The question I put to fundamentalists is: what 'divine perspective' is communicated here? I wonder whether Lambert is not tied too inextricably to the doctrine of inspiration of the whole Bible from the well-known passages in II Tim. 3:16 and II Pet. 1:20, which can be construed as asserting the doctrine of inspiration of whatever was regarded as scripture at that time, and, from such a presupposition, to carrying out his exegesis of Old Testament writings accordingly.

   'Progressive revelation' is commended by Lambert as the way out of the dilemma of accounting for the 'offending passages', but I cannot see that this resolves the problem—there is no systematic denouncing within scripture itself of those passages that are contrary to the Spirit of Christ.

   It might be counter-argued that such an interest would not have been of paramount importance to Christian authors generally, that the *kerygma* and its associated ideas were the all-important interest (the *offending passages* not being significant or relevant to the *kerygmatic* faith), but, considering that it was only the Old Testament that was understood as scripture during the formation of the New, and considering that the Old Testament was used liberally to authorise features of the early *kerygma,* the problem still remains.
3. I am not happy with Lambert's resort to the argument of setting up the wisdom of man against the wisdom of God (as though they must compete), for it discourages a critical outlook and an unprejudicial evaluation of the material. He writes, "Nor do we put ourselves in the position of those who know better and look down with a patronising superiority" (page 16), but then says in the same article, "Of course we must make decisions and act upon them . . .",

in the context of the need "to distinguish between clear and unambiguous biblical doctrine and passages capable of more than one interpretation", which is not altogether clear. He goes on to say, "The profession of knowing all the answers is usually a very human kind of pride, and it can be maintained only by parading much human misinterpretation as divine wisdom" (page 21). This, for me, encourages a superstitious constraint on objective enquiry upon a false premise that rational questioning sets oneself against the wisdom of God. He also says:

> One way of dealing with the situation is to cut out the offending passages as unworthy of Christ. The fault of this method is that those who share it set themselves up as arbiters pronouncing judgement on the Word of God. Another method essentially refuses to face the facts and by a most tortuous exegesis either asserts that the passages do not say what they do, or offers an attempted justification in the light of Christian principles.
>
> (page 16)

I am troubled with the second sentence of this statement, though I think the last sentence is sound. Can it be possible, I wonder, for exegetes attempting with integrity to understand passages which, at least on the surface, appear incongruous with other parts of scripture without, by that very exercise, setting themselves up as "arbiters pronouncing judgement on the Word of God", particularly if the exercise is one of attempting to arrive at what is meant by the expression, the 'Word of God'?

4. Origen's method of resolving the contradiction was by use of allegory. More recently students replaced allegory with typology. Lambert draws our attention rightly to the method of establishing the meaning of each particular passage as being that which the Old Testament author had intended, op., cit., pages 12–15.
5. Lambert, op. cit., pages 17–22.
6. D. Cupitt, *Taking Leave of God*, London, 1980, page 120.
7. J. Hick, *The Existence of God*, page 16.
8. The case is presented by C. H. Dodd, *The Bible To-Day*, London, 1968. pages 38f..
9. H. Küng, *On Being a Christian*, London, 1977, page 36.
10. Ibid., page 36–37.
11. Ibid., page 164.

7

GOD OF THE PSYCHE

Is there an objective God 'out there' that stands apart from us, or is he an invention of the human psyche (psyche as understood to be mind, as opposed to *psyche*, the metaphysical soul)? We must address this question before any analysis of the character of divine revelation through visions and auditions can be conducted. Centuries before Christ, philosophers had believed that the gods were the product of human projection. Xenophanes, the leader of the Eleatic school, is recorded to have said:

> But mortals think that the gods are born as they are, and have perception like theirs, and voice and form . . . Yes, and if oxen and lions had hands, and could paint with their hands and produce works of art as men do, horses would paint the forms of the gods like horses, and oxen like oxen. Each would represent them with bodies according to the form of each . . . So the Ethiopians make their gods black and snub-nosed . . .[1]

There are theologians, psychologists and philosophers, who are highly sceptical of a God operating outside the universe: J. Robinson in *Honest to God*; C. G. Jung in *The Archetypes and the Collective Unconscious*; D. Cupitt in *Taking Leave of God* (to mention just three).[2] They would deny the notion of God as a separate existent Being who directs the whole show and intervenes in human affairs. Robinson and Jung saw the need to make religion immanent and radically human, so as to remove all spiritual obstacles that stood in the path of man's full enhancement and self-consciousness. Cupitt appears to be continually pressing for a content-less God, which he describes as the "unifying symbol that eloquently personifies and represents to us everything that spirituality requires of us". Such a treatment, however, moves from the premise that there is no objective God 'out there', and that the gross demise of religion is a movement towards a heightened form of self-consciousness. Although people today appear to get by without faith in a Divine Being, it is another question whether his existence is to be explained by a lack of human self-consciousness in former times.

The pioneering psychoanalytical work of Jung presents a significant step forward in our changing awareness of God. He suggests from 'empirical evidence', that there are *archetypal images* within the psyche which determine and regulate human behaviour and feelings. The Genesis account describes for fundamentalists an omnipotent God creating human beings—'So God created man in his own image, in the image of God he created him, male and female he created them' (Gen.1:27 RSV)—but Jung reinterprets the biblical myth in psychological terms:

> Man woke up in a world he did not understand, and that is why he tries to interpret it.[3]

The religious question is this: *did God form man or man God?* The 'death of God' debate is largely closed today but a newer challenge is presented by the views of certain theologians and psychologists who subscribe to the notion that God is a creation of the human psyche. Having dispensed with an ontological existent God 'out there', it is suggested that man, as a conscious thinking creature, has given God his existence! One such psychologist is Julian Jaynes and in this chapter we shall examine this theory through his book, *The Origin of Consciousness in the Breakdown of the Bicameral Mind.*

THE BIRTH OF GOD IN THE BICAMERAL MIND

The bold and imaginative hypothesis of what Jaynes calls the 'Bicameral Mind' declares that men were not as conscious in earlier times as we are today. Beginning with laboratory studies of the brain, coupled with archaeological evidence, Jaynes speculates that ancient peoples from Mesopotamia to Peru could not think in the way that modern people do; consequently, they were not conscious. Unable to be introspective, they experienced auditory hallucinations—the voices of gods, as we find in the Old Testament and *The Iliad*—which, coming from the brain's right hemisphere, told a person what to do in novel situations and during periods of tension. This ancient mentality he called the bicameral mind. Only catastrophe and cataclysm forced mankind to learn consciousness, some 3000 years ago. Consciousness is ultimately grounded in the physiology of the brain's right and left hemispheres. The history of culture (rather than animal evolution) bears this out. Jaynes examines the human awareness of the bicameral or god-run man, the modern problem-solving man, and the contemporary throw-backs to bicamerality—hypnotism, schizophrenia, poetic and religious frenzy and the auguries of modern science. This is no bogus science, like Daniken's proposition—the gods in ancient times visiting planet earth and leaving behind evidence of their various exploits (*Chariots of the Gods*, 1969)—but a study worthy of serious consideration. Evidently this form of examination is the most insidious attack on biblical faith and religious belief there is, for it eats away at the very heart of the religious question of whether God is the creation of man brought about to satisfy his dreams and fantasies. In short, the question of whether God really exists at all?

Fundamentalists need to consider all the evidence of a non-theistic interpretation of the universe, and not to dismiss such contrary knowledge, however unpalatable it might be!

Jaynes states explicitly what he believes to be the case:

> The preposterous hypothesis we have come to . . . is that at one time human nature was split in two, an executive part called a god, and a follower part called a man. Neither part was conscious. This is almost incomprehensible to us.[4]

Of the bicameral god, he says:

> Some people find it difficult to imagine that there can be mental voices that are heard with the same experiential quality as externally produced voices. After all, there is no mouth or larynx in the brain! Whatever brain areas are utilised, it is absolutely certain that such voices do exist . . . it is highly probable that the bicameral voices of antiquity were in quality very much like such auditory hallucinations in contemporary people.[5]

Jaynes' thorough working knowledge of schizophrenia has obviously shaped his belief, and his predisposition is a retrospective evaluation of this pathological condition:

> Most of us spontaneously slip back into something approaching the actual bicameral mind at some part of our lives. For some of us, it is only a few episodes of thought deprivation or an instance or two of hearing voices. But for others of us, genetically lacking the enzyme to easily breakdown the biochemical products of continued stress into excretable form, it is a much more harrowing experience.[6]

It is common for schizophrenics to hear voices speaking to them in a most compelling fashion. "If that is not a real voice, then I can just as well say that even you are not now really talking to me", said one schizophrenic to his physician. "Yes, Sir. I hear voices distinctly, even loudly; they interrupt us at this moment. It is more easy for me to listen to them than you. I can more easily believe in their significance and actuality, and they do not ask questions."[7]

What is consciousness? We are not only conscious but are conscious of our consciousness! We are aware of our self, our 'I', the fact that we occupy this mind-space and not that one. The brain has twin chambers, neither of which function independently; the left dominant hemisphere (in right-handed people) is responsible for articulated language, and the right occupies our thoughts and reasoning faculties. The precameral mind was not like this, speculates Jaynes, for the precameral mind was automated by the voices of the gods in the right hemisphere. Being conscious, modern man has a heightened threshold to hallucinate, but not so early man. Neither is it so for schizophrenics, for their hearing of inner voices is very real indeed. Stress is the cause of the subject's 'openness' for hallucination—not the stress of facing trauma but that of having to arrive at a decision to face a life-threatening situation (as demonstrated by the studies of ulcers in rats[8]).

The brain, then, has two compartments. One is dormant but can take over if the other malfunctions, as in the case of injury. The dormant side can be stimulated with small electric shocks (sufficient to give tingling in the fingers), after which the patient hears voices.[9] The brain has many redundant areas,[10] but we cannot suppose that the brain functioned in a previous age as it does today:

> The hallucinated voices of the bicameral mind were amalgams of stored admonitory experiences that were somehow organised in the right temporal lobe and conveyed to the left or dominant hemisphere over the anterior commissures and perhaps the corpus callosum.[11]

From such physiological studies, Jaynes speculates on the mentality of what he calls the Precameral Mind?[12] *The Iliad* is a Greek poem of revenge written about 1230 BC. It is a psychological document of immense importance, for it bears testimony to the precameral mind. We shall examine the stages of Jaynes' thesis in more detail in order to do justice to the weight of his argument.

Stage 1 The Origin of Language

Jaynes challenges the conventional theories of anthropology by claiming that consciousness came after language, not before. With small groups of migrating tribes, visual gestures and signs would have been misleading as a means of communicating warnings of impending danger. In agricultural communities (essentially larger in size) sounds were needed, since visual signs would be inappropriate; they would not have been seen by all. So, language was born from stereotypical sounds designed to identify the type of threat, i.e., a sound for the tiger would be different from that of the bear. The warning sounds developed into nouns, and nouns became names, and so on in the progress of a more sophisticated language, all in order to identify the conscious 'I'. In time, the first god was born.[13]

Stage 2 The Dead King of Eynan Speaks

Jaynes sees quite significant stages in the development of the bicameral mind, and on to its breakdown with the arrival of consciousness. Archaeology has revealed some evidence to support his theory, which, although selective, seems fairly consistent. As we follow this evidence through, we note how Neanderthal man buried his dead king sitting upright as though facing his subjects and giving instructions and admonishments. The subjects heard the voices of the gods through the corpse of the dead king.

The skeleton of the king at Eynan is propped up to stare at mount Hermon, as though he were still speaking to his subject peoples.[14] Precameral man heard voices that were very real. The kings of Mesopotamia began as stewards of the god but became gods themselves (their divinity was signified by the eight-pointed star alongside their name). It is likely, argues Jaynes, that the voice of a powerful king was heard under hallucination—this was the precameral voice.

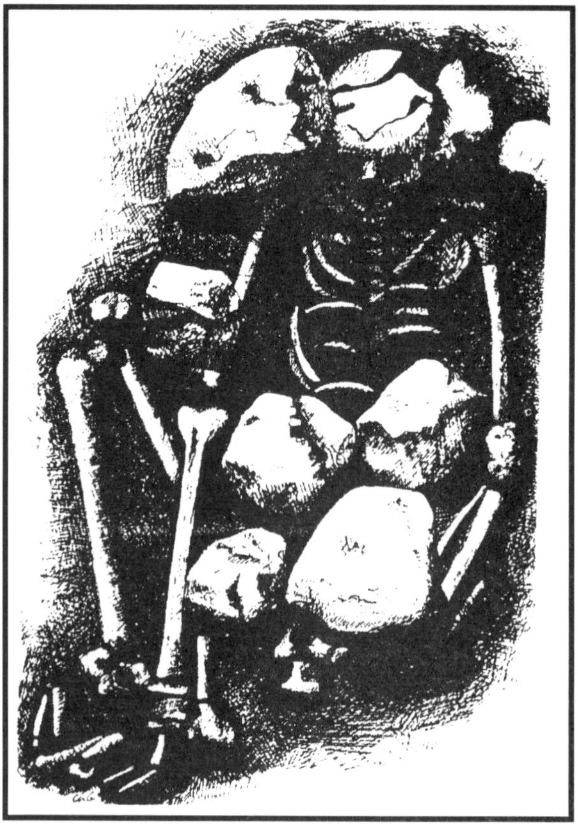

The first god, excavated in 1959: the dead king of Eynan propped up on a pillow of stones, about 9000 BC.

In the early period, man had a vastly different mentality to that which he has at present—part of his nervous system was divine. He was ordered about as a slave and was automated by a voice or voices which we today would regard as human volition:

> The gods were not 'figments of the imagination' of anyone. They were man's volition. They occupied his nervous system, probably his right hemisphere, and from stores of admonitory and preceptive experience, transmuted this experience into articulated speech which then 'told' the man what to do.[15]

The precameral mind developed from the ninth to the second millennium BC (Millennia are its units of time, not centuries). The royal corpse was supported with stones under its red parapet and was still ruling its Natufian village in the hallucinating minds of its subjects. The king of Eynan marks a highly significant transition then in mental development.[16]

Stage 3 Tukulti and the Beginning of the Breakdown of the Bicameral Mind

With the next stage, a change occurs in Mesopotamian mentality.[17] Tukulti stands and then kneels before the empty throne of his god. The breakdown of the bicameral mind has begun.

The gods have gone, and prayers are offered to regain the lost hallucinatory voice, just as in contemporary schizophrenic patients who are hallucinating. There is an abundant rise in divination and omens, and its process in all mammalian nervous-systems runs thus: if an organism experiences B after A, it will have a tendency to expect B the next time A occurs. This is the birth of religious language and practice.

Carving on the front of the Tukulti Altar now in the Berlin museum. Tukulti stands and then kneels before the empty throne of his god. Note the emphasis of the pointing forefinger.

The literature on the loss of the gods marks a change in Mesopotamia from Tukulti to the first millennium BC.

All through the Middle East toward the end of the second millennium BC there were large amorphous masses of half-nomadic peoples with no fixed grazing ground. Some were refugees from the Thera destruction (the legendary Atlantis) and the terrible Dorian invasions that followed. One cuneiform tablet describes migrations pouring down through Lebanon. The word for vagrants in Akkadian is *khabiru*, which, softened in the desert air, says Jaynes, becomes Hebrew. It is in the literature of the Old Testament that we see most graphically the process of the rise of consciousness from the breakdown of the bicameral mind.

THE RECORD OF PROPHETIC CONSCIOUSNESS IN THE OLD TESTAMENT

There is a considerable gap in consciousness between the books of Amos and Ecclesiasticus, between the prophet who feels his bicameral voice about to speak, 'Thus speaks Yahweh', and the writer who speaks with a consciousness in a mind-space, or 'I'. Those prophets and seers of the Old Testament who had a *direct* sense of the Spirit of God speaking to them were classified as *nabiim*. These were transitional men, partly subjective and partly bicameral, and the book of I Samuel is a fitting commentary on the process in action. There is "the gradual loss of the visual component, the growing inconsistency of the voices in different persons, and the increasing inconsistency in the same person, until the voices of the elohim vanish from history".[18] There is much confusion concerning the voice of the first gods, referred to in Genesis as *Elohim*.

The *Elohim* first tells Abraham to beget a son of promise, then he orders him to kill him, even as criminal psychotics might be directed to do today. Similarly, the bicameral voice has a sudden impulse to kill Moses for no reason at all (Exod. 4:24). Confusion for Balaam, too, whose bicameral voice first tells him not to go with the prince of Moab, then reverses the instruction (Num. 22:12, 20), then, when Balaam obeys, is furious—the visual-auditory hallucination sets out to kill him by blocking his way—and finally reverses the command again (Num. 22:35). The gods of many early cultures were regularly capricious.

Young Samuel was stirred from sleep to hear the bicameral voice of *He-who-is*.[19] The voices, we may suppose, continued through the period of his life to be heard by him who was marked as the last of the *nabiim*. The glimpses of precameral men persist until the downfall of the monarchy of Judah. They are referred to as the 'sons of the *nabiim*', indicating that there was probably a strong genetic basis for this type of remaining bicamerality. "It is, I think, the same genetic basis that remains with us as a part of the aetiology of schizophrenia."[20] In 835 BC, Ahab, the king of Israel, rounded up 400 of them like cattle to listen to their babblings (I Kings 22:6). Later, he and the king of Judah sat on thrones outside the gates of Samaria (I Kings 22:10) and had "hundreds of these poor bicameral men herded up to them, raving and copying each other even as schizophrenics in a back ward will do!". From time to time they were hunted down. In the ninth-century BC, a massacre of many is implied in I Kings 18:4, where Obadiah finds it necessary to hide a hundred *nabiim* in the caves. Another such slaughter was organised by Elijah a few years later (I Kings 18:40). They appeared to vanish at the downfall of Judah, apart from a few individuals ("the voices as a rule are no longer heard" at such a time[21]). Men still dreamed visions and heard dark speeches, perhaps, but by 400 BC, bicameral prophecy was dead:

> The *nabiim* shall be ashamed everyone of his visions: If parents catch their children naba-ing or in dialogue with bicameral voices, they are to kill them on the spot (Zech. 13:3–4) . . . If it was carried out, it is an evolutionary selection which helped move the gene pool of humanity toward consciousness.[22]

In conclusion, Jaynes' scheme of Man's intellectual history is simply this:

> In the second millennium BC, we stopped hearing the voices of gods. In the first millennium BC, those of us who still heard the voices, our oracles and prophets, they too died away. In the first millennium AD, it is their sayings and hearings preserved in sacred texts through which we obeyed our lost divinities. And in the second millennium AD, these writings lost their authority. The Scientific Revolution turns us away from the older sayings to discover the lost authorisation in nature . . . It is the Great Human Irony of our noblest and greatest endeavour on this planet that in the quest for authorisation, in our reading of the language of God in Nature, we should read there so clearly that we have been so mistaken.[23]

VESTIGES OF THE BICAMERAL MIND

Induced Possession

Oracles are not generally used by people in the modern world as a means of seeking guidance, yet there is a widespread attempt by some private groups to bring back the gods and have them speak through any one as a means of authorising a community's stance in life. The leaders, or initiates, of some fundamentalist sects and denominations attempt, unconsciously, to incarnate the god as though *possessed.* Such figures tend to come from unsophisticated backgrounds in the main. Historically, uneducated country girls were chosen to train as priestesses for the oracle at Delphi. Such induced bicameral possession was a learned activity, and we know from comments of Pythagoras of Rhodes in the third century that there was a period of training for this acquisition. The Gnostics invited common people to participate in divinity by accepting part of the divine within their being. Athanasius, the bishop of Alexandria, in the fourth century, began claiming that Jesus, the Messiah, should be regarded as being like Yahweh, a demigod, half human and half divine, in order to reflect his supposed parentage.[24] If Athanasius was right, then Jesus must have participated in Yahweh, since he was of the same substance. The consequence of such a teaching was that Christ was held to be divine, not only by Constantine but by the majority of Christendom throughout the Middle Ages.

This learning of an unconscious response was not like the learning of a practical skill; it was a wildly distinctive neurological state, quite unlike anything in ordinary life. Through various cues the initiate can reach this *reception of the god* and achieve a suspension of consciousness under hallucination, so that he or she may see or hear some divine message more *directly*.

Demon Possession

Illness brought about by emotional stress, says Jaynes, is a further vestige of the bicameral mind. The oldest, and most authentic, stratum of Gospel tradition preserves the idea that sickness is the result of demon-possession.

> Like schizophrenia, negatory possession usually begins with some kind of an hallucination. It is often a castigating 'voice' of a 'demon' or other being which is 'heard' after a considerable stressful period. But then, unlike schizophrenia . . . , the voice develops into a secondary system of personality, the subject then losing control and periodically entering into trance states in which consciousness is lost, and the 'demon' side of the personality takes over.[25]

Under such a condition (still in evidence today as in New Testament times), the attack is frequent but not persistent, lasting from several minutes to an hour or so. Between attacks, the subject is drawn into a loss of consciousness, when he or she seems someone other than his or her usual self, and the possessed has little recall of what happened after the attack. "In all cases I have studied", comments Jaynes, "it is rare to find one of criminal behaviour against other persons. The stricken individual does not run off and behave like a demon; he just talks like one."[26] In this condition, the voice is distorted, often guttural, full of cries, groans and vulgarity, against the institutional gods of the period. The induced possession of demons is a highly suggestible condition and the cure of the condition is by means of exorcism, which has not altered in form throughout the centuries (often by means of a contract). Exorcism is performed by a highly authoritative person speaking in the name of a more powerful god, and issuing a command of instant restoration to normal consciousness. Although most of the demon-possessed subjects of the New Testament were men, it is a curious fact that throughout the Middle Ages and thereafter the overwhelming majority were women.

Coming to the neurological question of what is happening during such trance-states of demon possession, it is likely, argues Jaynes, that the speech areas of the right non-dominant hemisphere are activated in spontaneous possession, as with the case of the bicameral mind. "Are not the contorted features due to the intrusion of right hemisphere control over the left?," asks Jaynes: "The fact that the majority of instances were women, and that women are (presently in our culture) less lateralized than men is somewhat suggestive."

Glossolalia

Induced possession is clearly a learned phenomenon and it is a vestige of the bicameral mind, just as in the case of *glossolalia*. *Glossolalia* is the 'speaking in tongues', an activity in which the worshipper was compelled under trance to utter a language of God that he or she did not understand, nor was conscious of. It is a practice not exclusive to the New Testament Church. There was no genuine precedent in the Old Testament; it was a phenomenon peculiar to Christian times. In the early period, it is likely that

Christians were practising the gift everywhere. Currently, it is encouraged only by Charismatic Christians, such as Pentecostals, who are actively looking for the experience. Various scholars have studied the phenomenon scientifically and the following factors have come to light:-

First, *Glossolalia* is initiated always in groups and always in the context of a religious service. The group factor is important for strengthening the collective cognitive imperative of the deep trance, often resulting from rousing hymns and exhortations of charismatic leaders: "If you feel your language change, don't resist it, let it happen."[27] Through repeated attendance at such meetings, and after watching others in *glossolalia*, the worshipper soon learns to enter into the deep trance-state of diminished or absent consciousness, in which he or she is not responsive to external stimuli. The trance is almost an autonomic one—shakes, shivers, sweat, twitches and tears. Then, the subject somehow learns to 'let it happen'. And happen it does, loud and clear, each phrase ending in a groan: *aria ariari isa, vena amira asaria!* [28]

> This quality of regular alternation of accented and unaccented syllables, so similar to that of the Homeric epics, as well as the rising and then downward intonation at the end of each phrase, does not—and this is astonishing—vary with the native language of the speaker. If the subject is English, Portuguese, Spanish, Indonesian, African, or Mayan, or wherever he is.[29]

After the glossolalia, the subject opens his eyes and returns to dusty reality, remembering little of what had happened, but he or she is told: "You have been possessed by the Holy Spirit. You have been chosen as God's vessel." It is the ultimate in authorisation, since the Holy Spirit is believed to take control of the individual:

> God has chosen to enter the lowly subject and has articulated his speech with the subject's own tongue. The individual has become a god—briefly.[30]

The cruel daylight of it all is less inspiring, comments Jaynes. Clearly *glossolalia* is not gibberish, nor can it be duplicated fluently. It has no semantic meaning whatsoever. John Kildahl has studied the tapes of twenty-six American *glossolalists* from Protestant denominations. When playing back the recordings before others in the same religious group, he discovered that the messages of 'tongues' were given thoroughly inconsistent interpretations.[31] Linguists have recognised that the metered vocalisations are similar across the cultures and language of the speakers, probably indicating that rhythmical discharges from subcortical structures are coming into play, which have been released by the trance-state of lesser cortical control.[32]

Finally, the ability does not last, it attenuates. More practice leads to a fuller consciousness of what is happening, which, in turn, destroys the trance. The more educated groups, who would have a weaker cognitive imperative, require the presence of a powerful charismatic leader to teach the phenomenon first. It is the resulting euphoric state that makes the acquisition of the gift desirable. Clinical tests on *glossolalists* (Thematic Apperception Test) reveal the subjects to be more submissive, suggestible and dependent in the presence of authority figures than those unable to demonstrate the gift.[33]

There are four factors of present-day *glossolalia* that suggest for Jaynes that this phenomenon is yet another example of a vestige of the bicameral mind:

a) the strong cognitive imperative of religious belief in a cohesive group

b) the induction procedures of prayer and ritual
c) the narrowing of consciousness into a trance-state
d) the authorisation of the divine Spirit and charismatic leader.[34]

CRITICISM OF THE BICAMERAL GOD

The stumbling block of Jaynes' theory is the variable nature of human consciousness. There are examples of people in modern times who still hear such guiding voices at stress points in their lives and who are clearly not schizophrenics. Many highly conscious people (by Jaynes' definition) are prone to hallucinate at times, and omens of diverse forms still occupy the attention of many intelligent people who are not necessarily of a religious persuasion. Further, particular archaeological artefacts and writings, which are used to characterise an age, ought not to be regarded as being the whole representation of human consciousness of that given age. Ecclesiasticus might represent the height of Hebrew consciousness, but for a long time afterward both Jewish and Christian apocalyptic writers can be claimed to have heard the bicameral voices. Conversely, Amos might have been subjected to the bicameral voice speaking through him, but the prophet was also capable of voicing an ethic of advanced moral insight, far beyond that which his environment would have fashioned, as we shall see. Jaynes would not refute this fact of diverse experience, but would turn it about, regarding it as evidence of a vestige of a bygone period. So, he devotes one third of his book to an examination of poetry, music, hypnosis, schizophrenia, religious practice and the auguries of modern science; he suggests that these demonstrate a vestige of the bicameral mind. This evidence, however, could equally be used to illustrate how certain individuals have an inclination or propensity towards such activities *at all times* of recorded history.

Fundamentalists cling on to some of these vestiges and see them as 'evidence of the divine'. Pentecostals endorse *glossolalia* and practise a belief in demon-possession and healing, along with Evangelicals and charismatics of the larger Church, and preachers of most denominations will become *possessed* by the Spirit in their oratory. The mistake is not one of discounting these experiences, but in seeing them as examples of 'absolute evidence' of divine interaction *per se.*

The theory of the breakdown of the bicameral mind with the development of consciousness is a programme which asserts that the notion of God intervening cannot be understood as a 'real happening'—as something objective, outside and independent of the human psyche—but which must be understood as an idea that came to birth and that had slowly evolved within the cultural consciousness of man. The quest of humanity is, for Jaynes, a relentless search for a lost better world:

> It said in a word that there is no authorisation from outside. Behold! There is nothing there. What we must do must come from ourselves. The king at Eynan can stop staring at mount Hermon; the dead king can die at last. We, we fragile human species at the end of the second millennium AD, we must become our own authorisation.[35]

Religion for Jaynes was a mere grasping after an illusive nettle, a frustrated attempt in multifarious forms to reach for something which had disappeared:

> After the collapse of the bicameral mind, the world in a sense is still governed by gods, by statements and laws and prescriptions carved on stelae or written on papyrus or remembered by old men, and dating back to bicameral times. But the dissonance is there. Why are the gods no longer there? The Psalms cry out for answers . . . Prophets, poets, oracles, diviners statue cults, mediums, astrologers, inspired saints, demon possession, tarot cards, Ouija boards, popes and peyote all are the residue of bicamerality that was progressively narrowed down as uncertainties piled upon uncertainties.[36]

Jaynes' whole thesis, and general line of reasoning, only holds true, however, if the assumption (assumption, not fact) is correct that there is no *otherness* aspect of God existing 'out there'. I would not presume to question Jaynes' knowledge of mental functioning, of the left and right hemispheres of the brain and so on, and much of his interpretation of archaeological data appears feasible—even though selective and nebulous in parts. It is his overall conclusion that I question, the belief that the *measurable part* of the human brain tells us all there is. I find it unconvincing that there can be nothing 'out there' communicating or intervening with us 'down here' from such data as presented by Jaynes. I question the 'God of the Psyche' because there is some contrary evidence, scanty though it may be, that suggests that there is *something* 'out there', which is distinct and apart from ourselves, that is trying to break through our finite boundary and 'communicate' with us in different ways.[37]

NOTES

1. A. K. Rogers, *A Student's History of Philosophy*, 1932, page 28.
2. J. A. T. Robinson, *Honest to God*, London; C. G. Jung, *The Archetypes and the Collective Unconscious*; and D. Cupitt, *Taking Leave of God*.

Considering the influence Cupitt has had in post-modernist religious philosophy, it might be useful to summarise his views, even though understanding him is not easy. His programme, as described in *Taking Leave of God*, recognises the need for an internalisation of our own spirituality, the need to reach for spiritual autonomy by appropriating to ourselves those values that are valuable to us (even "obedience is sin!", he says), and the need for a personal inner-transformation—the biblical New Covenant. Cupitt is against the 'realists" view of God, by which he means an objective reasoned faith upon tangible evidence and proof: "Theology must shift from an objective to a subjective and internalised interpretation of Christian doctrines." (page 92) "Christianity on an intellectualist interpretation is regressive in that it leads one back into a primitive and childish world-view, and it is heteronomous in that it projects the objects of religious concern as real beings, powers, influences, etc., to which one becomes subject." (page 155)

Cupitt's alternative programme to the traditional Christian one is described as 'Christian Buddhism—Buddhist in form, Christian in content'. He denigrates institutional religion as "belonging to a bygone age", and as something that will "invite us back into a childhood world". Cupitt presents a lifeline to drowning post-Enlightenment Christianity; a new way forward without rejecting the lot. He describes his programme as a *'movement'* of three interconnected themes: internalisation, autonomy, and the New Covenant. Cupitt's three-theme *'movement'* makes two *a priori* and unproven assumptions. First, that it is appropriate in describing the essence of spiritual life to people in the modern age to abandon completely any notion of a God 'out there'; second, that any form of communication as *something-given* cannot be valid unless it serves as a metaphor for a process that defies description, pages 8–14.

John Robinson, the author of *Honest to God*, has been described by religious realists as an atheist for promoting God in existential terms. He speaks of the *depth of life* in contrast to the

God 'out there', and the cosmos-transcending, almighty, individual Being. Robinson was a churchman and a preacher and, in spite of much opposition, his controversial book, in which he explored changed meanings, has converted many to Christianity. Cupitt is adamant that he is not an atheist: "If you judge my view atheistic please acknowledge also that it has an approximately equal claim to be judged orthodox and I shall be satisfied. Meanwhile I maintain that we have no way of judging that there is a god who is a person, who takes the initiative and so forth . . ." (page 94) In similar vein to Robinson, he holds on to the human as opposed to the 'out there' aspect of religion, suggesting frequently that it is inappropriate to promote a capricious God who acts differently today from what he did in biblical times: "In the Old Testament it was God who appeared to be posturing dramatically, and the believer hid in the cleft of the rock, kept his head down, remained very still and hoped that the divine storm would soon blow itself out. Today God keeps still—and I jump." "Freud himself led the way," says Cupitt, "for he notoriously thought little of the philosophy of religion and modern liberal theology. His mind was always drawn to the id of religion . . . In his own way he admired the ferocious, rampaging old patriarch who lurks somewhere at the back of theistic belief." (pages 59–60)

Cupitt's thought however, is not akin to Robinson's: "At this point I have to diverge from Bultmann because I think that he and Robinson and many others have somewhat confused the issue. The task is to overthrow a religiously bankrupt, because falsely objectified, dogmatism and to put specifically religious categories at the centre. The task is not to move from an objective and god-centred theology to a man-centred theology, as has too often happened. It is not primarily putting man and human psychology at the centre, but rather of putting the religious and the demand for its subjective appropriation by us at centre." (pages 43–44)

So, rather than run away from the subjective element in religious experience, he encourages Christians to live by it.

3. C. G. Jung, *The Collected Works*, page 31.
4. Julian Jaynes, *The Origin of Consciousness in the Breakdown of the Bicameral Mind*, USA, 1976, page 84.
5. Ibid., pages 85–6.
6. Ibid., page 404.
7. Ibid., page 95.
8. Ibid., page 93. Decision-making, which Jaynes regards as a non-conscious activity, is the stress-inducer rather than the facing up to something traumatic. If rats have to cross an electric grid each time to get food and water they develop ulcers; electrical shocks alone do not result in the same.
9. Ibid., pages 110f..
10. Ibid., pages 123f..
11. Ibid., page 428. Some modern research pointing to a strong relationship between schizophrenia and the bicameral mind is given on pages 429–30, and the neurology of the phenomenon is given on page 428.
12. Ibid., page 107.
13. Ibid., page 138.
14. Houses were built around one larger house—the temple; the gods are born and the voices are heard. The living 'dead' gods are outlined on pages 161, 174–175.
15. Ibid., pages 202–203.
16. Consciousness came about through this process:
    a) The emergence of writing weakened the divine authority, the law code of Hammurabi would allow the civil structure to become stable with an erosion of the precameral mind.
    b) The inherent fragility of hallucinatory control.
    c) The unworkableness of gods in the chaos of historical upheaval. In the second millennia half of the world's population became refugees, vast geological catastrophes occurred and civilisations perished. The Assyrian Empire rose.
    d) The positing of internal cause in the observation of the difference in others.
    e) The acquisition of the narratisation from epics.

f) The survival value of deceit.

g) A modicum of natural selection.

17. J. Jaynes, op. cit., page 224.
18. The loss of the visual component gives way to the bicameral voice, ibid., page 301.
19. Ibid., page 307.
20. Ibid., page 311.
21. Ibid., page 312.
22. Ibid., page 312.
23. Ibid., pages 436–7.
24. Ibid., page 347.
25. Ibid., page 348.
26. Ibid., page 349.
27. Ibid., page 358.
28. Ibid., page 358. From a tape of Dr Goodman's of a male *glossolalist* of Mayan descent, F. D. Goodman, *Disturbances in the Apostolic Church.*
29. J. Jaynes, op. cit., page 359. F. D. Goodman, *Speaking in Tongues: A Cross-Cultural Study of Glossolalia*, Chicago, 1972.
30. J. Jaynes, op. cit., page 359.
31. Ibid., page 359. J. P. Kildahl, *The Psychology of Speaking in Tongues*, New York, 1972.
32. J. Jaynes, op. cit., page 359. W. J. Samarin, *Language*, 1974, and *Tongues of Men and Angels: The Religious Language of Pentecostalism*, New York, 1972.
33. J. Jaynes, op. cit., page 360. J. P. Kildahl, *The Final Progress Report: Glossolalia and Mental Health.*
34. J. Jaynes, op. cit., page 360.
35. Ibid., page 438.
36. Ibid., page 320.
37. Ibid., pages 441, 434. It is not clear whether Jaynes is challenging religion or pseudo-religion at this point.

8

VISIONS AND VOICES

The departed spirit of Jacob Marley in Charles Dickens' *A Christmas Carol* is not only an amusing read, it is a fitting commentary on modern empirically based approaches to visionary experience:

> No, nor did he believe it even now. Though he looked the phantom through and through, and saw it standing before him; he was still incredulous, and fought against his senses.
>
> "How now!" said Scrooge, caustic and cold as ever. "What do you want with me?"
>
> "Much!" Marley's voice, no doubt about it.
>
> "Who are you?"
>
> "Ask me who I was."
>
> "Who were you then?" said Scrooge, raising his voice."You're particular for a shade." He was going to say "to a shade," but substituted this, as more appropriate.
>
> "In life I was your partner, Jacob Marley.". . . "You don't believe in me," observed the Ghost,
>
> "I don't," said Scrooge.
>
> "Why do you doubt your senses?"
>
> "Because," said Scrooge, "a little thing affects them. A slight disorder of the stomach makes them cheat. You may be an undigested bit of beef, a blot of mustard, a crumb of cheese, a fragment of an underdone potato. There's more of gravy than of grave about you, whatever you are!"
>
> At this the spirit raised a frightful cry, and shook its chain with such a dismal and appalling noise, that Scrooge held tight to his chair . . . .
>
> "Mercy!" he said. "Dreadful apparition, why do you trouble me?"
>
> "Man of the worldly mind!" replied the Ghost, "do you believe in me or not?"
>
> "I do," said Scrooge. "I must. But why do spirits walk the earth, and why do they come to me?"
>
> A Christmas Carol

This type of apparition is a visionary phenomenon which some people claim to receive today, in spite of the scientific-empirical outlook that overrides the modern way of looking at things. It is a common experience for the imagination to run free during restless sleeping hours, particularly if the subject is under stress or unwell. Hence, was this fictitious story a description of genuine apparitions that take place, or are such imaginings to be put down to stomach disorders or something similar? Are our senses to be trusted or are they misleading? Do spirit-apparitions really exist in the real world or are they all imaginary? This chapter examines the psychological process of the subject who receives visions and voices from God, both in biblical times and in our own day.

EBENEZER
SCROOGE

THEOPHANIES IN THE BIBLE

There is a clear precedent for modern charismatics who claim that they have experienced divine encounters—described loosely as theophanies—in both Testaments of the Bible. The Old and the New Testaments present theophanies as visions or voices, or as combinations of both. Although apparitions exist in biblical literature, in actual fact they are not as frequent as is sometimes supposed. Where they do exist, they are not written primarily as accounts of awe and wonder but are designed to serve some other theological purpose, both for the subject receiving the vision (pre-Oral Tradition) and later for the scribe documenting the event (Written Tradition). A large section of the Old Testament contains the books of the prophets, but the prophets are not to be understood primarily as forecasters or predictors of future events. In the main, the prophet's task was spiritual and moral. It was not one of divining what might be in the future but one of pointing out a higher ethic. Most of the writings of the prophets are geared towards drawing an indifferent and idolatrous Israel back to Yahweh. This point is not always recognised by fundamentalists however, yet the fact remains that there are very few passages in the Bible that are given as forecasts or predictions of historical events about to unfold. Of those texts that predict the future, the picture and imagery are largely obscure, which leads fundamentalist expositors to produce highly speculative interpretations.

The revealing of God's mind to man through apparitions involves a number of psychological and philosophical difficulties which need examining in at least three aspects:

a) the time and place of the apparition.

b) the concrete word or command issuing from it.

c) the character of the mediating phenomenon.

This study will be confined to the third aspect of apparitions, both to those encounters in the biblical records and to those visionary claims in modern times.

The foundations of Christianity would be unthinkable without its prophetic and visionary elements. Let us briefly consider a few types of apparitions found in the Bible that illustrate the broad range of religious theophanies to the worthies of old.

a) After receiving an apparition of God's glory within the cherubim, the prophet Ezekiel *hears the voice* of Yahweh:

> When I saw this I threw myself on my face, and heard a voice speaking to me: 'Man', he said, 'stand up, and let me talk with you . . . Man, I am sending you to the Israelites, a nation of rebels . . . '
>
> Ezek. 1:28–2:3

b) A second type is illustrated by Isaiah *having a vision*:

> The vision received by Isaiah son of Amoz . . .
>
> Isaiah 1:1

> This is the word which Isaiah son of Amoz received in a vision . . .
>
> Isaiah 2:1

c) In a third type, Jeremiah sees God's *revelation in pictures and symbols*:

> The word of the Lord came to me a second time: 'What is this that you see?' 'A cauldron', I said, 'on a fire, fanned by the wind; it is tilted away from the north . . .'
>
> Jer. 1:13

> This is what the Lord showed me: I saw two baskets of figs set out before the sanctuary of the Lord . . . . In one basket the figs were very good, like the figs that are first-ripe; in the other the figs were very bad, so bad that they were not fit to eat . . .
>
> Jer. 24:1

d) In a fourth type, *angels appear* to visionaries to give heavenly messages:

> There appeared to him an angel of the Lord, standing on the right of the altar of incense.
>
> Luke 1:11

> In the sixth month the angel Gabriel was sent from God to a town in Galilee called Nazareth, with a message to a girl betrothed to a man named Joseph.
>
> Luke 1:26

e) The divine communication has also come in *a dream*:

> An angel of the Lord appeared to him in a dream . . .
>
> Matt. 1:20; 2:19

f) Finally, it has equally taken place whilst the seer is in a *state of trance*:

> He [Peter] grew hungry and wanted something to eat. While they were getting it ready, he fell into a trance. He saw a rift in the sky, and a thing coming down that looked like a great sheet of sail-cloth . . .
>
> Acts 10:9f.

> After my [Paul's] return to Jerusalem, I was praying in the temple when I fell into a trance and saw him there, speaking to me . . .
>
> Acts 22:17 (II Cor. 12:2–5; Apoc. 4:2)

There is therefore *no unified form of divine communication* in the biblical narrative, and the letter to the Hebrews concludes the matter by summarising the various communicating forms of biblical revelations, such as we have previously considered:

> When in former times God spoke to our forefathers, he spoke in fragmentary and varied fashion through the prophets . . .
>
> Heb. 1:1f.

It is a relatively futile exercise to bring to ancient biblical documents the methods of psychological analysis that are employed in studying experience; only the historian can assess such literature composed in pre-psychological times. Yet, this leaves us with an unresolved problem: how else can the exegete make sense of such records? There is an interest in psychology and parapsychology in modern times, and fundamentalists are not slow in bringing pseudo-psychological interpretations to the recorded experiences of biblical prophets and heroes (one only has to sit through the average sermon or church exposition to note the practice). We cannot begin to understand the psychological processes behind biblical visions and to prophets and seers without resorting to a method of comparison with the claims of visionaries in modern times, even though many such claims may be dubious.

To help guide us through this highly subjective minefield, we shall refer to the work of a Catholic theologian, Karl Rahner, in his book *Visions and Prophecies*.[1] The choice is made because it is primarily within the Roman Church that current claims of apparitions are made.

The Spirit was revealed in the manner of visions and messages in the developing communities of the New Testament period, but it was not only evident in pro-Christian circles (Matt. 10:41; Acts 11:27–28; 21:9; I Cor. 12–14). Consequently, fundamentalists who are spirit-enthusiasts can make no legitimate claim to possess the Spirit in an exclusive sense.

Some modern-day apparitions are not merely visions to significant holy people for indulgent purposes; they are 'prophetic visions'. That is to say, there is a theological purpose for the visitation, namely, to guide the Church, or individuals of a church, through a practical or ideological matter. The Pentecostals and Evangelical Christians enjoy extravagant spoils of the Spirit's external manifestations—speaking in tongues, healing, visions and messages from God, etc.—but the phenomenon is not solely their possession. There are certain places of significant religious interest for the Catholic Church, where visions have occurred that have attracted very large crowds indeed. Places such as Lourdes and Fatima have gained their holy prestige as a result of appearances of the Virgin Mary. The subsequent healings that recipients claim to have received from their visits are open to auto-suggestive explanations, because neither the vision of the Virgin nor the subsequent healing 'miracle'—which, of course, is examinable—are likely to take place apart from the location of the shrine and outside the setting and context of the subject's heightened expectation. As to how we should evaluate the significance of the empirical fact that a miraculous healing has taken place is another question, and one we are not to ask here (religious authorities generally exercise considerable caution and restraint over disclosed miracle claims at such shrines). Our principal task is to examine the psychological basis for any such apparition— biblical or otherwise.

The case is more dubious with 'private revelations' than with 'public revelations', since the experience is primarily, if not exclusively, that of the devotee. As such, these phenomena are not accessible for critical investigation, unless a miracle or some message of testable forecasting accompanies the vision. In the case of private revelations, the function of the Catholic Church is not to endorse but to play down the extravagant claims of personal apparitions in preference for the 'non-prophetic', pure state of *infused contemplation* which is its origin.[2] The mystical theologians naturally reject this censorship, holding that any revelation has *per se* to be of a 'private character'. The consequences of the Middle Age abuse, however, where the exuberant free use of charismatic gifts took place with little self-control, were such that the

Catholic Church was right to commend a course of censorship and restraint over 'private revelations'.

The decisive issue, for our purpose, is to determine whether or not God is speaking through such private revelations, the answer to which would be difficult if the experiences were not open to external analysis. Some fundamentalist sects accept without question the authenticity of biblical visions, but rule the phenomenon of modern-day private revelations out of court; they see no place for such visions because God has revealed his word in full in the scriptures. This criticism is not consistent, however, for to such Christians, Rahner says: "Time is not a neutral dimension in which anything can happen and so anything can be revealed at any time."[3]

ESTABLISHING THE AUTHENTICITY OF A VISION

There are three objective criteria whereby a person standing outside another person's visionary experience can establish its authenticity. Authentic visions are as follows:

a) a vision accompanied by a miracle which can be verified empirically as an event suspending a law of nature.

b) a vision accompanied by a word of prediction of some future event, which has been clearly expressed before the event took place, and which does not conform to any human intuition, insight, or fortunate guesswork.

c) a vision accompanied by an experience which cannot be explained within the principles of hallucination, illusion or eidetic phenomenon (the psychology of images, where the ability to imagine an image is so vivid that it is believed to be objectively visible).

These criteria may help to clarify what stands as evidence for a phenomenon that is claimed to have come from an *other world*—a phenomenon, says Rahner, which cannot be accounted for by subjective indulgence, fraud, confusion or deception.

(a) Visions Accompanied by Miracles

As regards the first criterion of genuine visions, there are surprisingly few examples in the Old and the New Testaments (Gen. 32:22–32; I Kings 19:5–15; Acts 5:17–21; 12:6–11). Of those which do exist, we have no means of verifying their authenticity with empirical investigation. It remains the task of the historian to assess their validity by the use of textual criticism. There are, however, examples of visionaries living in later ages, who have boldly claimed to have received visions and witnessed miracles—the most striking being the visions of the children of Fatima and the supposed sun-miracle.[4]

With the second and third criteria, we can examine the phenomenon at much greater length.

(b) The Nature of 'Predictive' Prophecy

Rahner has identified five types of prophecy—which he understands as "a prediction or a foresight of a future event which could not be known by ordinary means".[5]

I. Superstitious Prophecy

The first might be described as 'superstitious', 'magical', or 'profane', prophecy. This category consists of techniques for wresting God's secrets; techniques that can be classified as one or other of the following: soothsaying, divination, oracle practice, astrology, chiromancy, palmistry, fortune-telling cards and necromancy. These manipulative devices were not unknown in Israelite history (Num. 23:23; Lev. 19:26, 31; Duet. 18:9–14) even though they were largely shunned (as also the Catholic Church: 'Occultism', etc., Decree of the Holy Office, 18 July, 1919, *Denz.* 2189). The well known case is that of Saul summoning the deceased Samuel by a medium at Endor. This example of necromancy was performed for the king to enquire a forecast for the outcome of a battle (I Sam. 28:3–25). These practices, while not unpopular today, leave the subject open to delusion and the risk of unbalanced mental state. The result of such practices is that the prophecies are "practically always infantile and primitive—befitting the intellectual and moral standards of their adepts—which of itself suffices to show that they reveal no source of 'higher' knowledge".[6] I think Rahner's judgement is a little strong here, for I have found some intellectuals involved in these arts (principally astrology), but I agree with him when he goes on to say that it is rare that the 'spirits' at seances reveal anything profound or significant to those around the table.

II. Clairvoyant Prophecy

The second type of prophecy belongs to the field of parapsychology, and includes prophetic dreams, second sight, clairvoyance, and a foreknowledge of the hour of death. Though this vastly underrated phenomenon is open to fraud and illusion, there is a residue of inexplicable events and foresighted auditions that defy conventional psychology and physics. Nevertheless, this is not to be understood as an intervention of God; though extraordinary, these abilities should be considered as natural faculties.

The borderline between parapsychological vision and an apparition of divine origin is unclear. A parapsychological vision of the future is usually just a vision, vivid and precise, and the seer is like a reporter or interpreter. By contrast, biblical prophecy is not so much a 'vision' as a 'Word'—a word that can be obscure, so as to leave within its scope freedom for the person to act. The seer is not a reporter describing his experience of being miraculously transported into the future. The message is not a remote forecast of the future. "Rather it will give the man to whom it is addressed the forward look into the future which he needs in order to endure his own present now with loyal confidence in God".[7] This is precisely what we find in the book of Daniel and Revelation; it is a message of hope for the seer's community to endure its current persecution and trial. Fundamentalist expositors do not view the matter in this way; they take such visionary books out of their *Sitz im Leben*. Those denominations, such as the Jehovah's Witnesses, the Seventh-Day Adventists and the Christadelphians, which search for a detailed programme of forecasts covering Christ's visible reign on the earth for the thousand years before the final Judgement and consummation of all things, have based their theologies on an arbitrary and literal interpretation of biblical revelation. They take the books of Daniel and Revelation from their respective settings and force the predictive visions into later periods than those for which they were intended.

III. Prophecy as a Philosophy of History

A third type of prophecy is an anticipation of the future in the light of a philosophy or theology of history. Most often this is a 'national prophecy', beginning with an embryonic insight of human genius into historical developments, and ending with a nationalistic hope or ideal. This may or may not be fulfilled, or it may be continually suspended until an unprescribed time of fulfilment—a methodology that can never be proved wrong! Some visionaries (inaccurately called 'prophets') have had uncanny intuitions of the future, quite separate from their particular historical settings, which have surprisingly turned out to be quite accurate (Rousseau, Nietzsche), whilst others have predicted short-term future events from the inklings of their own particular situations. I think the forecasts attributed to Jesus fit well this second category. He is reported to have predicted his own death from the historical pattern laid down for all the prophets of Israel, together with an intuition that the temperature was rising amongst the hot-headed zealots during the feast at Jerusalem. Again, it is recorded that he predicted the fall of Jerusalem from the stereotypical pattern of Israel's waywardness at a time when the Roman administration was becoming increasingly intolerant of Jewish fanaticism.

All such forecasts belong to the category of 'natural prophecy'. An important corollary is the observation that such predictions can work in the opposite direction:

> Many things will happen not because they were foreseen, but because they were 'predicted' of a future 'utopia', which will attract people as a new ideal and inspire them to realise it. Here the future is not foretold because it is going to happen, it happens because it has been foretold. The 'prophet' does not foresee the future, but sets the men of the present a new goal—sometimes even by warning against it . . . (as good Christians of our day who like to assume the mantle of Jeremiah and talk of impending doom should remember!).[8]

It is not clear whether the prophecies of Nostradamus fit this category, or into the parapsychological classification. Personally, I am not convinced that the forecasts of Nostradamus are an authentic or valid insight into the future. The detailed predictions are somewhat vague, obscure and imaginary, and it appears that commentators all too readily read a fulfilment into these predictions which involves a high degree of ingenuity.

IV. Mundane and Commonplace Prophecy

A fourth category of prophetic prediction is exemplified by those visionaries who place an exaggerated importance on the practical and specific leading of the Spirit in daily affairs (the charismatics of the Pentecostals and Evangelical Christians). The forecasting arises from the need to imitate what the earliest communities were doing for practical guidance under the superintendence of the Spirit:

> While they were keeping a fast and offering worship to the Lord, the Holy Spirit said, 'Set Barnabas and Saul apart for me, to do the work to which I have called them.'
>
> Acts 13:2 (Acts 16:6–10)

Often the visionary 'feels' a compulsion to move in a new direction, or issue a warning to an individual or group, or compel a decision over a matter where uncertainties exist, or claim an authority over a specific issue. The 'message' is rarely claimed to be auditory but intuitive (imaginative). It is normally practical and specific, and usually results from an activity of intense prayer and ecstatic worship.

This type of 'prophecy' is rarely self-critical and, as such, is naive; its predictions are not tested on a probability scale of success to failure, and its point of contact may be one of *infused contemplation* or may equally be accounted for by the laws of psychology and hallucination. This theology subscribes to the free leading of the Spirit, and since this involves an avoidance of any self-critical examination of the phenomenon, the activity is mechanically repeated to reinforce its validity, irrespective of failures on the way. It is attractive in that it gives a *direct* sense of the divine influence upon the individual and gives the recipient a feeling of warmth and spiritual infusion. In some instances, however, it cultivates an un-edifying spirit of elitism, resulting in sectarian schisms!

V. Genuine Supernatural Revelation

The final category of prophecy is described by Rahner as "genuine supernatural revelations of which God himself is the cause".[9] I have difficulty in accepting what Rahner says here. Naturally, in seeking criteria for genuine prophecy, we have, at least initially, to see the divine influence not fitting the previously outlined four categories of 'natural prophecy'. But, moving on, how are we to understand an omniscient God, first knowing the future, and second making that future known to the visionary without by that very same action jeopardising a free movement of history in the process? If the universe is wholly determined, there is no problem in a super-intelligence (God) being able to foreknow every sequenced event on a pre-programmed path—from the natural disaster of an earthquake in a given year at a given place to every human act and thought. Eminent physicists, theologians and philosophers see a conflict between a determined universe and the laws of probability and human freedom. How could God know the details that might occur at random? Can such details be predictable or programmable? It is not a question of complexity—God's mind being greater than the human mind, etc.—but a question of contradiction: God's knowing and man's freedom in acting and thinking arbitrarily. Rahner speaks of God as one who is "transcending time and history", as "omnipotent First Cause sustaining all creation", and he speaks of time as "an intrinsic modality of 'becoming'" where "for God the future is the present", etc., but this is meaningless to me unless he can demonstrate how the details of God's foreknowledge might work (at least by philosophical argument) in a universe which is not wholly determined! Foreknowledge and determinism are not quite the same thing, I grant (a child might behave in a manner that is predictable by his parents and in such a way that their foreknowledge does not of necessity preclude the child's freedom to act), but the fact that any action is calculable with certainty suggests a determinism of sorts. To claim that the belief has the testimony of scripture— "I reveal the end from the beginning, from ancient times I reveal what is to be; I say, 'My purpose shall take effect, I will accomplish all that I please' . . ." (Isaiah 46:10)[10]—and the support of the Catholic Church (*Denz.* 1707, 1790, 2145), only further begs the question of how this can be.[11]

(c) The Psychological Analysis of Visions

Under hallucination there is evidence of a heightened and refined form of consciousness by many who are not necessarily short of intelligence and controlled imagination. As we investigate the stimuli of the various prophetic insights, we notice no uniform process. It is feasible, argues Dodd, that Amos' vision of fire, and also the plumb-line (or 'lead'—an uncertain translation),[12] may plausibly be regarded as instances of creative imagination that had become vivid to the point of visual hallucination. In both cases, however, it is possible (and likely) that things actually seen in the real world have helped to determine the form of the vision. Physical objects in regular use, commonplace happenings, natural and social disasters and the like can all trigger the controlled imagination to perceive realities on a higher spiritual plane than that communicated by the events and objects themselves. Thus, the ravaging attacks of swarms of locusts leaving utter destruction in their wake, form a fitting image of what the seer might 'see' of the impending doom of the northern power (Amos 7:1–6). Jeremiah's visit to the pottery house, his staring eye on the craftsman's hands as he fashions the vessel from the shapeless lump, squashing the clay and then starting again until he has moulded the pleasing and acceptable form, triggers the controlled imagination to 'see beyond' the sensual world of appearances to the invisible world of Yahweh's dealings with Israel (Jer. 18:1–4).

In some cases (Amos' plumb-line), *the religious idea has projected itself upon the sensible image*, and the imagination has been invoked to give the object a symbolic meaning. In other cases (Jeremiah's potter), *a simple observation of an object is followed by a 'sudden intuition' which projects meaning on to what is observed.* On the one hand the object becomes a symbol of meaning, on the other the object stimulates an idea. In both cases, the object conveys meaning.

The case of the inaugural vision of Isaiah can be understood as a visual hallucination of a very different type (Is. 6:1–8). This young *nabi* is privileged to see the 'holiness' of Yahweh lifted up—a *numinous* presence of great intensity. We might imagine the pious seer worshipping in the temple court and musing over the visual seraphim-figures radiating before his eyes—those monstrous symbols which served as guardians of the divine Presence (much in the way that winged dragons stood watch at the entrances of Babylonian temples). Amidst the smoking perfumes of the altar of incense, and with the closing melody of the final chant ('Holy, Holy, Holy . . . ') ringing in his ears, the visionary becomes transfixed and caught up in a powerfully suffused *numinous* state of semi-consciousness, he sees Yahweh Himself, majestic and enthroned in His Temple. The trance-conscious musing over the symbolic creatures *draws the creative imagination to 'see' much more than the objective scene before him.* The seer's *mind has created meaning* even though other worshippers in the same setting have come away unmoved by it all.

From this moment on, the visual stimulus serves no further purpose as the imagination takes over and creates further symbols and images of a composite picture (some sensible, others non-sensible, much after the manner of our dreams). There is a further stimulus to Isaiah's vision that clearly comes from within the seer himself, and that is his mood. At reception, Isaiah's emotions and cognitive processes become suffused with the object before him and provide the stage for the drama to unfold: "Woe is me! I am lost, for I am a man of unclean lips and I dwell among a people of unclean lips" (6:6). There is melancholy here, there is humility and lowliness of spirit as the devotee kneels prostrate before the *numinous* Being, yet there is a commission too. A vocation comes from the encounter: "Then I heard Yahweh saying, 'Whom shall I send?' . . . And I answered, 'Here am I; send me . . .'" (6:8–9).

To say that the *nabi* might apprehend the 'Word of the Lord' through some measure of imagination is not to empty it of reality or to invalidate it, for there are other grounds than the statement of 'Thus saith the Lord' for determining truth from falsehood, as we shall see. Where an idea came from is of secondary importance to what that idea is, and psychology only partially helps us to understand the mechanism of how a 'revelation' might come. We are interested, now, in what might be claimed as a valid representation of Reality from 'revelations' that are illusory—elements of genius from elements of cleverness. There is no *a priori* reason for refuting the suggestion that a Mind outside our world might be telepathically communicating ideas to seers through some processes such as those outlined above. Even though psychology may provide us with a means of investigating the medium through which something has been 'revealed', this does not fully explain the phenomenon definitively, and we are left with more questions unanswered than those which are answered.

However, there is the need to distinguish the 'genuine' vision from the hallucinatory experience. The great mystical writers (St John of the Cross, St Theresa of Avila, et al.) have been notable for elevating the imaginative vision over the corporeal one.

Corporeal or Imaginative Visions

The mystics have been unanimous in agreeing that the imaginative type of vision is the more valuable and exalted. "Theresa of Avila expressly declares that she never had corporeal visions but only imaginative ones."[13] This acknowledgement removes for us a major difficulty, not so much for the person receiving the apparition—where the subject may be confused or deceived and it really doesn't matter—but for those of us wishing to establish the authenticity of the vision and message as of something from the 'other world'. For example, if the 'naive' recipient claims to have seen the corporeal Jesus, or the Blessed Virgin Mary, as an ontological object that is present in a spatio-temporal sense (that is, being perceived with the eyes in much the same manner as one might 'see' a friend beside one, in a two-way communication, and having their own individual consciousnesses), then there are difficulties. Of what substance are we to imagine the clothes which the heavenly figure might be wearing? Are they glorified clothes? If the recipient claims to 'see' Jesus as a child, since he cannot be a child after becoming an adult, how can this be? Again, how might it be possible for the vision or the message to be seen or heard by the recipient and not by those present at the same time (Saul's vision in Acts 9:7; 22:9)?

The fact that the visionary had the impression that the object of the apparition was 'real' is not of itself proof; hallucinations and eidetic phenomena are equally 'real' to the recipient. Should the heavenly figure 'speak', or 'move', or even let himself be 'touched', then, this again is no proof of their corporeality, for even this happens in natural purely imaginative processes.[14] Even if the visionary learns something surprising to him or her, or something previously not known to him or her, this again does not constitute proof. In the common experience of dreams we can experience a division of consciousness into two personalities, which, not infrequently, brings about a revelation of hitherto unknown material. Although the psychological explanation is complex, we do not think of an object in our dream as being corporeal. The location and activity of a person in a vision are no proof of corporeality, but are likely to be the product of the creative subconscious in the visionary, for even in dreams we will transcend the powers of natural consciousness; we imagine ourselves in strange situations and talking more intelligently than we do in reality (in dreams the creative free play of imagination is uninhibited).

Regarding mass-apparitions, is it not likely that there are principles of auto-suggestion at play in such cases, as in the case of mass-hypnosis, or in psychic disturbance (induced insanity)? In mass-apparitions the phenomenon must be considered as imaginary. Even though the subjects may witness the same stimulus, their apprehension of it may not be entirely identical.

In short, most visions are imaginative ones, above all else, argues Rahner, because they cannot possibly be corporeal ones. In attempting to work out a clearer understanding of imaginative visions, the divine and the human can be understood to work in harmony, as Rahner says:

> . . . such a vision must largely conform to the psychic laws determined by the intrinsic structure of the seer's spiritual faculties; secondly, to be authentic, the vision must be caused by God . . . For a vision to be truly the spiritual reality of a given person it must, metaphysically speaking, be the true act of this person, not only an act produced in him by God but also an act performed by the person himself.[15]

There is no absolute guarantee that the object is 'really there' then, only that it is 'perceived to be there', and there have been many mistaken judgements in modern times.[16] At some point there will need to be a valid assessment of a given vision and its content, of whether or not the object of the vision is felt to be 'seen' or 'imagined'. This will involve the making of a judgement. The judgement may be erroneous and may change with closer observation, theological reasoning, or altered predisposition. It is not invincible, and is not to be found in the senses but in the judgement following perception. Again, even if the recipient might be convinced of the vision's spiritual other-worldliness, how could the visionary convince another that he or she was not confused or deceived? There is no room for dogmatism but we must be consistent.

If we should choose to brush aside many of the above difficulties, and still seek some validation for visionary phenomena, there is only the evidence of clairvoyance that might account for the supranatural experience of apparitions. Parapsychology provides us with examples of telepathic communication through visions, such as

St Theresa's vision of 40 Brazilian martyrs being executed at the moment of the incident taking place.[17]

It is noteworthy how the genuine mystics have exercised caution and reserve over the objective accuracy of the imaginative content of their visions; they were eager to exalt the intense spiritual state whilst encountering the vision more than its content. The visionary content served as the mere aftermath of the visionary phenomenon. The imaginative vision, therefore, is only a secondary phenomenon, the central spiritual process being what the classical Spanish mystics described as *infused contemplation.*[18] Mystical ecstasy is a suspension of the senses, and the condition is the result of what is claimed to be the *central mystical process of God's self-communication.* The imaginative vision presupposes such *infused contemplation* and is a *radiation* or *reflex* of contemplation in the sphere of the senses.

In the narrative of The Transfiguration in the Synoptic Gospels (Mark 9:2–8 RSV and parallels), the story is related as *a corporeal event* rather than as a vision. The time and location are given ("after six days . . . led them up a high mountain"). A conversation is conducted between Jesus and Elijah and Moses—two prophets who, according to Jewish tradition in the first century, never died but lived in Abraham's bosom. Other details, however, suggest that a vision is to be understood ("and there *appeared* to them"), making the interpretation unclear. A further point of confusion is that the *corporeal* body of Jesus becomes *vision-like,* becomes transfigured ("his garments became glistening, intensely white, as no fuller on earth could bleach them") up to the point of receiving a message from his Father in heaven ("This is my beloved Son; listen to him"), after which, for those disciples undergoing the experience, Jesus is found to be alone.

IS THE SPIRIT STILL ACTIVE IN THIS WAY TODAY?

From this brief overview, a question naturally arises: Can the claims of some modern-day mystical Christians, who speak of receiving revelatory visions from God, be verified in the light of the fact that God is believed to have spoken in such a fashion in biblical times? If we answer this question in the affirmative, we might further ask whether there should be any cautionary criteria for distinguishing a genuine theophany from conscious (or unconscious) fraud or deception. If we answer in the negative, and deny the possibility of a theophany, what are our grounds for making such an *a priori* judgement?

Although the New Testament authorisation for visionary experience is not entirely conflicting, there are passages which encourage free reign of the Spirit and there are others which prescribe caution. Compare these two passages:

> Do not stifle inspiration, and do not despise prophetic utterances, but bring them all to the test and then keep what is good in them and avoid the bad of whatever kind.
>
> I Thess. 5:19–21

> But do not trust any and every spirit, my friends; test the spirits, to see whether they are from God, for among those who have gone out into the world, there are many prophets falsely inspired.
>
> I John 4:1.

At one extreme, there are pious Christians holding offices of influence, who are very judgmental in stifling the freedom of the Spirit by a form of 'orthodox conservatism'. They deny the possibility of spiritual encounter, and remain sceptical of the claims of current visionaries, and yet accept the phenomenon as practised in the New Testament with not an ounce of critical judgement. This is not consistent! Christadelphians and Jehovah's Witnesses, for example, are forward in pointing out Paul's reservation in giving status to this gift as compared with other gifts of the Spirit under the supreme ethic of love, and refer to Paul's wish to check its enthusiastic overemphasis and place of importance:

> . . . are there prophets? Their work will be over. Are there tongues of ecstasy? They will cease. Is there knowledge? It will vanish away; for our knowledge and our prophecy alike are partial, and the partial vanishes when wholeness comes.
>
> I Cor. 13:8

Yet, Paul did not ban the Spirit gifts. He did not seek to prohibit prophecy and *glossolalia* but he did seek to contain their abuse. Spirit gifts still had their place in the early Church for Paul because the Spirit was believed to be active. If we hold to the view that God revealed something to the 'worthies of old' through visions and voices, then why should he still not do so today? If we choose to be highly censorious of modern-day apparitions, then surely we should equally approach the biblical documents with the same measure of scepticism. Shouldn't the same rules of censorship and caution that are applied in post-biblical times be exercised for biblical periods too? If we conclude that current religious theophanies can be explained away with psychological and empirical reasoning, then, to be consistent, we have no choice but to subject the theophanies in the Bible to the same standards of criticism.

The advice of the mystical fathers of old was to play down the activity, and such would be the judgement of those of us today who take an objective empirical approach to these things. At the other extreme, there are liberal charismatics claiming to have received apparitions and other more 'observable' forms of 'spiritual gifts', such as speaking in tongues and healing, which have encouraged divisions and attitudes of élitism within some churches, and this is unfortunate. Caution and reserve are to be commended then, not merely for personal visionary experiences, but also for those communities that exercise a free rein of the Spirit. There are many Christian esoteric groups that actively encourage their members to indulge in unbridled spiritual euphoria, particularly charismatics, who would do well to take heed of the lessons of history.

Today, there is a far greater understanding of the complexities of the human psyche than that to which biblical writers would have had access. There is more insight into the 'tricks' that bring about illusions and confusions of sense-consciousness. Psychologists understand to a degree the nature of particular emotional states: feelings of exhilaration and ecstasy; beliefs of intense expectation; the mechanics of autosuggestion; mental imbalance; schizophrenia and hallucination. What is more, a vocabulary exists to describe these states and conditions. In short, there are abundantly more means of 'testing the spirits' than there were for those of the first century. I am not suggesting that we should regard every claimant as having a pathological disorder, or as being unbalanced, but I am prescribing discretion and evaluation before glib acceptance of that which is claimed. Having said this, the censorious Christian simply cannot apply one criterion for biblical visions and voices and a different one for a similar phenomenon in modern times.

Further to this, we cannot investigate everything by means of a philosophical reductionism, particularly those things belonging to a *spiritual domain*. There is a call for an open mind. The possibility of deception is there, but so also is the possibility of *direct communion*, just as in biblical times. Whatever the case, something extraordinary must be going on. In conclusion, it seems that there are as many grounds for accepting the genuine nature, psychologically speaking, of biblical visions and voices as an authentic message from God, as there are for accepting the same in modern times. A refusal to predispose oneself to the possibility of a visionary or auditory experience cannot by itself invalidate the case that such an experience is either possible or desirable.

NOTES

1. Rahner, *Visions and Prophecies*, London, 1963.
2. Ibid., page 20.
3. Ibid., page 23.
4. On Fatima, Rahner, op. cit., pages 103–5, (notes 132 & 133). A recent treatment of the visionary claims of the children of Fatima has been given by Francis Johnston, *Fatima: the Great Sign*, Devon, 1980. A series of monthly visions of the Virgin Mary is claimed to have been received by three Portuguese children, Lucia, Francisco and Jacinta, from 1916 to 1929, in a sheep pasture near the village of Fatima, 80 miles north of Lisbon. The predictions were given by the Virgin Mary around the holm oak and were confirmed by a number of 'observable facts': the purpose and ending of the war; the rise of Communism and the subsequent conversion of Russia; and the solar 'miracle' on 13 October 1917.

   To authenticate the visionary claims is difficult, since it is not easy to establish with certainty when the forecasts were committed to writing. Also, the writings appear somewhat vague and adorned with piety and sentimental adoration.

   What is interesting is that the children not only predicted that a firmament-shaking sign would take place at a certain time and location, but that the event was fully recorded by the media on a broad scale. Numerous newspaper reporters and authorities came cynically to the spot to observe what might take place, fully expecting to record a colossal fiasco. Tens of thousands converged on Fatima, despite appalling weather conditions and the opposition of armed guards at the Cova da Iria, to witness a ball of fire, resembling the sun, whirling in the sky amid a multitude of wavering colours flooding the landscape. The spectacle led many to believe that the end of the world had come. The event was recorded by the following newspapers: *Diario de Noticias*, 13 October; *O Secular*, 15 October; *Illustracao Portuguesa*, 29 October 1917; and many other professional accounts which are given in Johnson's book, op. cit., pages 53–66.
5. Rahner, op. cit., page 90.
6. Ibid., page 91.
7. Ibid., page 95. For this reason, Daniel 11 is untypical of biblical prophecy. It reads as a reporter's account, unlike the bizarre imagery found in Daniel's earlier visions. As a result, it is believed to have been written up after the event (*ex eventu*) by a Maccabean scribe. The account covers the wars of the Ptolemaic and Seleucid empires and the plundering of Palestine

by Antiochus Epiphanes in close detail. The account matches accurately other historical accounts, until we reach verse 40. The text of 11:40–12:4 was not fulfilled during this period, and is likely to be the point in history at which the seer lived. To claim this section is Messianic, is to read something into the passage from a New Testament perspective. For this seer, it was the time of consummation of God's kingdom, which the writer envisaged was around the corner; in this, his peoples' hopes were lodged.

8. K. Rahner op. cit., page 98.
9. Ibid., page 99.
10. Is. 41:22–29; 43:12; 44:7; 45:21; 46:10–15; Deut. 18:22; II Pet. 1:20; John. 13:19.
11. K. Rahner, op. cit., pages 99–106.
12. C. H. Dodd, *The Authority of the Bible*, op. cit., page 74. The 'plumb-line' in Amos vision may not be a correct translation. The word is Akkadian and has been translated as 'lead', but its meaning is unclear.
13. St John of the Cross, *Subida II*, 11; 16. Cited by Rahner, op. cit., pages 32–33.
14. K. Rahner op. cit., page 36, (note 31).
15. Ibid., page 41.
16. Ibid., pages 67–69; 86–88. In the catalogue of the history of visions, even by those who were claimed to be pious, there is abundant evidence of errors and distortions—historical, theological and aesthetic. A few brief examples will illustrate the point and will underline the need for caution and reserve in accepting the authority of visions at face value.

    a) Of *historical errors*, we may cite:
    St Norbert of Xanten who was absolutely certain that the Anti-Christ would appear in his generation; St Vincent Ferrer who declared with the authority of his visions that the end of the world was imminent.

    b) *Theological errors* in visions include:
    St Francis of Rome who received information from visions on the nature of the firmament, which cannot be correct; St Catherine of Siena who received revelations that Mary's conception was not 'immaculate' (a theological heresy for Catholicism); the visions of St Magdalene of Pazzi, St Brigid of Sweden and St Elizabeth of Schoenau which were contradictory concerning the life and death of Jesus (and the Virgin Mary) as recorded in the Gospels.

    c) *Aesthetic errors* of bad taste include:
    the Blessed Margaret Ebner being instructed by the child Jesus "how his holy circumcision was performed." She felt she had heard the voice of the Lord bidding her to suck the wooden statue of Jesus, which she kept in her crib; St Mary Magdalene who watched Jesus write his name on her heart with the milk of the Blessed Virgin (a fuller catalogue is given on pages 67–69).

    Of more recent apparitions, Rahner accepts only three as genuine from the thirty-one he cites, these being the children's apparitions of Fatima, Banneaux and Beauraing.

    The lists of fraudulent visions are numerous and it is to be noted how some of the apparitions which the Catholic Church condemned drew large crowds. In some cases, there were mass-hallucinatory phenomena:

    > In Lublin in 1949 the weeping Madonna had been visited by 100,000 people in one day. In 1939, 70,000 people gathered on Mount Ezquioga in the Basque country. Many such apparitions were found to be doublets of prior apparitions—the 'sun miracle' of Fatima. Many have been established as deliberate fraud—the revelations of Maria Rafols in 1853. The apparitions at Lipa in the Philippines were deliberately staged as a hoax; and the visions at Gimigliano were invented by the little visionary after seeing a film of Bernadette, though many people claim to have seen the sun-miracle during those visions, including a priest (pages 86–88).

17. Ibid., page 38, (note 34).
18. From the 'spiritual betrothal' to 'spiritual marriage'—the full mystical union. This 'experience' will be explored under a different term—the *numinous*.

9

THE NON-RATIONAL ELEMENT OF RELIGION

Rudolf Otto's classic book, *The Idea of the Holy*, presents a thorough treatment of the mystical side of religious experience.[1] This invaluable study attempts to restore the balance of the opposing extremes of objective reasoning and subjective experiencing. Many people in Western society can be classified as *creatures of a technological rationally objective culture, having no room for mystery and little tolerance for anything which is non-empirically based*, but is this a universal description of man?

After the Enlightenment, the categories of knowledge embodied in theology and philosophy drifted apart to become separate disciplines in their own right. The Enlightenment was the period of the seventeenth and eighteenth century, which was characterised by great thinkers like Hobbes and Hume in England, Lessing and Kant in Germany, and Rousseau and Voltaire in France. It had reduced the Christian faith to the rational proofs of God's existence, to natural theology, and to morality—there was no place for mysticism—but Schleiermacher challenged this new philosophical outlook by bringing the mystical element back to the fore. He defined the ultimate religious experience as the *feeling of dependence,* and he drew our attention to the essence of religion as that which is non-rational in character.[2] It is the type of feeling Abraham is imagined to have had when pleading with God for those of Sodom:

> May I presume to speak to the Lord, dust and ashes that I am.
>
> Gen. 18:27

Yet, Schleiermacher has been criticised for describing the 'result' of the feeling-state rather than the 'state' of the encounter itself. His definition, therefore, belongs to the rational side of the idea of God.

THE HOLY AND INEFFABLE

Mysticism is the lifting to prominence of the non-rational, or supra-rational elements of religion. Although mysticism has many varied expressions, two features occur in all forms:.

a) there is the feeling of *creature-consciousness*, or *creature-hood*—the consciousness of the puny state of every creature.

b) there is also the identification of the personal self with the transcendent Reality through *moments* of religious experience—to quote William James:

> The perfect stillness of the night was thrilled by a more solemn silence. The darkness held a presence that was all the more felt because it was not seen. I could not

> anymore have doubted that He was there than I was. Indeed, I felt myself to be, if possible, the less real of the two.[3]

Otto begins his thesis by coining a term to describe the ineffable part of religious experience, since most expressions we use to describe feeling concepts, such as 'Holy', cannot be stripped of the moral tones with which they have become associated. His term is 'numinous', from the Latin word *numen* meaning deity. He encourages us to consider *moments* of deeply felt religious experience, such as being rapt in worship, and to use this word to describe the 'pure' feeling-state. This spiritual and emotional feeling-state arises from reflecting upon *moments* of what he describes as *mysterium tremendum*:

> The feeling of it may at times come sweeping like a gentle tide, pervading the mind with tranquil mood of deepest worship. It may pass over into a more set and lasting attitude of the soul, continuing, as it were, thrillingly vibrant and resonant, until at last it dies away and the soul resumes its 'profane', non-religious mood of everyday experience.[4]

Mysterium denotes that which is hidden and esoteric, that which is beyond conception or understanding. *Tremendum* describes the feeling of shuddering in the presence of the divine. The 'History of Religions' school of thought has traced a development from a superstitious dread of spirits and demons to an awe, and to a state of what Otto describes as *fascination* for the spiritual and non-temporal. So, from earlier fears of malevolent spirits and a dread of the 'wrath of God',[5] there comes a confidence in that which is spiritual and a *fascination* with that which is divine. Elements of fascination, such as love, mercy, pity and comfort, have their rational parallels in the emotions and common psychical life, but in the non-rational sense they are thought of as absolute and complete:

> Things beyond our seeing, things beyond our hearing, things beyond our imagining, all prepared by God for those who love him," these it is that God has revealed to us through the Spirit.
>
> I Cor. 2:9–10

The *numinous* has parallels with the Buddhist teaching of 'Nirvana'. Nirvana is the theology of negation, the doctrine of Anatman which means 'entire emptiness'. Otto recalls a conversation with a Buddhist monk: 'What then of Nirvana itself?', he asked. After a long pause, there came at last the single answer, low and restrained: "Bliss unspeakable!"

> And the hushed restraint of that answer, the solemnity of his voice, demeanour, and gesture, made more clear what was meant than the words themselves.[6]

Mysticism must have its place within Christian living and experience. Mysticism has always been of central importance for Eastern Christianity, but for the West it has been acknowledged only with caution and reserve. Western Christianity has emphasised the importance of the rational elements of religion to the detriment of its non-rational features. Thomas Aquinas first brought Aristotle to the attention of the Church, with his rational apologetic of Christian faith, thereby conforming the Christian message to philosophically respectable reasoning. This process of defending the faith rationally has tended to preserve Christianity as a *rational faith*, at the expense of the non-rational elements of religion. (I use the term 'non-rational' in a neutral non-value sense, as opposed to the word 'irrational' which carries with it, I think, a pejorative undertone.)

THE RATIONAL AND THE NON-RATIONAL

Augustine and Luther are monumental figures in Church history. They both successfully retained the 'rational' as well as the 'non-rational' elements of religion in their writing. Augustine was a lecturer in rhetoric at the university of Milan. He was highly impressed with the great Bishop Ambrose of Milan—a master at preaching Christ in philosophical language—yet, he could be touched by the *numinous*, too. In page after page of his *Confessions* and *City of God*, he exposes his soul and describes a surrendering devotion to *something* much greater than himself—the *mysterium tremendum* of the 'non-rational' was clearly evident throughout his mystical reflections. During his conversion, he hears God calling him to service through the voice of a child:

> Lord will you never be content? Must we always taste your vengeance? Forget the long record of our sins.[7]

The *fascination* for the *numinous* had moved him to compose with passion:

> . . . it was as though the light of confidence flooded into my heart and all the darkness of doubt dispelled.[8]

Catholicism has put greater emphasis on the mystical side of religion compared with Protestantism, particularly in respect of the sacrament of the Eucharist, yet Protestants, nevertheless, have claimed to experience the *numinous* at times.

Luther was an academic in language, logic, geometry, arithmetic, music, astronomy, philosophy and biblical studies—achieving his Master's Degree by the age of twenty-one, on 7 January 1505.[9] He was a distinguished lecturer of the time at Wittenberg University, but his intellectual interests did not preclude him from being responsive to the *numinous*. During a period of depression and personal crisis, he expresses his gratitude to Dr Staupitz:

> If Dr Staupitz had not helped me out . . . I should have been swallowed up in Hell. I cannot forget, for it was through you that the light of the Gospel began first to shine out of the darkness of my heart . . . and he bore me in Christ.[10]

Luther could speak of the 'un-revealed', in contrast to the 'revealed face of God'. The *mysterium tremendum* was likewise evident in his writings:

> Then shall we learn how that God is a consuming fire . . . Wilt thou sin? Then he will devour thee up. For God is a fire . . . Yea, He is more terrible and frightful than the Devil . . .[11]

He was also humble enough to recognise in himself a *fascination* for the *numinous*:

> Christians are blissful people . . . If thou feelest it truly in the heart, it will be such a great thing to thee that thou wilt rather be silent than speak aught of it.[12]

Academics in modern times also have acknowledged the 'non-rational' and numinous aspect of religious experience. John Hick has radically questioned many aspects of Christian belief, such as the Incarnation, the Resurrection and Divine Providence, but, in spite of his rational approach to faith, he sees the validity of religious experience:

> It is rational to trust experience, unless there is reason to doubt it. Experience of God should be treated like this-worldly experience. Therefore it is rational to trust experience of God unless there is reason to doubt it.[13]

Paul Tillich, another radical philosopher of religion, says the following of religious feeling-states:

> Nobody can exclude the element of feeling in any experience in which the total personality is involved, and in religion this is perhaps more true than in any other realm.[14]

Don Cupitt asks whether religious experience is an 'extra sense' that some people have which others lack. Does the mystic gain knowledge in a way which is inaccessible for most others? Has he or she some special sense or faculty that is generally dormant in most of us? Pressing for stricter definition, he recognises that not every mystic is a visionary, and that there is no way of establishing authentic criteria for separating the subjective from the objective in *mystical experience.* Mystics, he says, do not produce consistent descriptions of the supernatural; such descriptions reveal metaphysical beliefs, such as 'reality being one', 'time being unreal', and so on, which is incompatible with modern experience. With 'interior' or 'introvertive mysticism' we *abstract away* from the senses and discursive thinking, and our thought becomes very still, absorbed and undifferentiated, but with the opposite kind of mysticism, known as 'extravertive', 'panenhenic' or 'nature mysticism', we gain a heightened awareness of the external world *through* our ordinary senses. "A good deal of intellectual interpretation is interwoven with the experience" in both cases, argues Cupitt. While he recognises that "mystical experience is very common, very diverse, and occurs in every religion and in people of no religion", he is doubtful whether it produces any valid form of knowledge.[15] The English philosopher, Bertrand Russell, would not have agreed. He felt the mystics had attained a universal experiential knowledge, and identified four characteristics of all mystics:

a) they place greater store on *knowledge through intuition* than reason.

b) they see a *plurality of meaning* behind the universe—tending towards pantheism—with no division.

c) they view *time as being unreal.*

d) they see *the division between good and evil as not being ambiguous.*

Although his treatment of mysticism is a 'rational study' of its logical validity, and, therefore, a reasoning of the unknown by an inappropriate form of rational knowledge, he still commends the 'non-rational element' as a valid form of wisdom:

> On all four of these questions, while fully developed mysticism seems to me mistaken, I yet believe that, by sufficient restraint, there is an element of wisdom to be learned from the mystical way of feeling, which does not seem to be attainable in any other manner. If this is the truth, mysticism is to be commended as an attitude towards life,

not as a creed about the world. The metaphysical creed, I shall maintain, is a mistaken outcome of the emotion.[16]

THE NUMINOUS EXPERIENCE OF THE HEBREW *NABI*

Turning to the Bible, we discover that the Old Testament has a rich store of the *numinous*. The stock of Israel's folklore is full of easily discernible *numinous* episodes, even though the prophetic writers have worked over the early narratives to give the Old Testament a 'modernised' outlook.

As Jacob awakens from the ordeal of his horror-stricken nightmare, he cries: "How awesome is this place! This is none other than the house of *elohim*!" (Gen. 28:17 RSV). He encounters a 'nameless Being' in a wrestling match, alone at the haunted ford and in the deep black of the night. In the morning light—when the spirits are known to flee—he is amazed to find himself still alive and fully conscious. He is compelled to name that holy site in central Palestine, *Beth-El*—the presence of *El* (*El*= God).

At a later stage, the *numinous* object is no longer a vague *El*, but the distinctive Yahweh. The divine name represented by the Hebrew consonants YHWH, though conventionally vocalised as Yahweh, is by no means a certain rendering. Various other names have survived the recasting of the patriarchal narratives by the prophetic schools—*El Elyon, El Shaddai, El Gibbor,* etc., which are very different from the titles of Yahweh and *Baal*. The early Israelite went to 'seek the face of God' at places where encounters had previously taken place, such as at sacred wells, holy trees, desert regions, high places—particularly the summit of Sinai. It is not clear how *El* or *Baal* was understood in early times, whether as a distinct 'personality' or a plurality—*Elohim* or *Baalim*. Neither is it clear how far the spirit was understood to inhabit the sacred sites, as opposed to merely visit them at odd times. It is not essential to establish the precise mechanisms of those early encounters to recognise their significance. Later on, under Moses, the religion of Yahweh became much more clear-cut. He may still retain features of a 'nature deity', as the stormy God of Sinai, yet he is distinctively a person, a 'man of war', a 'living God' and a 'jealous God', albeit a transcending God and one having 'majesty' and 'holiness'.

With the arrival of the Prophets during the monarchy, there came a new phase of authority figures in Israelite history. These 'men of God' had more status than the priests of the 'high places'. Israel had a copious number of officially approved ministers of the cult, like her neighbours, but these charismatic prophets had no pedigree; they were authorised by impulse rather than heritage. They possessed uncanny insights and had remarkable gifts of clairvoyance—they were 'seers'. They were 'charismatic' figures who were not averse to putting even the king in his place when it was expedient so to do. They were prone to enter trance-states and bouts of ecstasy periodically, and would claim that their pronouncements were indeed divine utterances—speaking 'the word of Yahweh' (or as the fundamentalist would say, under the 'inspiration' of God). They were moved by a supernatural force, by the 'breath' or *ruach* of God! The Hebrews called such 'men of God' *nabi* (a word derived from the incoherent babblings of the ecstatic person).[17]

A problem arises for the exegete when attempting to establish which of the many and varied oracles should be accepted as being truly 'inspired' by God, as opposed to those impersonations of auto-suggestive superstitious forces. Drawing such a distinction is not easy, for both—*nabi* and charlatan alike—claimed to speak under the influence of God's *ruach*. Apart from periods of revival (such as Elijah on mount Carmel, I Kings 18:20–46), this was an age where the task of discriminating the genuine *nabi* from the impostor was not always easy.

Modern psychology presents us with a means of diagnosing this peculiar psychic phenomenon of suggestibility, but these were times when no such science existed. We know that the *nabis* were capable of grasping ideas and ideals of profound moral and intellectual significance, far superior to the conditioning factors of their environment, even though their environment would have prompted the requirement of such ideas and ideals. Our records have undergone extensive editing by the prophetic schools, from a more advanced spiritual perspective. Nevertheless, the reports preserve the tales of *nabis* like Samuel and Nathan in the early period, who were remarkable leaders and reformers. According to tradition, it was under the direction of a *nabi* that the revolution from the tribal federations of Israel to the dynastic monarchy was achieved (I Sam. 8–10). Further, it was a *nabi* who had the brash audacity to confront the King of Israel, a "man after God's own heart", with a poignant parable designed to point to a higher ethic from which he could not exempt himself. With lucid simplicity the lesson was brought home to king David by the *nabi*, Nathan, that he had sinned against Yahweh (II Sam. 12).

A giant *nabi* arises in the next age, who was ranked as the highest amongst all the prophets of Israel, and his name was Elijah the Tishbite. Yet this was also a period of confusing authorities. Ahab had a band of *nabis* that served as court soothsayers—all claiming to speak the "word of Yahweh" —and we have no reason to suspect that the grotesque antics of Zedekiah ben Chenaanah, with his iron horns (II Chron. 18:9–11), were a deliberate ploy at play acting. As C. H. Dodd has said, "He was doubtless powerfully inspired, but there was no sort of ballast to it all".[18] Clearly, Elijah's credentials as the greatest *nabi* stand tall: he is 'possessed'; he sees visions; he hears voices; he reads the thoughts of the heart; he can appear and disappear in a moment; he is a rain-making medicine man and a worker of miracles; when the *ruach* is upon him he performs the most amazing feats of endurance. The account of his vision on Horeb seems an authentic record of an intense and immediate sense of the presence of God—a deeply *numinous something* revealed in the mystery of silence. In common with other Israelite *nabis*, Elijah fought the *Baalim* tooth and nail, and consolidated Israel's formal allegiance to Yahweh, but after him and his successor, Elisha (II Kings 2:9–10), there came no *nabi* of any real religious genius. Dodd's comment does not seem too far amiss:

> From this time onwards the nabis as a body appear rather as a degrading than an elevating influence. They became the 'false prophets' of the time of Isaiah and Jeremiah. Their 'inspiration', in the formal sense, never fails . . . If therefore inspiration is to be considered as in any way a condition of the authority of the biblical writers it must be something more than a function of abnormal psychology as we meet it in the primitive ecstatic.[19]

In the eighth and seventh centuries, the great prophets, Amos, Hosea, Isaiah and Jeremiah, put less emphasis on being 'inspired' by God's *ruach* or 'spirit' as an authentication of their message being the 'Word of Yahweh' (Ezekiel was an exception).

There was derision for the body of *nabis* by the great prophets ("the foolish *nabis* who follow their own spirit . . . they say, 'Says Yahweh,' when Yahweh has not sent them!"—Ezek. 13:3, 6; Amos 7:14; Mic. 3:5; Is. 28:7; Jer. 23:13–17; Zeph. 3:4). Although 'visions' in the books of Amos and Isaiah are what psychology describes as visual hallucinations ("I saw Yahweh seated on a throne", Is. 6:1), the authority with which they speak appears to rest more on the spiritual content of their message than on God's *ruach*, while self-claims of speaking the word of Yahweh carry no weight at all. There is a lesson here for charismatic fundamentalists. Jeremiah is forward in criticising the purely ecstatic *nabi* and appeals to a criterion other than that of being 'inspired' by God's *ruach*:

> Let the *nabi* who has a dream tell the dream, but let him who has my word speak my word faithfully . . . Therefore, behold I am against the *nabis*, says Yahweh, who steal my words from one another. Behold, I am against the *nabis*, says Yahweh, who use their tongues and say, 'Says Yahweh'. Behold, I am against those who prophesy lying dreams, says Yahweh, and who tell them and lead my people astray by their lies and their recklessness, when I did not send them or charge them; so they do not profit this people at all, says Yahweh.
>
> Jer. 23:28–32 RSV

> If we are to follow Jeremiah's lead we shall refuse to find the test of inspiration in the psychological mechanism by which it is mediated; we shall seek it in the value of the inspired utterance itself.[20]

PERSONAL CHRISTIAN EXPERIENCE

Many Christians of all persuasions will have delighted in the biblical episodes of awe and wonder from early Sunday School days; those *red-blooded* tales that titillate interest and underline the passions of humanity still prompt the imagination for most of us. The stories of Yahweh thundering his Law from Sinai and the opening of the Red Sea have filled young minds with a sense of excitement for that which is fantastic, 'non-rational' and *numinous*. The imaginative mind has marvelled at the 'men of God', who authorised the celestial orbs to stand still in their place, caused axe heads to float upon water, raised the dead to life, and so on. These stories are passed down and accepted by the young with little or no discrimination or discernment, until each individual becomes of age and begins to question such things. I am not saying that this is wrong or unethical, for such stories (historical, mythical, metaphorical or imaginative) are the backcloth of valuable religious experience, but I am saying there are disadvantages.

There are drawbacks in accepting Bible stories at face value, in that they paint fantasy pictures of the past and encourage a detachment from the present. While these stories open up the possibility for genuine *numinous* encounters with God, they also obscure his place in daily life. Like it or not, with the advent of science, we are schooled in a methodology that seeks explanations other than spiritual ones in accounting for life's regular and irregular experiences. Even the most 'spiritual' would have to concede, that, apart from major crises points in life, events are not generally governed by pseudo-spiritual superstitious forces, but by empirical factors of cause and effect. The transferring of biblical motifs to today's thought-forms, without any interpretation or translation, has rendered the Church open to incredulous dogmatism and shallow sentimentality. Here lies the role for preachers and theologians: *the art of communicating ancient ideas and idioms in modern thought-forms and meaningful expressions.*

Textual criticism aids us in understanding the original literary forms of biblical narratives that describe the divine encounters of the 'men of God'. We might understand in part the nature of their various spiritual encounters, but technical studies do not help us one jot to have the experience of apprehending the divine in any first-hand way. For Christians, the *numinous* is understood as being moved to see Christ in a mystical way. Paul claims to have been 'in Christ', because he found Christ—or more precisely because Christ found him—and it is pertinent to ask of each Christian whether the *numinous* has been 'experienced personally', or whether their faith has only its 'formal' and 'rational elements'. There has to be a mystical element in the experience of what Paul describes as 'living in Christ'. It is only to be expected, considering the spiritual *milieu* of Paul's environment and the importance that mysticism had in his day.

The notion of the spiritual dimension is retained only on a theoretical level today. It does not figure largely within people's world-view, and it hardly dominates daily activity to any great extent, certainly not as much as it did for those in biblical times. Educationalists speak of the 'spiritual need' of young people, as though such a need was distinctive and easily discernible from others, but they would be very suspicious of pupils receiving an 'experiential lesson' aimed at encouraging them to receive a *numinous* experience, or a divine encounter, personally, at a non-Church school. So, in secular education, religion is accorded lip-service, faith is formal and theoretical, and *spirituality* is largely none existent—apart from watered down forms in poetry, drama and art.

In Church, the preacher is required to translate the 'spiritual experiences' of men like Paul, Augustine, and Luther, into meaningful language and expression, in order that men and women of our own day may see *the essence of the challenge of the Gospel* apart from its many 'churchified' abstractions. Some fundamentalist Christians lift this idea of the Lord's all-pervasive directing and its associated language indiscriminately from its sources, and apply it as the norm by which all should live. They talk persistently of the Lord affecting their 'every thought' and 'every action', and, as such, I cannot but feel that this experience comes over as counterfeit and artificial. The Evangelical emphasis on divine intervention requires the individual to sacrifice his cognitive reasoning and let go his inhibition, so that the imagination and emotions may take complete control. This is a diversion from true *numinous* experience. I recognise, of course, that I am making a value-judgement here; I am expressing an opinion offensive to those attempting to live as they judge the first-century Christians had lived, but I feel this is not what is expected of the enlightened believer.

At the other extreme, there are Christian 'realists'. The problem with the 'realist' interpretation of religion—as found in the doctrines of fundamentalists like the Christadelphians—is that it cannot come to terms with the mythological. In dispensing with the myth we lose the *numinous*. The 'realist' faith is a formal and theoretical faith, in that it prescribes a matter-of-fact and almost mechanical approach to life's dilemmas rather than an open-ended journey of discovery. A biblical verse is sought for every conceivable problem. There are no riddles to solve and the personal leadings of the Spirit are played down. Like it or not, we cannot dispense with myth, but neither should we fail to recognise it for what it is. The *numinous* cannot be experienced in a *tangible* sense without an emotional attachment to *something* in mythological form—it was the case in biblical times, and it is the case today. It was said of David that 'he was a man after God's own heart', a description, no doubt, of an emotional love-bond with Yahweh, the God of Israel, but, while the experience may be genuine, the language is anthropomorphic—God has no heart, and emotional attachments to divine beings can only be imaginary, not factual. Christians attempt to love one another with the divine love—*agape*. This is the love by which God loved Jesus and Jesus loved the disciples. The term *agape* encompasses the deepest form of love without the sexual component, but a word is only a label. The passion of the believer for Jesus is the emotional attachment experienced by the believer for a glorified figure, and, as such, the language has to be mythological even though the experience may be valid and meaningful.

I was privileged to make a visit to Israel a few years back with a small party of friends. We travelled light and put up at various Youth Hostels at places of biblical interest. One of the group became sick during the early part of the holiday and the others were tired. It was decided that we would make a change of plan by stopping an extra night in the hostel at Tiberias instead of keeping to our itinerary, but I was keen to visit a hostel overlooking Galilee. So I went on alone. I sat on the grassy slopes and looked over the serene blue lake. I pondered the visual images before me—stalks of thistles and wheat at my feet, farmers and vine growers busy at work, industrious fishermen on the water, and bedouin shepherds going about their daily business—and I thought of Jesus' parables. I mused for a moment on the close bond Jesus must have had with God, through the verse of a well known hymn:

> O, Sabbath rest by Galilee;
> Beside the Syrian Sea,
> Where Jesus knelt to share with Thee,
> The silence of eternity,
> Interpreted by love.

At that place, and at that moment, I willed a *religious experience.* I attempted to engineer an encounter with Christ, but, alas, it did not happen! I was not able to provoke a *numinous* theophany even in the very land where Jesus had once knelt. I failed to meet him amongst the vast array of visual images that must have prompted his fertile mind. God was not real in that situation!

On a different occasion, I was driving to Barmouth in South Wales to join up with a group of friends on a Christian camp. I felt low at the time; I think it was because I was unable to get the full week off work to help run the camp. I was also tired and a little upset over letting a friend down with a failed promise or something, I can not quite remember the details. I felt very miserable within myself, estranged, and a little disheartened. My mind reflected on the text of Romans 8, and the contemplation of the sentiments of that scripture hit me with such irresistible force that tears began to trickle down my cheeks. For a moment I had to stop the car:

> For I am sure that neither death, nor life, nor angels, nor principalities, nor things present, nor things to come, nor powers, nor height, nor depth, nor anything else in creation, will be able to separate us from the love of God in Christ Jesus our Lord
>
> Rom 8:38–39

I was speechless, I was shaking for a while, and then an incredible sense of *closeness* and *warmth* came over me: *there is nothing that can separate me from the love of God in Christ Jesus our Lord.* I was exhilarated and at peace with *something*, I don't know what. I felt drawn into a divine encounter, and I think I understood for the first time the power of the living Christ, something of the *numinous* presence, some form of theophany.

NOTES

1. R. Otto, *The Idea of the Holy*, New York, 1958.
2. The "feeling of unconditional dependence", is what he later wrote. For an analysis of Schleiermacher's thought see P. Tillich, *Perspectives on 19th and 20th Century Protestant Theology*, London, 1967. Tillich sees Schleiermacher as the father of modern Protestant theology, in that he tried to combine piety with philosophy—the deepest philosophical thoughts are completely identical with my most intimate religious feeling. His use of 'feeling', however, left him open to attack by psychologists, wishing to demote faith as having no sound philosophical base, but it is clear, argues Tillich, that Schleiermacher means 'intuition' by the term, not empty sentimentality, pages 90–114.

'Existentialist' is the term used by modern philosophers to describe the current situation and outlook. Its style permeates every branch of the self-expressive arts—great literature, drama, the visual arts, poetry and the modern-day novel. In short, we are unable to think than to think existentially. Existentialism is a branch of philosophy that originated during the nineteenth century with thinkers such as Sôren Kiekegaard (1813–1855) and Martin Heidegger (1889–1976). Briefly, it is a doctrine of man in terms of his nature within the universe. It puts its emphasis upon the human subject within his predicament, in time and space, and sees an essential conflict between what exists and what is given. How have we arrived at this point?

First, we begin in Germany with Immanuel Kant (1724–1804). Kant followed the English philosopher, David Hume (1711–1776), with a criticism of Natural Theology (i.e., the idea that God's existence can be verified in the natural world). For Kant, there is an unbridgable gulf between God and man, between man's finite nature and God's infinitude. We are imprisoned by being finite and we are unable to break out!

An attempt at bridging the gulf was made by Georg W. F. Hegel (1770–1831), with his programme of philosophical synthesis: first we begin with *thesis*, then comes its criticism—*antithesis*, and finally its compromise—*synthesis*. Hegel saw the point of identity between God and man within the philosopher's mind: God becomes real in the self-consciousness of man, and the essential nature of man belongs within the inner life of God.

Kierkegaard would have nothing of this. The world might be reconciled in Hegel's mind, he said, but it certainly was not the case in experience. The world might be reconciled in essence (Hegel), but the system of essences is not the reality in which we are living, argues Kierkegaard; we are living in the realm of existence. He understood man to be living in a tragic situation. Although Hegel coined the words 'estrangement' and 'alienation' to describe man's situation, it was Kierkegaard who put man within the frame of that situation! One of the consequences of the unreconciled world of post-Existentialism is that man is a lonely individual: here lies the despondency of the modern age (P. Tillich, *Perspectives on 19th and 20th Century Protestant Theology*, London, 1967: Kant, Moral Religion and Radical Evil, page 64; The Universal Synthesis: Georg W. F. Hegel, pages 114–136; Kierkegaard's Existential Theology, pages 162–180). This was not a very optimistic picture, but it was the way the existentialist philosophers saw the human situation.

Philosophers of religion have not helped in checking this landslide of human hopelessness. Don Cupitt, in trying to reformulate Christianity for the modern age, describes two factors of modernism that have led to the demise of traditional faith (*Taking Leave of God*). In cosmology, he says, there has been a change from the "old sacred, highly wrought, finite cosmos to the new 'meaningless', boundless mechanical universe", from a universe that was rich, complex and populous like a very rich literary text, full of hidden symbolism, values, purposes, omens, portents, occult forces, to one of disenchantment. "For us the world is what the sciences of nature have shown it to be—morally and religiously neutral and without magic." Secondly, there has come a corresponding change in the nature of knowledge. "In the old order, 'knowledge' meant pre-eminently a fixed body of sacred traditional material which it was vital to keep intact." It was a knowledge which preserved a communion with the divine. Modern knowledge is quite different—it is man-made, critically established, unmysterious, ever-expanding and subject to revision. Unfortunately there is another kind of strength that it lacks, and that is the distinctive kind of strength that the old religious knowledge did have. Such knowledge gave pre-modern societies an intense religious happiness (D. Cupitt, *Taking Leave of God*, London 1980, pages 17–18).

3. W. James, *Varieties of Religious Experience*, page 66.
4. R. Otto, op. cit., page 12.
5. *Orge of God* is normally translated, 'Wrath of God'. We are to imagine a non-personal principle of retribution; we cannot set an angry God in opposition to the merciful Jesus, I Chron. 27:24; I Thess. 1:10. For a study of Paul's understanding of the 'Revelation of God's Wrath', see G. Bornkamm, *Early Christian Experience*, 1969, Ch. 4; and C. H. Dodd's *Commentary on Romans*, Rom. 1–3.
6. R. Otto, op. cit., page 39.
7. Augustine, *Confessions*, Middlesex, 1973, page 177.
8. Ibid., page 178.
9. J. M. Todd, *Martin Luther*, London, 1964, page 20.
10. Ibid., page 76.
11. R. Otto, op. cit., page 99.
12. M. Luther, *Erlangden ed.*, xi, 94, cited by R. Otto, op., cit., page 103.
13. Michael Goulder challenges this view upon the basis that we cannot wholly trust this-worldly experience, M. Goulder & J. Hick, *Why Believe in God*, London, 1983, 'How Dependable is Experience?', page 50.
14. P. Tillich, op. cit., page 104.
15. D. Cupitt, *Taking Leave of God*, London 1980, pages 29–31.
16. B. Russell, *Mysticism and Logic*, page 18.
17. G. von Rad, *Old Testament Theology*, Vol. II, London, pages 6–32. C. H. Dodd, *The Authority of the Bible*, Revised Edition, 1960, page 53.
18. C. H. Dodd, op. cit., page 56.
19. Ibid., page 60.
20. Ibid., page 65.

10

THE INTERVENTIONIST GOD

Much of my reflective Christian thinking has been taken up with the question of God's intervention, or involvement in life, set against the balance of chance.

During my adolescence there was an over-inflated ego which held the notion that God had called me to a mission of earth-shattering importance. I went through that appealing evangelistic phase which contends that God is operative in every detail of existence, from manipulating events and decisions as to a vocation to suit his purpose, to his tampering with the ignition coil of my vehicle in order to prevent a pile up on the M6 motorway. While I do not scorn this expression of faith—owing to its means of giving Christians impetus and a sense of vocation—I do feel there ought to be a growing up from this type of belief, whereby we place so much unmerited onus on God's activity and so little on human endeavour and accomplishment. It seems appropriate to ask whether this form of divine intervention matches everyday experience, and answer such a question with honesty and humility.

This leads me on naturally to say what I feel is often lacking in many Evangelical Christians today—the virtues of sincere honesty and ruthless objectivity. That is not to say that such Christians deliberately falsify the facts, but to acknowledge their reluctance to match personal belief-systems with objective experience. If one is genuinely committed to a search of God's ways and methods of working in a world of multiple explanations, then cherished presuppositions, handed down belief-packages, fanciful thinking, and a wish to cast the divine into the human mould, should all be thrown into the melting pot of honest and critical evaluation. Not only is this essential for personal growth and development, it is the only way of establishing the essence of 'true' Christianity for those remaining interested in Christ but still outside the Church.

Our Christian evaluation of what is a *real happening* or a *meaningful occurrence* is decided not only by our predisposition over such a religious issue as divine intervention, but by our interpretation of random, albeit significant, events in life over which we have little control. Such data, however, can be contradictory and misleading. For example, when David Jenkins was appointed Bishop of Durham in April 1984, there was considerable dismay from the lay community to the extent that those opposing him brought a petition of 12,000 signatures to the Archbishop of York. They claimed that Jenkins was unfit to have been made a bishop for holding radical views on much traditional Church doctrine—including the Virgin Birth, the Resurrection narratives, and the Gospel miracle-stories. Within three days of his enthronement ceremony, York Minster was struck by a thunderbolt and many felt that this 'natural event' was a demonstration of God's wrath! This is all very plausible, we may conclude, if God works in such a way, but these very devout, yet not very discerning, church folk overlooked one factor: the same David Jenkins had an omen earlier on in his life that directed him to join the Church when he had every intention of choosing an alternative career. Now if we are attempting to be objective over everyday occurrences, whether mundane or spectacular, how are we to interpret such events in life which on the surface appear random?

With such a question in mind, the reading of philosophy can aid one in seeing the distinction between an 'objective reality' and *an experience* of that so called 'objective reality'; what might be real and what might the judge *perceive* to be real?

The question before us, then, is how we are to understand the nature of God's intervention in the grand affairs of world politics and in the petty affairs of everyday living. The biblical precedent for divine activity is unmistakably clear. Both Testaments provide countless examples of God's absolute and thorough-going intervention in human history. The Bible indeed provides us with a *red-blooded* theology, but do our own personal experiences and reflections over significant events in life bear this out? Is God active in an observable way in the daily affairs of our day as he was believed to have been in biblical times?

I found fresh insight on this fascinating topic after reading two books, and partial answers to many long-term questions began to emerge. The books were, *Why Believe in God,* a debate between Michael Goulder and John Hick, and *Transpersonal Psychologies* by Charles T. Tart.[1]

In chapter five of *Why Believe in God*, Goulder cynically deposes the arguments of the 'for God's intervention' school with illustrations taken from the Falkland War:

> One might think that an Exocet missile had been launched from an Argentine aircraft and was homing in on HMS Invincible; but at the crucial moment God deflected the electronic device so that it missed the carrier and fell harmlessly in the sea. Those with such a theology can certainly say, 'Thank God' . . . We also find it hard to explain why God should spare the Invincible but not the Sheffield or Atlantic Conveyor, if he monkeys about with the electronics. It makes him seem arbitrary or favouritizing—are those sailors on these ships the greater sinners? [2]

Again, when Pope John Paul I was elected (on democratic voting principles) by the Vatican, Cardinal Hume declared: "We have elected God's candidate", to which Goulder replies:

> I am not privy to the secrets of the Vatican election chamber, but the situation is easily imagined. Forty-five percent of the cardinals, let us say, arrive determined to vote for Cardinal Conservativo of the Vatican Curia. Forty-five percent have come to give their vote for Archbishop Liberale of Brazil. Prayer is said, and hearts are made open to the Holy Spirit; and it at once becomes clear that God's man is the charming light-hearted Venetian, who is duly elected. But then, alas, the job kills him off in a month. Ah, the inscrutable will of God! How unsearchable are his judgements and his ways past tracing out! [3]

This is a heads-I-win, tails-you-lose theology. Such a glib theodicy of equating disaster with God's punishment of the wicked first began to be questioned in the modern period with the great earthquake of Lisbon in 1755, when hundreds of people were killed in a church while celebrating the Mass. Being the Age of Reason, this catastrophic event marked a turning point in the philosophy of religion.

In John Hull's personal reflections on blindness in *Touching the Rock*, he speaks of *retrovidence* rather than *providence*. He says that "It is only when we look back that the fortuitous is endowed with meaning. Meaning is conferred after the event". Providence suggests that a path is laid out for one, along which God will lead. Should I have been born a century ago, I would have lost my sight earlier, if I were to be born a century from now, I no doubt would never have become blind:

> A trackless waste is laid out with paths once it has been crossed . . . My blindness was the result of thousands of tiny accidental happenings . . . Blindness does not make me happy. I did not choose it, nor was it inflicted upon me. Nevertheless, as an accidental event it could become meaningful. Retrovidence is a visionary gift of the Holy Ghost.[4]

This is an interesting perspective, in that it suggests that meaning can be gained through an infinite range of accidental possibilities. While it is not deterministic, it still betrays a predisposition to accept that events are endowed with meaning. Let us broaden the discussion by considering first how past religious people have taken upon themselves an unselfish vocation from a call, before moving on to examine its process.

CALLS TO MISSION

There have been many outstanding figures in the history of Christianity that have lived remarkable lives from calls that could be described as 'mystical' or *numinous*. Some have become responsive in a mystical way to the beckoning draw of scriptural verse, whereby the 'written word' calls out to them from the printed text and compels them to move in a given direction during a moment of personal trauma, not as a prophetic fulfilment but as a motivation for action and mission. However, the 'written word' was not the only means of such *numinous* calls:

1) Albert Schweitzer's call to the African mission (to forsake careers in Divinity and Music) *came from the text of the parable* of The Rich Man and Lazarus. The physical miseries of the natives in the forests were, metaphorically, Lazarus, and we of the prosperous West were pre-figured by The Rich Man[5]:

> How many disciples recognise that the one they profess to follow was a healer, and that his last command to his disciples was: 'Preach the word, heal the sick, cast out devils. Freely ye have received, freely give'? [6]

This exercise is highly imaginative and suggestible if used without a balanced sense of judgement. An Old Testament lecturer once gave an amusing anecdote of a young man wishing to seek God's direction at a cross-roads in his life. He took a pin and placed it on a verse of scripture. It read, "and he went and hanged himself" (Matt. 27:5 RSV). He repeated the exercise after feeling not a little dismayed by his first attempt, only to leave him in further trouble, for the pin randomly rested on the verse, "Go and do likewise!" (Luke 10:37 RSV). The practice of biblical verse-selecting for divine guidance is not the only means of arriving at decisions through crises' points in people's lives.

2) Simone Weil's mission came from *musing over a mundane event* at a tiny Portuguese fishing village. She sensitively became aware "that Christianity is pre-eminently the religion of slaves". This insight arose from rapture in a place of solitude when totally exhausted. During an evening under a full moon she observed a group of women visiting ships and chanting hymns in a vigil.[7]

3) Others have become commissioned to service after hearing the divine call *through the medium of another person*. Martin Luther's sense of mission came from an intuitive word of a close friend. Augustine of Hippo renounced his worldliness at the voice of a child.[8] Elizabeth Fry was commissioned by the thought-provoking comment of a Quaker: "Thou shalt be a light to the blind, speech to the dumb, and feet to the lame."[9] William Wilberforce was stirred to carry through his reform of slavery from a casual comment of the Prime Minister, William Pitt: "Wilberforce, why don't you give notice of a motion on the slave trade?"[10]

4) Finally, some have felt commissioned *through the writings of spiritual people*: John Wesley's heart was warmed after reading Luther's Preface to Paul's letter to the Romans.

Scripture, therefore, is only one of many other means of stirring the hearts of men and women to vocations and missions. Does the end result of nobly led lives validate the *numinous* call that has set them off? This can barely be true, for there have been many 'secular' reformers that have lived impeccably self-less lives that were not motivated by religious conviction.

Some suggest that the notion of God communicating something to people (or even the notion of God's existence at all for that matter), is a psychological 'prop'—a belief that satisfies a psychological need. If this is so, and in fact there is no God 'out there' communicating with human beings, it would leave not only fundamentalists but all other Christians, out in the dark of nihilism! We considered the question of God's existence in chapter seven, here, we wish to expand the question by asking whether his existence is supported by evidence of what might be called *divine intervention*. So, is there any evidence of a more empirical and historically objective kind that can give us greater assurance that there is more going on in the universe than meets the eye?

THE GOD 'OUT THERE' AND THE CALL AS SOMETHING 'GIVEN'

In chapter four of *Why Believe in God*, John Hick has a penetrating article on 'Prayer, Providence and Miracle.' He abandons the notion of a God intervening in history at set periods of time (the biblical picture), either by monopolising events, or by influencing the human psyche, and, instead, he promotes the thesis that God is always transmitting some unknown type of communication to man in a continuous and consistent form. He is eager to resolve the inconsistency problem of God's intervention. Hick argues that the only reason why this mechanism of God's perpetual calling appears not to be the case is because human beings are rarely sensitive to this *continuous call*. When we become open to this initiative of God, as at certain periods of time religious people have done (during the ministry of Jesus, for example), then, remarkable events have taken place. In this way any arguments about God's inconsistency are ruled out and the potential for men to become divine, or like Christ, is within everyone's grasp.

In *Transpersonal Psychologies*, Charles Tart discusses the newly developing (and grossly underrated) branch of 'science' known as Parapsychology. There is now abundant evidence, he says, for the paranormal phenomenon of telepathy, clairvoyance, psychokinesis and premonition.

- Telepathy is the mind-to-mind link, regardless of intervening space or objects which obstruct the two subjects that are giving and receiving some form communication.
- Clairvoyance is an awareness of events at a distance, which is normally applied to the practice of summoning up the dead by means of a trance medium.
- Psychokinesis relates to the practice of exercising an energy of the mind to effect the movement of physical objects through space. The mind energy can have effect within the body by accelerating the *natural* healing process.
- Premonition, or Precognition, is the fairly common experience of having an uncanny feeling that something is about to take place. It is not necessarily being able to predict the event clearly and unmistakably, but it is the inner-sense that when something has occurred the subject had felt that there had been a prior awareness, if only in retrospect.

This evidence is collected together and collated in the libraries of the Royal Society of Psychical Research, and some of this evidence has been subjected to the most rigorous of laboratory testing. There is also accumulating evidence for the phenomenon known as 'out-of-body-experience' (OOBE).

Whatever the physical process of God's communication might be, it appears likely that the phenomenon of extrasensory perception (ESP) will belong to the same category of mental processing as that of our 'normal' mental activities. Secondly, it is possible that we, as complex beings, can discover innate powers *within ourselves* which are products of God's essence—the psychology and physiology of which might still elude us. If this possibility is accepted at a cognitive level, there may result a growing awareness of innate human powers *within each of us* to achieve things which formerly our self-doubt had judged impossible.

Some form of parapsychological energy (biblically, the Holy Spirit) had evidently flowed through Jesus, enabling him to heal and foresee things his environment would not have made accessible to him. The healing is brought about by the patient's own mental processes being turned in upon their own physical ailment—psychokinesis. This process cannot work, however, without some powerful psychic energy taking control from another mind outside, as in the case of Jesus, the healing physician—telepathy.

Naturally, we have not begun to understand the mechanics of this process, and some may feel that we should not make any attempt to do so, but twentieth-century thinking people expect of Christian theologians an objective examination of all possible factors when accounting for abnormal phenomena. A typical model of perception and motor responses may help here, to illustrate how the mechanism of action resulting from perception works, and to aid us in speculating as to how ESP might fit this process.

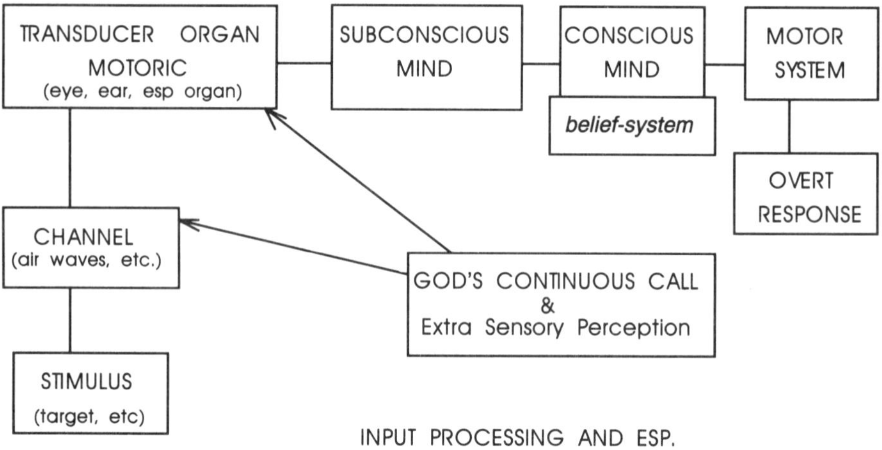

INPUT PROCESSING AND ESP.

In the above model, the input processing stage is where any stimulus is either accepted and made use of, or rejected and discarded; it is the belief-system that collates these varied experiences. This is why a given experience, such as the decease of a loved child, can bring about quite contradictory results in different people—reinforcing in one the belief in God, whilst reinforcing in the other atheism or the contention that God is passive, non-interventionist, or totally uninterested in human suffering. If there are good scientific grounds for accepting the phenomenon of ESP as an operative force in human experience, is there no equal viability for the acceptance of a God 'out there' transmitting *something* of his Being to us 'down here'? Tart is eager to make a science of states of consciousness and altered states of consciousness, such as the condition under meditative trance, in order to bridge the gulf between religious and scientific enquiry.

We are presently examining the nature of *intuitive experience* as opposed to 'deductive reasoning'. Yet the two are not mutually exclusive, for all knowledge is experiential knowledge. I know gravity exists by experience every time I drop a ball. I don't need to understand its physics! One of the major problems is that when scientists use the word 'mystical' they do so in a pejorative sense. What Tart challenges is the particular scientific method of 'physicalism' that assumes that all reality can be measured by empirical observation. This is a necessary challenge because the mystics claim to know things not by empirical reasoning but by *intuitive experience.*[11]

DIVINE FORESIGHT AND THE FUTURE

Fundamentalists are forward in pointing out that the fulfilment of predictive prophecy is an empirical piece of evidence that God has communicated information to the prophets. This is, as we have pointed out earlier, a misuse of the Bible. It is a misconception to regard the few prophetic forecasts as spanning considerable periods of time, stretching on into future ages far beyond the horizon of the seer's coherent imagination. The opposite is in fact the case; *their forecasts sprang from their current historical contexts.* They were projections of an immediate future, an imminent tomorrow. Even the stereotyped 'foreshortening of days' lay only around the corner, for there would have been no other way of presenting a vision of sufficient potency to lift the morale of people without by the same token suggesting that its fulfilment was not far away. There is a major philosophical problem entailed in the notion of *divine prediction*, not merely over the erroneous means of communicating the *divine mind* to the human recipient, but principally over the possibility of predicting a future event in a universe which is not deterministic but random, *unpredictable* and not causal in a mechanical way. It is beyond the scope of this study to pursue this philosophical issue here, only to draw attention to the complexity of the process and to acknowledge that *divining the future* is an unresolved phenomenon, both for theologians and physicists. The study of history reveals few convincing examples of *intuitive minds* being able to forecast the future with any consistent accuracy.

In Arnold Toynbee's monumental work, *Study of History,* he draws our attention to that 'which is measurable' from the lessons of the past. He traces three common factors that have prevailed in those civilisations that have not become extinct. He sees a pattern of 'challenge and response' as the model upon which civilisations either develop or decline, survive or become extinct:

1) The first factor he titles 'Archaism', by which he means the idealisation of the 'good old times' of yesteryear. Thus, Fascist Italy romanticised the Roman Empire, and Nazi Germany glorified its national past before the Jewish doctrines of Christianity had corrupted its pure ways.
2) The second factor he coins as 'Futurism'. This is the escapist philosophy that abandons any responsibility for changing the present by seeking only those utopias that lie around the corner.
3) The third is 'Detachment', which describes the attitude of those who all too readily 'throw in the towel'. No responsibility is taken for the present, all is beyond hope, all beyond retrieving (our age has devised a considerable range of escapist means, ranging from the vast array of intoxicating substances to the most sophisticated and pseudo-mystical religious cults).
4) The final and liberating factor is what Toynbee has called 'Transfiguration'.[12]

'Transfiguration' shows itself in a regular rhythm of withdrawal from a situation (not in the sense of truancy or detachment), followed by a return to that same situation, in order to transform it by engagement and action. The biblical revelation is rich in presenting this rhythmic pattern of God and the spirit-led man: God's Word goes out to Moses in calling the Hebrews from serfdom; Isaiah lifts the morale of Israel to withstand the Assyrian forces; Ezekiel inspires hope for an exiled people; the Gospels portray Jesus of Nazareth going out to meet sinners and calling them into fellowship with God; the *Logos* doctrine of the Fourth Gospel has the descent of that which was of the very being of God to earth to save a lost humanity by drawing the Sons of God into his home; Paul travels to the 'end of the world' to win converts for Christ. These are not examples of *divining the future* in the classical sense; the images of a future utopia are not ends in a literal sense, but the means of a further end, namely, the raising of morale.

The pattern of transfiguration is effected, therefore, by the Word of God:

> For as the heavens are higher than the earth,
> so are my ways higher than your ways
> and my thoughts than your thoughts;
> and as the rain and the snow come down from heaven,
> and do not return until they have watered the earth,
> making it blossom and bear fruit,
> and give seed for sowing and bread to eat,
> so shall the word which comes from my mouth prevail;
> it shall not return to me fruitless,
> without accomplishing my purpose,
> or succeeding in the task I gave it.
>
> Is. 55:9–11

> "Do not my words scorch like fire?" says the Lord. "Are they not like a hammer that splinters rock?"
>
> Jer. 23:29

THE NATURE OF THE 'WORD' OF GOD AS A CALL TO MISSION

We have reached an impasse in our studying regarding the authority of the Bible. If:

- there are no theological grounds for accepting that the Bible is inerrant or infallible, yet we have good grounds for understanding its existence as being more than the product of human processes;
- we cannot adopt the world-view that the Bible supports as being compatible with our own, yet we recognise that truths can be separated from their cultural and environmental contexts;
- we cannot appropriate for ourselves the scheme of biblical pre-history and extra-history, yet we can identify a *numinous* call of God operative in life, just as it was with the prophets compelling them to respond to the challenges of their own situations;

What, then, is the universal message for us to take for ourselves?

We are driven to accept only one theological interpretation of the Bible that fits the facts: *the Bible is not the Word of God, per se.* The Bible is the *record* of the Word of God, in past ages. Its *numinous* category, through the medium of the 'printed word', may still compel men and women today to rise to the spiritual challenge before them. The Bible indeed *contains* the 'Word of God', but we have little recourse but to accept the fact that *the Bible is not, in its entirety, the Word of God for man.*

I am aware, of course, that there are passages in the New Testament on which fundamentalists base their claim that all the books found in the canon of the Bible are to be regarded as the 'inspired' scriptures in a summary sense, but this belief we are forced to regard as untenable.

The 'printed word' has proved to be a creative factor in history, and the power for renewal and regeneration is embodied in the 'Word' of biblical revelation. Here is the universal relevance of the Bible, not in a fixed world-view, or an abiding message, or an unalterable teaching, or an ultimate philosophy, but in the eternal process which transfigures men and women to become spiritually like God.

If we accept that there might be a God 'out there' who is continually sending his 'Word' to us 'down here'—whether it be through scripture, people, writing, intuition or significant events—as he did in the first century with the coming of Christ, then we might begin to realise for ourselves the possibility of becoming one with him in the Spirit. Our part is to allow ourselves to be receptive to the possibility of a 'Mind' calling to us; and to recognise that we have within ourselves the potential to become like Jesus. We need to recognise our own human potential and become in tune with that which is God-given. We should not be overcome by negative and nihilistic reasoning in holding that God once spoke loudly in first-century Palestine but whispers almost inaudibly in our own time! The invitation to be drawn into communion with the divine is there to take up—the choice is ours.

NOTES

1. M. Goulder & J. Hick, *Why Believe in God*, London, 1983. C. T. Tart, *Transpersonal Psychologies*, London, 1975.
2. M. Goulder & J. Hick, op. cit., pages 81–83.
3. Ibid., page 85.
4. J. Hull, *Touching the Stone*, London, 1990, pages 148–149.
5. A. Schweitzer, *On the Edge of the Primaeval Forest*, London, 1922, Ch. 1.
6. A. Schweitzer, *Albert Schweitzer The Man and His Mind*, London, 1955, page 39.
7. R. Rees, *Simone Weil: A Sketch for a Portrait*, London, 1966, page 40.
8. Chapter 9, The Non-Rational Element of Religion.
9. E. H. Hayes, *Yarns on Social Pioneers*, Surrey, 1960, page 28.
10. Ibid., page 51.
11. There is much similarity between the thought of 'mystical' *intuitive knowledge* and eastern mysticism. A brief examination of two schools of Eastern teaching will underline the basis upon which *intuitive knowledge* differs from reasoned deductive knowledge.

    For the followers of Yoga psychology, *magic* is a grossly misunderstood term by which we tend to imagine conjuring tricks performed on the stage. For Eastern people however, "Magic is properly 'magistery', or mastery, in the sense of mastering one's own self-state before contemplating control of anything else". (page 434) The mastering of the mind and the subjugating of the body characterises much Yoga psychology. The Cartesian dualism of mind and body as heterogeneous substances gave rise in Western psychology to all kinds of fantastic notions regarding interactions between them both. Descartes thought the interaction took place in the pineal gland, ignoring the fact that the pineal gland was part of the material body, not of the immaterial mind. In Yoga psychology, mind and body are not heterogeneous but homogeneous. They are different evolutes, or modes of manifestation, of the same fundamental creative energy.

    The goal of Zen Buddhism is enlightenment, which is a wisdom derived from *intuitive insights*, a transformation of personality, and a new life style finding the 'real-you'. This is indescribable self-realisation, which is not systematically analysed, just experienced—an absolute unselfishness of which the subject did not know himself or herself to be capable. It is not esoteric, just exoteric; it is a diminution of the ego. By contrast to Platonic deduction, the Buddha said that *intuition*, not reason, is the source of ultimate truth and wisdom, for the *intuitive mind* is capable of partaking of the universality of the universal Mind—that which Jung called the *Collective Unconscious*. Here we see the differing insights of the East and West. Enlightenment means 'seeing things as they are', beyond the world of appearances. What the Buddha saw under the bo tree was the true-self—intrinsically perfect. He discovered that all men were inherently perfect, that is, that every man possesses the potentials of perfection, merely waiting to be actualised. Clearly, this is not the state of the Christian fallen man; it was the state of *Nirvana*—a term derived from the negative prefix *nir* with the root *vana* meaning 'to burn'. It was the extinction of all forms of becoming: desire, attachment, ego, etc.. Under the altered state of consciousness, the normal consciousness of desires is abandoned, never to rise again. *Nirvana* destroys 'defiling' aspects of the ego—hatred, greed, delusion. With the problem of suffering, an analysis of the symptoms of suffering shows that in each of them our desire is in conflict with the laws of existence and, as we are not able to change these laws, the only thing that remains is to change our desire.

The Christian *Mystical experience* is typified by such sentiments as those of the *Confessions* of St Augustine: "My mind in the flash of a trembling glance came to Absolute Being—That which is". It is the consciousness of direct contact with Transcendental Reality. Evelyn Underhill speaks of the deep centre or the *pivot of the Christian position*. A deep centre which is not God but rather that *point where God touches us*. This is a centre lying dormant in most people, precisely because they limit their life to the superficial self, with its limited sets of perception through cognition and sense.

12. Cited by C. H. Dodd, *The Bible To-Day*, London, 1968, pages 126f..

II

CRITERIA OF 'REVELATION' IN BIBLICAL MORALITY

At this point, the reader might naturally assume that the Bible should be relegated to other groups of literature that are merely the products of human genius, and that is all. He or she might conclude that the Bible has no rank or divine status for conveying the mind of God any more than other literary work. We shall now see that this is not the case, as we search for criteria of genuine 'revelations' of God through the 'inspired' *scriptures*.

A friend once remarked: 'I think Jesus would be less impressed by our singing hymns about him than by us carrying out what he asked.' Such a statement brings up for discussion the place of ritual and ceremony within Christian living. What purpose does the rite of baptism or the celebration of the Eucharist serve, or the elaborate display of costume and symbol in Christian liturgy? How important is liturgy in relation to morality and the practice of Christian ethics? Does Christ, in fact, wish us to worship him in any conventional sense at all? Might he not just want us to follow in life what he taught us, without any formal expression of commitment, without singing praises, without communal prayers in a place of worship? Is it axiomatic for the Christian to be a Church attender and a regular worshipper, as opposed to being a moral person? Let us explore the relationship of liturgy to ethics.

Hinduism sees ritual and symbol as serving as pointers for directing the attention of the devotee towards the divine. There is no longer any need for the pointer once the eyes have been turned towards the spiritual. In Indian thought, then, while ritual is continually practised by the worshipper, it is a means to a nobler and more spiritual end rather than an end in itself. Now, is this the case with Christianity, or do ritual and celebration for those worshipping in Church have intrinsic meanings in themselves?

Throughout history, human beings have practised the most abhorrent ceremonies as a requirement of the cult. Take for example, the summer Corn Rite of the Pawnee Indians:

> In the Pawnee confederacy in the Mississippi basin as late as 1817 a Comanche girl who had been taken prisoner by the Skidi was rescued from being offered to the Morning Star by a Chanti warrior who dashed into the assembly, seized the victim and carried her off to her tribe on his horse. This daring deed was followed by other attempts at rescue, but it did not prevent a Sioux girl in her early teens being dedicated to the Morning Star for six months in 1838 and treated as sacred in the manner of the Aztec young divine victim. Two days before she was due to be sacrificed she was led from wigwam to wigwam accompanied by the chiefs and warriors. At each she received wood

> and paint, and on April 22 she was painted half red and half black, tied to a sort of ladder, slowly roasted over a slow fire, and then shot with arrows. The chief sacrificer tore out her heart and devoured it while the rest of her body was cut into small pieces and placed in baskets to be taken to a neighbouring cornfield. There, the blood was squeezed on the new grains of corn to fertilise them. The implements were burnt in the fire and the ashes strewn on the fields for the same purpose.[1]

This gruesome ritual not only offends our Christian sensibilities, it sharpens our critical judgement too, to such a degree that we find it impossible from our own situation to imagine what magical forces could have been manipulated by such practices. The Aztec Calendar Rites similarly illustrate the depravity of a religion without a morality. As a means of securing a successful August maize harvest, the hearts of prisoners of war were torn from their smoke-charred bodies and publicly devoured by the priest of Xiuhtecnhtli, the god of fire.[2] Now, the fundamentalist might feel assured that at least such atrocities would never have occurred in Israel, but he would be wrong.

Archaeologists have discovered a number of children's skeletons in the foundations of Palestinian buildings. This Canaanite rite was not uncommon in the ancient world. At the high place at Gezer, skeletons of new-born infants have been unearthed that were buried in the foundations to establish the permanence of the city. It is not always acknowledged by fundamentalists, but it is a fact that such a superstition was not confined to the Canaanites—Hiel rebuilt Jericho in the reign of Ahab (c. 880 BC) by laying the foundations on his first-born son, Abiram, and the gates of the city on his younger son, Segib (I Kings 16:34). Other deplorable rites of human sacrifice were not unknown in Israelite religion, and some are even known to have been integrated within the very worship of Yahweh, with no clear statement of prohibition.[3]

THE MORAL PROPHETIC INSIGHT

A religious cult is the natural outgrowth of the non-rational *numinous* feeling, and the early cultic rituals of Israelite religion bear the marks of its impulse. A holy sense of awe was expressed in ritual, which gave the feeling of joy, serenity, and peace to the worshipper when practised rightly. It is not always easy to see the relationship between the place of the cult and ethics in the history of religion. C. H. Dodd has examined this relationship in detail.[4]

There is a tension between the putative will of God regarding the 'perfect soul' and what we today would regard as a 'morally upright citizen', and there are examples in the Bible in which an aspect of the superstitious *taboo* (or '*profane*' for Durkheim) was the most important requirement of God. In the case of Uzzah, a 'good man' was struck dead for an instinctive response in steadying the slipping Ark of the Covenant (II Sam. 6:6–9); it was a pious action, but, 'according to scripture', it was one that was penalised by God's wrath! From our moral position, God's judgement (if indeed it was) appears unreasonable—Uzzah's reaction was well intended. The net result was that of a more cautious King David placating Yahweh with burnt-offerings and peace-offerings, all correctly and in order—"there must be no more playing with fire!", says Dodd.[5]

The elaborate ritual and liturgy of Israel's festivals were written up in meticulous detail. Technically referred to as the Priestly code, this ritual has been preserved in the books of Leviticus and Deuteronomy. The codes are ascribed to the dictation of Yahweh to Moses, engraved, it is said, by the very *finger of God* on slabs of stone, but this cannot be so. There is no doubt, that, as the narrative stands, these legislative requirements—honoured and enforced by the priestly guild of the Levite clan—were not all original to Moses (some laws have counterparts which antedate the Mosaic period by many centuries). The Law of Moses, as found in the Torah, is the work of the Deuteronomistic school of scribes in the times of the monarchy. It was produced to satisfy the need for a more precisely defined liturgy. Though a skeletal form is likely to have been very old, there can be little doubt that later cultic requirements have been read into the early period, for there is an unmistakable clash between the book of Leviticus and the form of Israelite liturgy denounced by Amos. The distinctions between Yahweh, the God of Sinai, and the *Baalim* of Canaan were not at all clear in the early period. The Israelites celebrated a ritual observance not too dissimilar to the *Baalim* cults at times, at the sacred sites of the 'carved stones' of Gilgal, the well of Beersheba and the bull-temples of Bethel and Dan. It is noteworthy that an early form of the Ten Commandments (Exod. 34:14–26) has little moral content to it, but is almost entirely concerned with religious festivals and rules of taboo. Amos speaks out in uncompromising style against the religious syncretism of the Baalim cult:

> Resort to me, if you would live, not to Bethel;
> go not to Gilgal, nor pass on to Beersheba . . .
> If you would live, resort to Yahweh,
> or he will break out against Joseph like fire
> fire which will devour Israel with no one to quench it.
>
> I hate, I spurn your pilgrim-feasts;
> I will not delight in your sacred ceremonies.
> When you present your sacrifices and offerings
> I will not accept them,
> nor look on the buffaloes of your shared-offerings.
> Spare me the sound of your songs;
> I cannot endure the music of your lutes . . .
>
> Amos 5:4–6, 21–23 (4:4–5; 10:1, 4)

This language—along with the plain statement in Amos 5:25: "Did you bring me sacrifices and gifts, you people of Israel, those forty years in the wilderness?"—denouncing the sacrificial cult is so strong that some theologians wonder whether Yahweh ever prescribed expiatory rites and sacrifices at all. Amos was far from being a fanatical nihilist, but he was no less radical for his day The *numinous* is preserved throughout his prophecies, and his conception of 'holiness' was directed not so much against the breaches of irrational taboo, as against the immoral social relations of the Israelites towards their fellows:

> They grind the heads of the poor into the earth,
> and thrust the humble out of their way.
> Father and son resort to the same girl,
> to the profanation of my holy name.

Men lie down beside every altar
on garments seized in pledge,
and in the house of Yahweh they drink liquor
got by way of fines.

Amos 2:7–8

Listen to this, you who grind the destitute and plunder the humble, you who say, "When will the new moon be over so that we may sell corn? When will the sabbath be past so that we may open our wheat again, giving short measure in the bushel and taking overweight in the silver, tilting the scales fraudulently, and selling the dust of the wheat; that we may buy the poor for silver and the destitute for a pair of shoes?" Yahweh has sworn by the pride of Jacob: I will never forget any of their doings.

Amos 8:4–7

Similarly, in the south, Isaiah condemned the most appalling rites of expiation used to protect men from the wrath of 'holiness'; they offered no protection, it was social justice and 'righteousness' that was required.

Hosea says the same; in crisp style, the prophet declares:

For I desire steadfast love and not sacrifice,
the knowledge of Yahweh, rather than burnt offerings.

Hosea 6:6 RSV

Again, Micah, a century later, pours contempt on empty cultic practice:

What shall I bring when I approach Yahweh?
How shall I stoop before God on high?
Am I to approach him with whole-offerings or yearling calves?
Will Yahweh accept thousands of rams
or ten thousand rivers of oil?
Shall I offer my eldest son for my own wrongdoing,
my children for my own sin?

Micah 6:6–7

Finally, to make it crystal clear, Micah follows by describing the true requirement of service:

He has shown you, O man, what is good;
and what does Yahweh require of you?
but to do justice, to love kindness,
and to walk humbly with your God.

Mic. 6:8 RSV

In reaching the zenith of prophetic insight, we begin to see a criterion coming to light of how we might establish a genuine utterance of God's 'Word' from one of human judgement. *What was remarkable about the prophets of the eighth and seventh century was how epoch-making their oracles were in the times in which they lived.* We tend to forget this today in an age where secular morals take precedence over religious and spiritual values, but, in earlier times, the religious cult had little to do with what we would call morality.

One criterion for determining a genuine revelation of God will be a consensus of agreement over a biblical saying, requirement, or action, supporting a lofty moral ideal, such as that of recognising one's obligations to the poor.

It is hard to see how the environment exclusively could have fashioned the moral insights of the Hebrew *nabis*. Now, while some may hold that a 'revelation' to a receptive soul might not be so much the result of human intuitive reflection but the reception of *something* coming from a mind outside our world, it seems more plausible for others to search for criteria as to how we might prove this, for the *divine telepathy* model is not easy to accept. The later prophets opened up new ideas of moral conduct and saw more clearly into the nature of what it means to be *holy*. True *holiness* was not getting requirements of the cult right, but acting righteously. Indeed, as we have said above, there are some prophetic statements which suggest that sacrifices and the offering of gifts were never really wanted by Yahweh. Jeremiah, particularly, contends that obedience to Yahweh's commandments is much more important than cultic ceremony.[6] What is not in dispute in the great prophets, is the issue of the precedence of morality over cultic practice.

> It is the Hebrew prophets who most clearly and uncompromisingly asserted that the holy is the righteous, and worship itself a sham apart from the intention to be and to do good.[7]

They took the momentous step, then, of making 'holiness' a moral ideal.

I am claiming that a higher revelation—even an exclusive revelation—can be interpreted by such prophetic statements that we today would see as spiritually and morally excellent. I would not suggest, however, that all the *nabis'* words were equally profound and true, even from those making profound utterances elsewhere. Since 'inspiration' of the biblical authors can in no way preclude them at times from human error or imperfection—both in their records of required conduct and their understanding of metaphysical truths—it is difficult to see how we might give much weight to 'inspiration', other than that of seeing the term as describing a *zeal* and *passion* for recording the things 'believed' to be of God. So, the word 'inspiration' carries not so much an authority as an *inclination* towards God in the practice of writing, and inerrancy is not precluded. In seeking universal values in the Bible, we have to judge by the content of each particular utterance. We have no choice, therefore, but to be selective in setting out biblical authors' ideas in a hierarchy of excellence by the use of criteria other than the belief that these things are of God because they are contained in the 'inspired' Bible.

There are unsavoury comments and pronouncements by the great prophets of Israel found in the Bible. For example, we cannot hold as true or valid the bitter cry of Isaiah that portrays a preferential God favouring some orphans and widows while disfavouring others:

> Therefore Yahweh showed no mercy to their young men,
> no tenderness to their orphans and widows . . .
> For all this his anger has not turned back,
> and his hand is stretched out still.

Isaiah 9:17

Whatever sentiments led to the composing of these words, they are certainly far removed from what we understand of the loving 'Heavenly Father' of the Gospels. Such examples of 'unchristian' values can be multiplied in the prophets and Psalms. Dodd sums up the situation:

> Any theory of inspiration of the Bible which suggests that we should recognise such utterances as authoritative for us stands self-condemned. They are relative to their age. But I think we should say more. They are false and they are wrong . . . Inspiration therefore does not imply moral perfection or intellectual infallibility.[8]

> No one not blinded by a superstitious bibliolatry could possibly accept for truth, as they stand, many elements in Old Testament prophecy.[9]

THE NON-PARTISAN SPIRIT OF THE HEBREW *NABIS*

Amos in the opening chapters turned his figure of justice towards an arrogant Israel after dismissing the nations of Damascus, Gaza, Tyre, Edom, Ammon, Moab and Judah. In artful irony, he moves in on Israel just as the hearers are applauding the prowess of their national God:

> For crime after crime of Israel
> I will grant them no reprieve . . .
> For you alone have I cared,
> among all the nations of the world;
> therefore will I punish you
> for all your iniquities.

Amos 2:6; 3:2

Isaiah courageously claims that the Assyrian invader was Yahweh's instrument in carrying out justice upon the evils of Judah (Is. 10:5). Equally, Micah predicted that Zion should be a "ploughed field" (Mic. 3:12). Again, Jeremiah suggested that it was Yahweh's will for Judah to go under (Jer. 9:11; 10:22). It is not that the *nabis* of the period were losing their religious passion and national pride—indeed, their passions drew them into greater engagement—it is just that they were able to see more than their contemporaries that nationalistic zeal had to take second place to morality, and that God must care more for a *universal right* than for the 'rights' of a particular nation. There are lessons we have to learn here in the light of a century that has witnessed two World Wars and the Jewish Holocaust. What an amazing discovery this was, then, by the *nabis* of the eighth century.

A further criterion for a political philosophy emerges for us, whereby we might weigh up an attitude as being truly a revelation of God, namely, *a righteous deed must take precedence over the 'rights' of a national cause. A deity who cannot demonstrate a non-partisan spirit in his dealings with all people cannot indeed be God.*

TOWARDS A UNIVERSALISTIC CONCEPT OF GOD

There was a period in Canaan when Yahweh had all but lost his personal identity, when, as Dodd says: "He was identified or confused with local Els and Baals whose 'personality' was a fluctuating quantity, till no one knew whether there was one Jehovah among a multitude of Baals, or a multitude of Jehovahs who were also Baals."[10] In the light of this confusing religious syncretism, the Deuteronomistic reformers pronounced the uncompromising doctrine of monotheism: "Yahweh our God is one Yahweh" (Deut. 6:4 RSV). The environment might have helped shape the concept of the monotheistic God but it certainly could not have produced it—the 'natural' forces were against this outcome. The implications are clearly evident. Since Yahweh is the only God, his plan must be to make himself known to all peoples. The calling of Israel was not to grant it a state of privilege or arrogant prestige over other nations, or to procure any exclusivity, but to be his 'servant', to tutor it for a role throughout history, so that it might become a missionary nation and bear witness to the righteousness of God amongst all peoples. It is Yahweh's will that all nations should be saved:

> Come forward and urge your case, consult together:
> who foretold this in days of old,who stated it long ago?
> Was it not I Yahweh?
> There is no god but me;
> there is no god other than I, victorious and able to save.
> Look to me and be saved,
> you peoples from all corners of the earth; for I am God, there is no other.
> By my life I have sworn,
> I have given a promise of victory,
> a promise that will not be broken,
> that to me every knee shall bend
> and by me every tongue shall swear.

Isaiah 45:21–23

Thus the seeds of universalism were sown and a *nabi* was to grasp something which his environment could never have revealed, namely *the monotheistic character of the Hebrew God and his universal interest in all peoples.*

THE LOVE-ETHIC OF THE HEBREW *NABIS*

There is evidence of another criterion of revelation found in the way the *nabi* conceived the character of God. It is not clear whether the changing conception of the character of God was prompted by the growing awareness of man's need for improved relations with his neighbours, or whether the *nabi's* new moral outlook was arrived at as a natural progression of a new understanding of God. Perhaps, the features of cause and effect are not as important as the realisation that Yahweh was a God inextricably bound up with human relations and the ethic of love.

Some of the tenderest and most touching human traits are ascribed to the Hebrew God by the eighth-century prophets. Hosea, particularly, becomes aware of the love of Yahweh through his bitter experience of losing his wife. Though she had left him, he could not cease loving her. How then could Yahweh abandon his people? "When Israel was a boy, I loved him (Hos. 11:1)." He had grasped something else of the *holiness* of God. He learned that indeed there must be something eternal and unqualified in the love of God, and that, within the very nature of love, there must also be the property to show mercy and forgiveness.

Jeremiah is regarded as being pessimistic when exposing the corruption of his own people, yet nevertheless he speaks of the hope of a 'new covenant' in which sin would be forgiven and God's law engraved upon men's hearts:

> The time is coming, says Yahweh, when I will make a new covenant with Israel and Judah. It will not be like the covenant I made with their forefathers when I took them by the hand and led them out of Egypt . . . I will set my law within them and write it on their hearts; I will become their God and they shall become my people.

Jer. 31:31–34

Ezekiel's rigid "plagiarism might seem to have left no loophole for unmerited mercy", in that he thought it was not possible for men to hope for mercy unless they were prepared to repent.[11] But what if they would not, was that the end of the matter? Ezekiel goes that little bit further, by describing how God would intervene and create in them a 'new heart', so that they would repent:

> I will sprinkle clean water over you, and you shall be cleansed from all that defiles you; I will cleanse you from the taint of all your idols. I will give you a new heart and put a new spirit within you; I will take the heart of stone from your body and give you a heart of flesh. I will put my spirit into you and make you conform to my statutes, keep my laws and live by them.

Ezek. 36:25–27

Although this was conceived as a crude supernatural overriding of human will, it bears a conviction that there must be something in God beyond retributive justice. This was an advanced insight for the time.

This awareness of the loving nature and limitless mercy of the Hebrew God, which by far surpassed any retributive justice, forms a further criterion of universal 'truth'. It is the loftiest ideal of revelation found in the Old Testament.

PROGRESSIVE REVELATION

We are not justified in seeing these moments of prophetic insight as being evidence of a *progressive revelation* within the biblical text, if we understand *progressive* in a periodic-sequential sense. There is a slow progress clearly visible in a general way, but in the particular it is not very evident. For example, there is a development in the requirement of sacrifice in the Bible, through internalisation and moralisation of the crude cult—from human sacrifice to animal offerings, from animal slaughter to linguistic acts expressing self-surrender to God, and from linguistic acts to the modern value of altruistic conduct. Other ideas show a regression, or an oscillation from one extreme to the other, such as pietism: from 'puritanism' to 'secularism', and vice versa. Having reached the high water-mark of spiritual ascendancy during the eighth century BC, we witness a falling away up to the Christian era of revelation in terms of moral relations. We see reversion to nationalism from snippets of universalism, retrogression to cultic means of placating an angry deity from the elevation of a unilateral morality, and sectarian feuds of 'puritanism' aimed at designating the 'true' people of God. The prophets taught us that God was not capricious or contingent, but consistent and trustworthy in his dealings.

When the Deuteronomistic writers amended and re-wrote the pre-prophetic literature, they left intact some examples of a very capricious God: Cain's sacrifice was rejected in favour of Abel's, just to suit what appears to be an arbitrary whim of God (Gen. 4:4–5); Moses was called into the desert, shown favour, given a fantastic commission, etc., only to find at one point that "Yahweh met him and sought to kill him" (Exod. 4:24 RSV); Elijah reproaches God for killing the son of a good widow to whom he had been sent, resulting in his later appeal to bring the boy back to life (I Kings 17:17–23).

Early biblical narratives preserve many examples of amoral traits alongside those of higher conceptions of Yahweh's deeds—clearly, the incongruent features were never seen, either by the original scribes or by those later editors electing not to amend the narratives. Since later editors were forward in changing other elements of the biblical narrative that did not comply with orthodox belief, we may reasonably presume that they were not too unhappy or embarrassed by some of the amoral projections of the capricious dealings of Yahweh.

At a later stage of Israelite history, and during a time of fear that Israel's heritage might be lost, we see in the Jewish Apocalyptic literature a return to meticulous liturgical rites and the practice of puritanism (as evidenced in Daniel and the books of Maccabees). The Apocalyptic writers appeal to God's *ruach* (or *pneuma*) as the authorisation of their visions, just as the *nabis* had done in the past. They exploit ecstatic trances of a wholly irrational kind, they are fantastic and rich in fantasy, they are bizarre and highly imaginative. Yet they are, in my judgement, less advanced in spirituality than the giant prophets of the eighth century whose insights we have been considering. If the prophets of Amos, Isaiah and Jeremiah were *progressive*, then the Deuteronomists and many of the Apocalyptic writers were *retrogressive*.

I know there are passages in Daniel that commend a virtuous religious attitude. They represent a faith that resolves to cling on to God regardless of how the situation might turn out (Dan. 3:17f.). The general tone, however, qualifies the book to be seen as typical apocalyptic prophecy.

THE LOVE-ETHIC OF THE NEW TESTAMENT

The New Testament moves towards the ultimate moral goal of the altruistic love-ethic. There are however, some immoral elements found in the New Testament, to which some fundamentalists give unwarranted importance. A few practical injunctions are promoted at the expense of the love-message as a whole. Dodd cites the story of a

Calvinistic preacher who said: "the Almighty is compelled to do many things in his official capacity which he would scorn in his private capacity."[12] This form of hypocrisy can be seen in some of the decisions of leaders of fundamentalist sects! No doubt this dilemma arises from the futile attempt to marry some of the detestable and immoral dealings of Yahweh in the Old Testament with the loving Father of the New—a problem which exists only for those who hold the whole Bible to be infallible. The highlighting of a few spurious verses as a code of sectarian practice—in ignorance of their moral implications—is a case of not seeing the ethical wood for the ecclesiastical trees!

I call this a feigned ethical theology, in that it practises love because the Christian is *commanded* to love his neighbour as himself, even his enemy likewise, not because he *understands it as being the only way to live*—an ethic as effectively practised by the non-Christian. The love act is demonstrated in a formal sense only, for behind the love-mask beliefs and practises are retained that in their essence are clearly uncharitable and unchristian! Take the following as examples:

a) those Christian sects which excommunicate a member for marrying out of the Faith—a lead taken from ambiguous statements of Paul, completely out of context.

b) those doctrinally exclusive communities which refuse to share the Eucharist with Christians of other churches.

c) those clerics who promote the war-ethic in the 'name of Christ' as a means of bringing about political or ecclesiastical revolution.

d) on an individual level, those Christians who address another as "Brother" and yet behave toward him as though he were worse than an enemy!

All the above may be an unwitting response resulting from an obsession with carrying out the *commandment* of biblical verse 'to the letter', but it is a misguided ethic, it is psuedo-love, and it is no less uncharitable and unchristian for being done in ignorance!

We have suggested above that a teaching that promotes a high ethical ideal might serve as evidence of it being a revealed truth, indeed, as a criterion for an utterance being a valid *revelation of God*. In the Gospel of Mark, Jesus gives the principle upon which the 'man of God' must now base his life:

> Love the Lord your God with all your heart, with all your soul, with all your mind, and with all your strength . . . Love your neighbour as yourself . . .
>
> Mark 12:28–34

In the Sermon on the Mount, this principle is explained in unmistakable detail:

> Anyone who nurses anger against his brother must be brought to judgement.
>
> Matt. 5:22

> Love your enemies and pray for your persecutors.
>
> Matt. 5:44

> If someone slaps you on the right cheek, turn and offer him your left . . . Give when you are asked to give; and do not turn your back on a man who wants to borrow.
>
> Matt. 5:39–42

> How blessed you are, when you suffer insults and persecution and every kind of calumny for my sake. Accept it with gladness and exultation, for you have a rich reward in heaven . . .
>
> Matt. 5:11–12

> There must be no limit to your goodness, as your heavenly Father's goodness knows no bounds.
>
> Matt. 5:48

The Johannine corpus also preserves the ethic of love:

> I give you a new commandment: love one another; as I have loved you, so you are to love one another.
>
> John 13:34

> But if a man says, "I love God", while hating his brother, he is a liar.
>
> I John 4:19

These sayings put together describe the unconditional transcending nature of the love of God, as taught by Jesus. The love-ethic has no limits, and is in no way to be understood as the counter-balance of the 'wrath of God', as found in Paul (Rom. 1–3). The phrase "the wrath of God is revealed from heaven" forms a linguistic parallel to the expression, "the righteousness of God is revealed through faith for faith" (1:18/17). Both describe the message of the Gospel as an eschatological salvation-event. Although the term "is revealed" connects the two opposing ideas together, 'God's wrath' is not to be understood as being contained within the Gospel itself, or as serving as a complement to it, neither is it to be understood as a part and product of God's essential nature and being; rather the term is used as a means by which the ungodly world is subjected under sin—the pre-condition of the Gospel.[13]

On the relationship of liturgy to ethics, there is a saying of Jesus that demotes the place of ritual observance to that of having right relations with other people:

> If, when you are bringing your gift to the altar, you suddenly remember that your brother has a grievance against you, leave your gift where it is before the altar. First go and make your peace with your brother, and only then come back and offer your gift.
>
> Matt. 5:23–24

It is on these principles that the Christian is to base his or her own morality. This is not to say that the ethic comes from within man, or that it may not be *something* that is God-given. This is the point at which I part company with those philosophers of religion, such as Cupitt (*Taking Leave of God*) and quite recently Goulder, who appear to promote an enlightened morality without a base, for, as I believe Prince Philip once remarked: "Education without religion makes clever devils!"[14]

The biblical verse does not give us the definitive answer to all our ethical questions; it cannot, for it is conditional to the age in which it was written. These moral injunctions and imperatives are in a sense quite absolute because they are principles, but the applications of principles in the nuts-and-bolts issues of everyday moral dilemmas are conditional. Paul, an apostle of first rank, wrestles with the ethical challenges of his own day and, although he claimed to have received divine insight—"and I believe I too have the Spirit of God" (I Cor. 7:40)—it did not give him infallibility over a moral pronouncement that will stand for all time and for every occasion.

We can distinguish various modes of thinking in Paul's writings. Like a rabbi, he draws conclusions from a traditional authority, principally the Old Testament, but he also bases his authority on a saying of Jesus, the tradition, and even on the indelible law of nature. He is a philosopher when making logical and coherent deductions from first principles, or when making a deduction from experience. Sometimes he casts reason and argument aside and declares with prophetic conviction that his judgement is the 'word of the Lord'. We do not find him exploiting the gift of ecstatic utterances (in fact, he plays it down), and we do not find him issuing instructions under the 'inspiration' of God's *pneuma* either. In Paul, we find a devout disciple of the Lord, who is by no means short of intellect, knowledge and wisdom, working at the love-ethic in the particular moral dilemmas of his day. Unlike the fundamentalist, we do not find him searching for scriptural authorisation as the sole means of carrying the argument, neither do we find him issuing *ex-cathedra* statements over contentious issues, such as the rights of women for the priesthood, sisters wearing head-coverings in worship, the right to exclude some from the Eucharist, the nature of the 'God-head', or the correct form of the service, etc..

The Bible can be understood to be the *record* of God's 'revelation', then, by virtue of the following criteria:

1. moral relations are of greater importance to God than cultic or liturgical observances.
2. in the eyes of God, righteous deeds must take precedence over the rights of a national cause.
3. the truest picture of God is that which presents him as a non-partisan spirit: he shows no favouritism, he is not the exclusive God of Israel or of the Church, but he is the Lord of all peoples.
4. God is a supremely ethical Being, who wishes men and women to be equally ethical in their social relations; to love the unlovable, and to love one's enemies as oneself, and to forgive without limit.

Our Christian task is one of translating the ethic of love into the many daily responses we are called upon to make in our various social relations. As to the importance of ritual and worship in Christian living, I cannot see any place for being dogmatic; it must be an individual decision. There is no divine injunction, it is a matter of choice. If a study of religion over the centuries shows us anything at all, it is the fact that the development of religious consciousness has led us to see that the requirement of the cult has had to give way to an exalted moral code of man's relations towards his fellows; the symbols and rituals have no intrinsic values and meanings in themselves, but only those that have been ascribed to them.

The Christian love-ethic presupposes 'Christ', and the 'Christ-figure' presupposes Jesus. It remains for us, then, to consider the most remarkable person in religious history who is claimed to have been the *fullest revelation* of God, the man Jesus of Nazareth. What can be known of Jesus of Nazareth?

NOTES

1. E. O. James, *Sacrifice and Sacrament*, 1962, pages 84–85.
2. Ibid., pages 77–83.
3. The passing of children through the fire of Moloch was forbidden under judgement of the death penalty (Lev. 18:21; 20:2). Ahab and Manasseh ignored this indictment, however (II Kings 16:3; 21:6; 17:17). There is evidence of a spate of child sacrifice at Topheth in the valley of Hinnom, just before the exile (Jer. 32:35; Ezek. 16:20; 20:31). These first-born victims were mainly dedicated to *Moloch* and *Baal*, but, in this age, the cultic practice was conjoined with the worship of Yahweh (Jer. 19:5; 32:35; Ezek. 23:39; Num. 18:15f.). Following the example of Abraham offering his son to Yahweh (even though the editor has used the story to denounce child sacrifice), Jephthah, Hiel and Ahaz are set a precedent in this early source of ancient Israelite practice, E. O. James, op. cit., page 95.
4. C. H. Dodd, *The Authority of the Bible*, 1929.
5. Ibid., page 91.
6. The text runs thus:

   > When I brought your forefathers out of Egypt, I gave them no commandment about whole-offering and sacrifice; I said not a word about them. What I did command them was this: If you obey me, I will be your God and you shall be my people. You must conform to all my commandments, if you would prosper.
   >
   > Jer. 7:22–23

   We cannot conclude with certainty that this was the general prophetic viewpoint, owing to the contrary evidence of the Deuteronomists and Hosea, who sought to purify the cult from abuse. All we can say is that there appears to be ambiguity within the sources over the place and importance of ritual observance, and whether or not Yahweh ever prescribed this form of cultic practice as the means of obeying his commandments.
7. C. H. Dodd, op. cit., pages 96–97.
8. Ibid., pages 129–130.
9. Ibid., page 129.
10. Ibid., page 101.
11. Ibid., pages 108–109.
12. Ibid., page 100.
13. See C. H. Dodd's *Commentary on Romans* (1:17f.), 1949, and G. Bornkamm, *Early Christian Experience*, 1969, chapter 4, 'The Revelation of God's Wrath: Romans 1–3', pages 47–70, London, 1963. Dodd demonstrates on linguistic grounds that 'God's wrath' cannot mean an emotion of anger being vented by God. Bornkamm shows the literary dependence of the ideas found in Romans 1–3 on the Stoic terminology of Hellenistic Judaism.
14. D. Cupitt, *Taking Leave of God*, London, 1980, writes in the Preface:

    > Modern people increasingly demand autonomy, the power of legislating for oneself . . . In philosophy there is a class argument to the effect that unless we claim and exercise this radical kind of freedom we are not being truly moral at all . . . I must appropriate, internalise and truly make my own the standards I live by . . . If I do obey a good God whose commandments are good, my obedience is only meritorious in so far as I freely and rationally judge for myself that God's commandments are intrinsically good and deserving of adoption as principles of conduct, so that I would freely choose to obey them in any case whether God commanded them or not.

    Much of what Cupitt says is true, in the sense that we must internalise and appropriate to ourselves a received moral principle in order that we may be moral. What I am unsure about is whether any such dependable moral conduct can be arrived at through one's own mental reasoning and power of choice, to the extent that the individual might legislate for himself. Could not the murderer self-justify his villainous act if he so believed that his action was the right one for him, or if he claimed to have been so instructed by God?

12

CRITICAL STUDY OF THE HISTORICAL JESUS

Was there a *real human being* called Jesus? One German scholar, George Wells, has argued that if one considers impartially the lack of information about Jesus in the Pauline corpus, we would have to conclude that Jesus was an invention from Jewish sources which speak of a heavenly redeemer who would die on earth and rise up to heaven. There is no mention of any of the following historical details of Jesus in the letters of Paul:

- His parents, his place of birth, where he lived, or even when he lived.
- John the Baptist, or Judas Iscariot, or Peter's denial of his master.
- His miracles or parables, in fact, virtually any indication of ethical teaching at all.
- His trial before Pilate, or Jerusalem as the place of his execution.

This observation, while not absolutely correct, prompted Wells to conclude that there is no sound evidence that Jesus ever existed as a real person. He is not saying that Paul personally disbelieved in the historical Jesus; he is claiming that we are not compelled to accept *per se* that Jesus existed in the flesh.

Few scholars would discount the existence of the historical Jesus on the basis of Paul's silent witness to him in his letters, but this is not to say that they would concede that any authentic information about him can be found in the Gospel narratives. The fundamentalist is committed to the conservative view, namely, that in the Gospels there is a witness to the Jesus of history that is dependable. Now, what is the correct solution?

THE QUEST OF THE HISTORICAL JESUS

When Albert Schweitzer attempted to close the debate on *The Quest of the Historical Jesus*, he caused a considerable stir amongst conservative Bible students. When examining the work of radical historians, Schweitzer showed how each writer had fashioned his respective 'Life of Christ' in accordance with his own personal stance. Christ was painted from palettes of personal religious prejudice. He concluded that there was not much objectivity in the exercise. Some time has now passed since the writing of *The Quest*, yet if we look again at some of those earlier historians he reviews, such as David Friedrich Strauss or Ernest Renan, we shall not find many of their conclusions too far removed from what the main body of scholarship today has regarded as 'orthodox' critical opinion.[1] The problem is that we need time to adjust to radical conclusions that question our beliefs. Given a little time, most fair-minded Bible students have grown to live with a scepticism with regard to the historicity of the birth narratives, the resurrection records and the traditional Church teaching on the Incarnation, even though there is still unease about such questions in some quarters!

When critical scholars and historians begin to examine some of the details of the life of Christ that are preserved in the New Testament, there is considerable disquiet amongst fundamentalists. With this topic, I am conscious of treading more heavily upon the toes of fundamentalists than in previous studies, yet we must conduct such a study because I think fundamentalists are reluctant generally to emphasise the incongruity between the 'historical Jesus' and the 'Christ of the *kerygmatic* faith'. Studies in the historical Jesus have rendered him virtually impossible to find, say the critics, yet the fundamentalist replies: 'Turn to the Gospels, read, accept, and just believe.'

Such a resolute standing in the trenches by fundamentalists is adopted wholly in derision of biblical criticism. This apologetic relies not only on an uncritical acceptance of the 'printed words' of the New Testament, but on an erroneous implication that the critics know not the scriptures (John 5:39)—in fact, the converse is true. Critical scholars, of necessity, have had to commit themselves to a painstaking study of such matters as literary form, linguistics, aetiology, narrative comparison, contemporary situation, and to consider all possible meanings and relevances of the texts before arriving at any personal theory.

JESUS—THE EVIDENCE [2]

There is a non-Christian testimony to Jesus in the writings of the Jewish historian, Josephus, which has sometimes been used in support of the Christian assertion that the Jesus of the Gospels can be verified by independent historical witness. However, many New Testament scholars have recognised for some time now that this record as it stands must be an interpolation by a Christian monk; the early manuscript must have been doctored for *kerygmatic* purposes, since a Jewish Pharisee like Josephus would never have made such propagandist claims for Jesus. The passage runs thus:

> Now, there was about this time, Jesus, *a wise man*, if it be lawful to call him a man, for he was a *doer of wonderful works*—a teacher of such men as receive *the truth* with pleasure. He drew over to him both many of the Jews, and many of the Gentiles. *He was (the) Christ*; and when Pilate, at the suggestion of the principal men amongst us, had condemned him to the cross, those that loved him at the Wrst did not forsake him, for *he appeared to them alive again*, as the divers prophets had foretold these and *ten thousand other wonderful things* concerning him; and the tribe of Christians, so named from him, are not extinct at this day.
>
> *Antiquities of the Jews* book 18 Ch. 3:3[3]

It is not likely that Josephus would have made such statements as those italicized. While the argument of a doctored text appears sound on a first reading, a Jewish scholar, Geza Vermes, has recently suggested that the whole section need not be regarded as an interpolation. He has argued from the basis that much of the phraseology and language is typically that of Josephus.[4] Vermes has reconstructed on Form Critical grounds what he believes to have been the original passage of the report of Jesus:

> At about this time there lived Jesus, a wise man . . . he performed astonishing feats (And was a teacher of such people as are eager for such novelties). He attracted many Jews and many of the Greeks . . . Upon an indictment brought by leading members of our society, Pilate sentenced him to the cross, but those who had loved him from the very first did not cease to be attached to him. The brotherhood of the Christians named after him, is still in existence.

What is significant about this reconstruction, is that it represents an unbiased record of the life and execution of the Jesus of history without any pro-christian additions. It is a reconstruction on sound exegetical principles—there was indeed, then, a man called Jesus, an influential teacher who was executed by Pilate, and so on.

There can be little doubt, therefore, that a remarkable Jew by the name of Jesus once lived in Galilee during the first century.

A copy of a second-century letter has been discovered at Masada which suggests that there had been in existence a secret Gospel of Mark. It was used by an inner-circle of first followers of Jesus, and it shows us that what became the orthodox Church may not have been the only community committed to Jesus of Nazareth.[5]

The new quest of the historical Jesus looks not so much at the New Testament witness but at the rival sectarians of the Judaean desert, and it presents a very different Jesus from the one preached in the Bible. Why, however, should we lightly discard the Gospel narratives as an *ipso facto* account of who Jesus was and what he did?

THE CONTEXT OF THE DEBATE

Constantine summoned the bishops together to resolve conclusively the issue which had unsettled his previously secure empire; the Council took place at Nicaea in 324 AD.[6] The Emperor issued the Creed after weeks of discord, and the teaching of the eternal nature of the Son of God became settled for a short while till Chalcedon. Constantine's successors systematically destroyed rival Christian documents that were contrary to the Creed, and non-conforming Christians were eliminated. Rival documents survived, nevertheless; some having been discovered only in recent times.

Did the Roman Church get its understanding of Jesus right? What had happened in the three centuries between Jesus' crucifixion by a Roman Governor and his confirmation as the Co-Creator and Co-Ruler of the universe by a Roman Emperor?

The established Church order brought about by Chalcedon had remained intact for almost twelve centuries until 1517, when a German theologian called Martin Luther put up for discussion ninety-five criticisms of the Roman Church. His protest heralded the Protestant Church. He claimed that there was no decreed authority of the pope as the supreme interpreter of the Bible, and that the only authority was the 'Word of God' embodied in the Christian scriptures. Luther himself produced the first popular translation of the Bible in the vernacular, and the German tradition of biblical criticism began—a tradition which would eventually lead to conclusions of which Luther would never have dreamt. Luther inherited the belief that the Bible was a sacred text, and that the Gospels were first-hand accounts by faithful eyewitnesses, but within two centuries both these assumptions would be challenged.

SIGNIFICANT STAGES IN THE SEARCH FOR JESUS

1. The first challenge came when medieval belief in the supernatural was eclipsed by science, rationalism and the age of enlightenment. Rational explanations were sought for miracles of all kinds. Inevitably, the miracles of the Gospels came under careful scrutiny: Jesus walking on the water was a stunt performed by standing on a sand bank; healings were done by special ointments, etc. Once the process had begun, scholars began examining the Gospels, not as sacred texts but as historical documents. It was demonstrable that not only did the Gospels contain discrepancies and contradictions, they also had straightforward mistakes. Mark's Gospel, for example, has Jesus travelling through Sidon on his way from Tyre to the Sea of Galilee. Not only is Sidon in the opposite direction, but there was no road from Sidon to the Sea of Galilee at that time, only a road from Tyre; whoever wrote it, was not familiar with this part of first-century Palestine. Why did the Gospels contain such indisputable mistakes?

By the middle of the nineteenth century, one eminent German scholar, D. F. Strauss, upset Christian orthodoxy by promoting the idea that the Gospels were not written by first-hand eyewitnesses. He showed that they could not have been written by the apostles, Matthew and John, or by the disciples of the apostles, Mark and Luke, but must have been composed by anonymous second-generation Christians.[7]

2. The authors of the Gospels remain unknown to us, then, but when were they written? One significant event provides us with a clue—the destruction of the temple in Jerusalem by the Romans in 66 AD. There are frequent hints and indirect allusions in the Gospels to the plundering and demolition of the temple, forty years or so after the crucifixion of Jesus:

> The king was angry, and he sent his troops and destroyed those murderers and burned their city.
>
> (Matt. 22:7)

> And Jerusalem will be trodden down by the Gentiles.
>
> (Luke 21:24)

How long, however, after the overthrow of Jerusalem were the Gospels written? By the middle of the nineteenth century the hunt for the earliest Gospel texts was on.

A German monk and scholar, Tischendorf, entered St Catherine's monastery in the Sinai desert in 1859 and discovered *Codex Sinaiticus*, a treasure that had remained hidden for 1400 years.[8] The codex was an almost complete copy of the Old and New Testament in Greek, and was made soon after Constantine's council in the fourth century. As the Gospels were written in Greek, it was possible to match the text with fragments of the Gospels discovered earlier from the dry sands of Egypt. Many of these fragments were almost identical to *Codex Sinaiticus*, proving that there had been very little tampering with the Gospels since they were first written. One passage written on both sides of papyrus from the Fourth Gospel matches Codex Sinaiticus, and has been dated reliably to around 125 AD. Upon thematic and Form Critical grounds, it is reasonable to conclude that the Synoptic Gospels must have been composed and completed much earlier than this date, and, since Mark's Gospel has fewer allusions to the taking of the temple, it seems reasonable to date this book before 66 AD.

3. Although the date of the composition of the Gospels might be early, how reliable are they as records of events that *actually happened*?

When Napoleon went to Egypt in 1798, he took with him a group of scholars to study the buildings and inscriptions of the times of the Pharaohs. They discovered startling similarities between the myths of ancient Egypt and the stories in the Bible. Not only were there myths in which men were transformed into miracle-working gods and divine heroes, but there were also stories of virgin births and resurrections. This recognition prompted the study of other ancient religions having mythological themes, themes that also run through Christianity.

The rationalists tried to explain the miracles as natural events, but now a new wave of scholars became convinced that the miracles never really happened at all; rather they were myths the early Christians had used as a way of expressing their belief in Jesus' divinity. Again the work was pioneered by D. F. Strauss.

The Church had maintained that Jesus came as a fulfilment of Old Testament prophecy, but Strauss disputed this by suggesting that the Christians simply used these forecasting predictions to fill in the unknown details of Jesus' ministry. He cited passages from the Old Testament which were formerly used as proof-texts for genuine historical details of the ministry and evidence of divine prediction:

> Behold a young woman shall conceive and bear a son.
>
> Isaiah 7:14 RSV

> But thou Bethlehem . . . from you shall come forth for me one who is to be ruler in Israel.
>
> Micah 5:2 RSV

> A star shall come forth out of Jacob.
>
> Num. 24:17 RSV

> They shall bring gold and frankincense, and shall proclaim the praise of the Lord.
>
> Isaiah 60:6 RSV

> Even my bosom friend in whom I trusted, who ate my bread has lifted his heel against me.
>
> Psalm 41:9 RSV

> My God, my God, why hast thou forsaken me?
>
> Psalm 22:1 RSV

> Yet he bore the sin of many . . . he shall prolong his days.
>
> Isaiah 53:12, 10 RSV

And they made his grave with the wicked and with a rich man in his death.

Isaiah 53:9 RSV

After his work was published, Strauss was dismissed from his university post and never again was allowed to hold a teaching position. Today, however, his work is regarded as a landmark in New Testament studies.

4. One result of Strauss' work was the special interest in Mark's Gospel, since it contained the least mythological content, but even Mark has unusual features that one would not expect to find in a straightforward narrative of history. One of these is the theme of secrecy, which runs throughout the Gospel. Wilhelm Wrede drew attention to this in his notable work, *The Messianic Secret in The Gospels*.[9] Some examples are:

> Jesus forbade them to tell anyone. 7:36 RSV
>
> Jesus sent him home saying, 'Do not tell anyone in the village'. 8:26 RSV
>
> Then he gave them strict orders not to tell anyone about him. 8:30 RSV

If Jesus had performed such a spectacular miracle as raising someone from the dead, how could it be kept a secret, for every one of the subject's acquaintances would be aware that the person was alive again? Jesus seems to have been preoccupied with secrecy. Dennis Nineham has made a special study of Mark, and has concluded, that, according to this evangelist, Jesus took steps not to publicise his actions where in practice it was not possible to keep them secret.[10] Wrede's solution was that the sources Mark relied upon contained no references to Jesus being the Messiah, yet the evangelist had believed that Jesus had been the Messiah, so Mark explained the absence of such reports by inventing the theme of secrecy.

The crucial thing about this realisation is that it tells us a lot about the purpose of the Gospels. A Gospel is not a biography but a work of theology, or propaganda, designed to get across certain religious points, as Nineham shows. How much can be known then about Jesus? It is a pertinent question indeed when we bear in mind that the evangelist's emphasis was designed to build faith rather than satisfy historical curiosity.

The first theologian to consider the implication of New Testament analysis up to the time of Wrede was Schweitzer.[11] He addressed himself to the traditional image of Jesus, who was born of a virgin, who walked on water, and who rose to heaven. This is what he said:

> The image has not been destroyed from without, it has fallen to pieces, cracked and disintegrated from the historical problems which came to the surface one after another. We must be prepared to find that historical knowledge of the personality and life of Jesus will not be a help but perhaps even an offence to religion. He will be to our time a stranger and an enigma.

The Church's adherents were largely ignorant of nineteenth-century damage done to the image of the historical Jesus; scholarship was restricted to the cloistered world of academia, and several factors conspired to keep it there.

As a response to this new wave of criticism, the Catholic Church initially fought fire with fire, but then Leo XIII encouraged the Catholic theologians to adopt the methods of German historical criticism. As a result, the Catholic Modernist movement was born. It was centred in Paris and England. The ultimate reaction of the Vatican was swift, with excommunication and censorship brought in to check the new movement, and Catholics had to swear an anti-modernist oath. Protestants, on the other hand, continued in the forefront of critical study.

Later on, further archaeological discoveries in the Near East began to open up a fresh understanding of what could be known with certainty, but only for those who didn't feel threatened by such open-ended enquiry.

5. In 1896, members of the British-based Egyptian society went in search of ancient papyri and found in the dry Egyptian sands a rubbish tip at Oxyrynchus that revealed hundreds of papyri from the second, third, fourth and fifth centuries AD. One of these writings was an early Christian document containing fragments of a collection of known and unknown sayings of Jesus, many of which are not found in the New Testament. What was of interest and great significance to scholars was that there was nothing else. There was no connecting narrative of places or times. This absence prompted the German scholar, Carl Ludwic Schmidt, to carry out the experiment of removing the linking phrases from the Gospels which connected the various sayings and events of Jesus, so that they too could be reduced to a collection of sayings and deeds with no chronology.[12] He then examined the linking phrases that he had removed:

> It happened at this time . . .
>
> When he had gone a little further . . .
>
> Once he was approached by . . .
>
> He went away to a lonely place . . .
>
> When after some days . . .
>
> Once more he went away . . .

Such links were devoid of detail, just vague lines joining Jesus' words and actions together. Schmidt concluded that these links were constructed by the evangelists themselves to create a continuous narrative. He further maintained that their sources must have come down to them as an unconnected list; the narrative passages had no historical validity. Much of this remained speculation, however, until a discovery was made at a village in upper-Egypt called Nag Hammadi by two Bedouin Arabs collecting top-soil for their vegetable patch.[13] In one they discovered a vessel in which was found a parchment having a much longer collection of unconnected Gospel sayings and deeds—the Gospel of Thomas.[14] This supported the theory of an original unconnected source document underlying the Gospels. It also proved that lists of Gospel sayings continued to circulate long after the Gospels had been written, and that Schmidt's theory was likely to be right. Schmidt set the stage for the person who was to lead the field for the next fifty years, the German theologian, Rudolf Bultmann.

6. The mythological content of the Gospels had been revealed to be secondary by Strauss; the framework of the narrative that knitted together the various sayings and deeds was shown by Schmidt to be artificial, but what about the sayings and

deeds themselves? If the Gospel authors could invent material to suit their respective individual theological purposes, it seemed reasonable, according to Bultmann, that we should disregard anything the early Church had an obvious motive to invent.

Bultmann searched for anything tailor-made to serve the needs of the early Church. A good example was the incident at Ceasarea Philippi of the confession of Peter. He regarded this story as suspect because the passage venerates the claim of Jesus to be the Messiah and the status of Peter as the leader of the early Church. He demonstrated that rabbis uttered similar words long before Jesus was born, and suggested that the early Church could have borrowed these along with the many other Jewish sayings and prophecies. Bultmann concluded that many of the earliest sayings of Jesus were attributed to him by the early Christians and that these sayings were being developed until the evangelists strung them together like beads to produce the consecutive Gospel story. Not only were the stories of Jesus' birth, infancy, miracles and resurrection mythological, so too were many of his deeds and sayings. The 'baptism' and the 'preaching about the kingdom' were the only details he could accept to be genuine, the latter because this message brought about the crucifixion. An immediate controversy broke out with the publication of his book, *Jesus and the Word*,[15] a work in which he kept separate the notion of faith and the study of the historical Jesus. He argued that 'historical research' must not be restricted by any sentimental devotion to the 'Christ of faith'.

7. Earlier this century, travellers in Syria encountered isolated communities that still spoke in Aramaic—the presumed or accepted native tongue of Jesus. The common written language of the first century was Greek—the language in which the Gospels were written. Some scholars began to detect traces of Aramaic behind the Greek text of the Gospels, traces which they felt could indicate the original words that Jesus would have spoken.[16] In the same way that 'On the bridge of Avignon' translates as 'Sur le pont d'Avignon', so a few phrases in the Gospels seem to form poetry when translated back to Aramaic, as if they had once been fashioned and designed by a teacher to be learnt by heart. Could that teacher have been Jesus? These researchers said yes, but Bultmann's followers pointed out that the earliest Christians also spoke in Aramaic. Consequently, traces of Aramaic might show a given passage to be early but not that it necessarily represented a genuine utterance of Jesus.

British scholars contend that since Jewish rabbis expected their disciples to commit their teaching to memory, it is highly plausible that Jesus—as a highly influential charismatic teacher—would have done the same, and that what we have in the Gospels are genuine records of the words of the historical Jesus that have been committed to memory and reinforced by fresh and repeated application. However, this cannot be wholly supported by the evidence. The theory rests upon a number of assumptions which, if pressed too far, run foul of the known facts. The Lord's prayer and the words at the Last Supper, for example, should, on the basis of Aramaic originals, have been preserved identically, but some records do not quote Jesus' words at all, and those that do preserve them in very different forms. The translation from Aramaic to Greek might account for some of the minor differences but it cannot account for the major ones. We should not expect identical phrasing in the light of what is known of the Oral Tradition. It must be remembered that the oral transmission was not infallible.

It is clear, therefore, that the words of Jesus were not committed to memory and recalled in quite the way the theory suggests.

8. English scholars like C. H. Dodd have used a much broader criterion to establish authentic events and words of Jesus.[17] The entry into Jerusalem, for example, is recorded by each evangelist. It is known to be of Jewish practice and custom, and the event seems consistent with Jesus' proclamation of the kingdom of God—even Bultmann felt this story was reliable. Using such a criterion, a more authentic picture of Jesus began to emerge. Even so, the details of the story are not dependable—did Jesus ride on a donkey as a king (Matthew) or on a horse as a priest (Luke)?

The results of critical biblical scholarship have re-established confidence in some of the Gospel narratives of what Jesus said and did, but there is no current direct evidence that Jesus ever thought of himself as God, which is the basis of the Nicaean Creed.[18]

NOTES

1. David Friedrich Strauss' first *Life of Jesus*, 1835, of over 1400 pages, was a mythological interpretation of the life of Jesus. He developed his method from Hegel's philosophy of thesis, antithesis and synthesis. Formerly, the life of Jesus was understood as being wholly supernatural—this was *thesis*. Following this, counter explanations proliferated in translating all events as intelligible and natural—this was *antithesis*. Hence, a solution was found with his mythological interpretation—which was *synthesis*. In practice, this involved a radical discounting of much of the ministry as verifiable history. With the stories prior to the baptism, everything is myth; the narrative of the baptism is certainly unhistorical. The story of the temptation is unsatisfactory, and the call of the disciples could never have happened as it has been narrated. He was not sure whether the cleansing of the Temple and some of the healings had ever happened, though others clearly cannot be disputed once their Messianic attachments have been removed. The miracle-stories have a much larger legendary content to them, and the transfiguration narrative is a further appearance story of the risen Christ. In all cases, the narratives are myth. (*The Quest.*, chapter VIII)

   Ernest Renan's *Life of Jesus*, first published in 1835 (Walter Scott, Ltd., London), is a very readable account of a humanist's life of Jesus, written by a veritable French historian. At times, the author attempts a psychology of Jesus' motivations and development from (by his own admission) the scantiest of legendary Gospel sources. On the divine side of the coin, he said of Jesus that "he never argued about God, for he felt him directly in himself" (page 30). Again, when describing all venerated men of God, he said, "the breath of God was free within them". (page 282) Several miracles are not even mentioned, while others are demythologised, making the reader feel quite at home in modern thinking and spirituality as he follows the narrative. The resurrection event was an apparition of the Master to a devoted group of disciples, and to the power of a woman's love:

   > For the historian, the life of Jesus finishes with his last breath. But such was the impression he had left in the heart of his disciples and of a few devoted women, that during some weeks more it was as though he were still alive and consoling them. By whom had his body been taken away? Under what conditions did enthusiasm, always prone to credulity, create the group of narratives by which faith in the resurrection was established? In the absence of contradictory documents this can never be ascertained. Let us say, however, that the strong imagination of Mary Magdalen played an important part in the matter. Divine power of love!" (pages 271–272)

2. The basis of this chapter is taken from a BBC television programme called 'Jesus—the Evidence'.

3. *Josephus*, translated by W. Whiston, London, 1960, page 379.
4. G. Vermes, *Jesus the Jew—A Historian's reading of the Gospels*, 1973.
5. The Secret Gospel of Mark.
6. J. N. D. Kelly, *Early Christian Doctrines*, London, 1959.
7. D. F. Strauss, *Life of Christ*, 4th. edn, 1840.
8. Count Tischendorf entered St Catherine's monastery on three occasions to retrieve the complete codex in spite of considerable obstacles—see *6000 Years of the Bible*, G. S. Wegener, London, 1958, Ch. 16, pages 275–293.
9. W. Wrede, *The Messianic Secret in The Gospels*, 1901.
10. D. Nineham, *The Gospel According to St Mark*, New York, 1963.
11. A. Schweitzer, *The Quest of the Historical Jesus*, London, 1936, page 396.
12. Carl Ludwic Schmidt, *Der Rahmen der Geschichte Jesu,* (The Framework of the Jesus Story). The principal texts were the following: Mark 1:14–15; 1:21–22; 1:39; 2:13; 3:16–19; 4:33–34; 6:7; 6:12–13; 6:30.
13. R. M. Grant, *The Secret Sayings of Jesus,* London, 1960.
14. *The Gospel of Thomas*, trans. A. Guillaumont et. al, London, 1959.
15. R. Bultmann, *Jesus and the Word*, London, 1962.
16. M. Black, *An Aramaic Approach to the Gospels and Acts*, 2nd. edn., London.
17. C. H. Dodd, *New Testament Studies,* Manchester, 1953. See H. K. McArthur's, *In Search of the Historical Jesus*, London, 1969, Ch 11, for a criticism by C. H. Dodd of C. L Schmidt's work.
18. If, in Mark 2:7, only God could forgive sins, and yet Jesus does so in vv 10–11, is there not here a possible claim of Jesus to be God?', asks Michael Green. The problem, as I see it, is that this passage, and others which are similar (e.g. Luke 5:25–26; 7:17) make no explicit claims of Jesus to be divine. The inference is there admittedly, but the passages could equally be used in support of the view that God's authorisation of Jesus' work was evident throughout the ministry.

13

THE SCANDAL OF JESUS

THE HISTORICAL JESUS AND THE CHRIST OF THE POST-PASCHAL FAITH

The bedrock of historical certainty is the acceptance that with the coming of Jesus there was scandal! When Paul preached the cross of the risen Christ to the Corinthians, the message he proclaimed was a gospel of "foolishness" to the Greeks, and "scandal!" to the Jews (I Cor. 1:24—'scandal' = *scandalon,* literally, the movable stick or trigger of a trap, meaning something that trips men up).[1] Historically, the *scandal* of the Christian Church was not identical to the *scandal* of the historical Jesus. The Church from the beginning became an organised system and in every sense a brotherhood, whilst the call of Jesus was quite different: it was a challenge for response and decision for people in their living situations to enter the kingdom.

In one of the earliest New Testament documents (I Cor. 5:7), Paul gives a sacrificial interpretation of the death of Jesus: "For besides, our Passover lamb (*Pasche*), Christ, has already been sacrificed." (C. K. Barrett). Obviously, the death of Jesus was not merely understood as the demise of a good man, or the prelude to resurrection, but was interpreted theologically—it was a sacrifice. The faith of the earliest Christian community was a faith after and in the light of the crucified Jesus; it was a 'post-paschal faith'. Hans Küng's study, *On Being a Christian,* begins from the premise that historical criticism must give us a truer picture of the real Jesus than the figure coming out of a glib reading of the Gospels. Not so for the fundamentalists! They avoid the conclusions of historical criticism, and refute the idea that there is any significant difference between the 'historical Jesus' and the 'Christ of the post-paschal faith' of the early Christian community.

The *scandal* of the historical Jesus becomes a little clearer when we consider a series of contrasts: when we contrast Jesus with other religious founders; when we contrast Jesus with his contemporaries; when we contrast the 'Jesus of history' with the 'Christ of the post-paschal proclamation'. We are asking what it was about the coming of Jesus that was so distinctive, particularly when Jesus had such an exceptionally short life, as compared with the Buddha or Mohammed, in which to form a following, to exert an influence, and to make his mark. *The special feature of Christianity,* says Küng, *is that it considers that this Jesus is ultimately decisive, definitive, and archetypal for man's relations to God.*[2] This is a bold assertion indeed, and one in need of much qualification. To claim that Jesus is the archetypal figure of man's relations to God is to claim more than that Jesus was one amongst many other prophets declaring God's way; it is to affirm that Jesus was *the man.* In the context of the world religions, the claim being made, then, is that Jesus was not merely 'a way' and 'a path' to God, but *the way* and *the path* to God!

In our examination of the historical Jesus, we cannot ignore the emergence of the sociological phenomenon of the Christian Church, purporting, as it does, to follow in his name, since the Christ of the Gospels is a presentation from and through the faith of the earliest Christian community. When Mark describes Jesus proclaiming the good news of the kingdom of God in the opening verses of his Gospel (1:15), he is not presenting Jesus as the founder of a community or society. The kingdom was not a religio-political theocracy or democracy, as the Zealot revolutionaries believed; it was not an avenging judgement in favour of an élite group of perfect people, as the Essenes and the Qumran monks contended; it was not a kingdom constructed by men through an exact fulfilment of the Law and a higher morality, as the Pharisees prescribed. The kingdom of God, in accordance with the prayer of Jesus, was a situation where God's name was truly hallowed and his will absolutely carried out on earth; it was a situation in which all sin was forgiven and all evil overcome, and it was a situation primarily *for the individual.* As the Gospel of Matthew is read however, it is evident that this writer has an interest, not only in individual discipleship but in the relevance of the kingdom *for the Christian community.*

The task at this point, however, is to sketch, as best we can from all the available historical evidence, the man Jesus of a first-century village in Galilee—*the figure independent of the community's faith and interpretation.* From this point onward, we shall describe the Christ of the Gospels—the Christ of the proclamation, the interpreted Christ of the community's evangelism—as the *Christ of the post-paschal faith.* We shall describe the Jesus that has to be gleaned from the Gospel sources—the Jesus before Oral Tradition, the Jesus untangled from interpretation and dogma, the Jesus of historical criticism—as *the historical Jesus.*

JESUS OF NAZARETH

The first point to make is that all the best and unprejudiced historical critics accept the evidence to be sound that there was a real historical figure by the name of Jesus; he was not an invention of the early Hellenistic Church. Rather, there was once a man called Jesus who was a Jew of his time, who conformed in the main to typical religious customs, and who spoke in Aramaic. Even the most radical of New Testament scholars, Rudolf Bultmann—who believes that "what the sources offer us is first of all the message of the early Christian community, which for the most part the church freely attributed to Jesus"—has said:

> Of course the doubt as to whether Jesus really existed is unfounded and not worth refutation. No sane person can doubt that Jesus stands as founder behind the historical movement whose first distinct stage is represented by the oldest Palestinian community.[3]

It is impossible to bring the 'God of the philosophers' and the God of Israel and of Jesus into any superficial harmony. Jesus' concept of God was a feature of undoubted historical authenticity. His was an understanding of God which did not dwell on biblical terminology or handed down tradition. Jesus does not speculate on the nature of God's being, his essence, or his attributes, neither does he construct any new concept of him in metaphysical or philosophical ways. He simply assumes the *reality of God* from the Old Testament—his heritage—and speaks of him in different and radical ways. He proclaims the irrevocable closeness of God, he testifies that the divine will is bound up with the well-being of man, and he has no hesitation in addressing him as his 'Father'. He frequently uses terms such as 'the highest' and the 'king'—a practice shunned more as blasphemy than disrespect by contemporary Jewish scribes—but the favoured form of address he used of him was *Abba*. The intimacy of his child-like relationship with God was anything but childish, and the child-like trust he personally cultivated was extended to all. Children can say *Abba*: "Unless you turn round and become like children you will never enter the kingdom of God!" (Matt. 18:3). This was a way of addressing God unparallelled in the whole of Jewish literature.[4]

The 'Father' in the Lord's Prayer is linguistically a new non-sacramental address, not in the sacred Hebrew language but in the Aramaic vernacular. It is direct, affectionate, untypical and intimate, and far too existential for Jewish usage. This freedom and licence of Jesus describe God as an advocate, and such an address is unmistakably pre-paschal. The character of God as 'Father', in the allegory-type parable of The Lost Son, is an affectionate metaphor. God is not the father in the parable but was *like the father*—the returning son says, "Father, I have sinned against heaven [God] and before you [his father]" (Luke 15:21). He is a father who lets go without a fuss, without chase, then rushes back and accepts the prodigal before any gesture of repentance is voiced—impetuously, he interrupts his son's admission of guilt. He is the Father of the abandoned, the God of the godless, the one who prefers the prodigal to the son that stays at home, the tax-collector to the Pharisee, the prostitute to her judges, and the lawbreakers and outlaws to the guardians of the law. This Father-God is nothing like the God feared by Marx, Nietzsche or Freud—a God who is partisan, having a lust for power, or one existing as the superego instilling burdensome feelings of guilt. He is concerned for every sparrow and every hair of our head, he knows our needs before we ask, and he puts our worries into their true perspective.

Beginnings

We cannot avoid seeing Jesus as an itinerant preacher, as one having a novel message of God which upset many of his contemporaries—good news that was evidently *scandalous*! There are no sound historical grounds for not accepting that Jesus learned the trade of carpentry, but clearly he had abandoned the work of such an artisan craft in support of himself in the latter part of his life. He would have received his religious instruction through the village synagogue, along with every other pious Jewish boy of the time. He received no formal training in any of the devoutly religious sects around him. He found no home within the two schools of the Pharisees. He was not privileged to belong to the aristocratic Sadducees. He was not compelled to flee to the Judaean desert and escape for solitude in the Essene monastery at Qumran. He did not submit himself to the party of the revolutionary Zealots in the hills of Galilee, local to where he lived. This was not because his *scandalous* message was not concerned with any of their concerns—with purity of heart, with a passion for the scriptures, with an interest in faith of the most personal kind—and certainly not because his teaching was not revolutionary either!

The story of Jesus' visit to the temple when he was twelve is not a very dependable historical recollection. The only factual details we have of his youth are the names of his parents and brothers—James, Joses, Judas and Simon (Mark 6:3). The names of his sisters are not given.

The Baptism

There are no sound historical grounds for not accepting the fact that the Baptism by John had quite an effect upon the young Nazarene during his rise to public prominence. Some additions have undoubtedly entered the tradition of the baptismal accounts, as well as some legendary motifs—the voice from heaven, the Holy Spirit descending like a dove, and the intuitive insights of the Christ and the Baptist. Narrative comparisons reveal how each evangelist has given the Baptism story a Messianic content quite differently, but it is still likely that Jesus was baptised by John in Jordan. What is unmistakable is the sharp contrast in the teaching of the two prophets. The *scandal* of John's preaching was judgement-centred (upon the 'sons of Abraham'), while the *scandal* of the good news of the kingdom was opportunity-centred. John might say, "Already the axe is laid to the roots of the trees; and every tree that fails to produce good fruit is cut down and thrown on the fire" [i.e., the time is ready for cropping] (Luke 3:9), but Jesus, by contrast, would reply in the parable of the Fig Tree: "Leave it, sir, this one year while I dig round it and manure it" [a practice not necessary for a fig tree, i.e., this is the time for reprieve, for the judgement is as yet stayed—this is the time of opportunity] (Luke 13:6–9).

Although a following of the Baptist continued well into the second century (some have been discovered in Iraq in the twentieth century), the message of Jesus carried within it the seeds of a universal and lasting following. Judgement or opportunity, both were a *scandal*, both interpreted an urgency of the time, both were promulgated to stimulate individual action and response, but the contrast was clearly there, a contrast that left an imprisoned Baptist not a little dismayed later on.

The Ministry in Galilee

The call of the disciples is not inconsistent with what an itinerant rabbi of the time would have done. The names of the twelve in the accounts vary slightly but not significantly. The number twelve could have been a post-paschal tradition, for it appeared necessary for the early Church—who saw herself as the 'New Israel'—to have twelve apostles (one to represent each tribe). They found it necessary to replace Judas the traitor with Matthias, a figure not noticeably prominent in the early community (Acts 1:23–26), like others of the twelve. The legendary motif of the miraculous catch of fish in Luke, may have originally been a post-paschal 'appearance' story (Bultmann), since the Fourth Gospel uses the story thus and the Gospel of Peter, and neither Mark nor Matthew knew of it in this context. This does not mean, however, that the call to catch men (i.e., as a fisherman catches fish) is not historical.

The call to leave all behind and follow in the way was not extended to everyone, for Jesus clearly found support from many who remained in their ordinary situations in life. The immediate disciples were not an élite group drawn out of the world to take up an ascetic life-style, but they were called for a particular purpose. The kingdom was offered to all, but some refused to become part of the missionary group, such as the wealthy man recorded in Mark 10:17–22. Some exclusive sayings were designed for the inner-band only (such as the cost of 'building a tower', Luke 14:28–32, in spite of the fact that Luke presents it as being addressed to the crowds, 14:25), others were designed for the masses (the Sermon on the Mount was probably delivered to the crowds). Some discriminating exegesis is called for when interpreting in practical terms what Jesus called the populace to give up as the condition for entering the kingdom.

The *scandal* of Jesus was not only in what was said but in what was done. *The fellowship with all common folk—women, children, prostitutes, tax-swindlers, outcasts, bandits, outlaws, law-breakers, irreligious and disease ridden—marked him as an extraordinary charismatic, a quite unique rabbi* (I do not use the term charismatic in a pejorative sense but to describe one who was Spirit-led). Forgiveness and acceptance for Jesus would not require the precondition of penance and repentance (*metanoia*); it was offered by him without qualification and irrespective of merit. Jesus indulged in such mealtime 'worldliness' because God is a forgiver of sinners, an acceptor of misfits, and a lover of enemies. The tax-collectors, vagabonds, lawbreakers and outlaws differ from the pious and religious in that their sins are more open and public, and far less subtle. The *scandal* was not in the mere acceptance of the lower religious echelons, for there have been many who have similarly cast in their lot with and preferred the rejected classes. Jesus had the audacity to proclaim that such were God's preference too; that sin, which had carved an unbridgeable gulf between God and his people, could no longer be used as the barrier dividing the Father from his children; that such a reunion was not academic nor technical, but was being demonstrated by the hordes coming out from the hills to dine with him, without qualifications and without selection and without favour. *What was happening, in actual fact, was that those ordinary folks who were fraternising and indulging in good food and wine with the rabbi heralded as the "glutton and drunkard" were in practice eating and drinking with God.* Sin was not merely forgiven by his daring word and authority, there were visible signs of forgiveness and pardon being demonstrated by the invitations going out and the guests coming in. This was the *scandal* that offended the religious sensibilities of the sectarians; this was *scandal* indeed!

Jesus taught not like the scribes, "he taught with authority". *He taught in parables, and it was through his masterfully constructed parables that he proclaimed the coming of the kingdom of God*, that he challenged human nature at its root, that he revealed to the non-religious what the 'Heavenly Father'—as *Abba*—was like, and that he made clear to everyone his *scandalous* teaching (the secret element in Mark 4:9–12, 33–34 is a literary device of the 'Messianic Secret'). With the teaching in parables we are in the earliest and most authentic tradition of the historical Jesus.[5] Again, this is not to say that the evangelists have not in some instances altered the original forms of the parables, as a means of clarifying the post-paschal faith. The parable of the Vineyard in Mark 12:1–10, for example, has clearly been altered in retrospect by Matthew and Luke to fit the details of the crucifixion (Matt. 21:33–46; Luke 20:9–19). The parables of The Talents, Sheep and Goats, The Ten Virgins, The Thief in the Night and The Banquet (Matt. 25:14–30; 25:31–46; 25:1–13; 24:42–44; 22:1–14, resp.), have been adjusted to encompass the early Christian expectation of the imminent *Parousia*. The Sower, The Wheat and Tares, The Dragnet and The Lost Sheep (Matt. 13:3–23; 13:24–30; 13:47–50; 18:12–14 resp.) have been modified to suggest that ideas of Church practice were clearly present in the mind of the historical Jesus. Yet, who can doubt the poignancy of the parable of The Lost Son, The Lost Sheep, and the Lost Coin (Luke 15:11–32; 15:3–7; 15:8–10 resp.), for disclosing what God was truly like in respect of sinners? Who can doubt the sound psychology lying behind The Unjust Judge, The Good Samaritan, The Pharisee and the Tax-collector, The Good Employer, The Unmerciful Servant and The Wicked Husbandmen (Luke 18:1–8; 10:25–37; 18:9–14; Matt. 20:1–16; 18:23–34; 21:33–46 resp.), as a most powerful medium for the individual in seeing his own situation for bringing about personal change? Who can fail to understand the nature of Jesus' mission after listening to The Mustard Seed, The Seed Growing Secretly, the Lost Sheep, The Unfruitful Fig Tree and the parable of The Sower—without the key (Mark 4:30–32; 4:26–29; Luke 15:3–7; 13:6–9; 8:4–8 resp.)? Here was the pre-paschal message of Jesus.

In this highly original and authentic material, the historical Jesus cut deep within the heart of human nature to leave men and women in want and in thirst of God's provision. A story cannot be improved upon by abstract ideas, nor images by concepts; the experience of being stirred is more potent than intellectual apprehension, for words may teach but examples carry us with them.[6] Here again, the *scandal* of the good news of the kingdom is demonstrably made clear, not necessarily in the Gospel narratives as they have been handed down to us through transmission, but as the parables would originally have been heard by the audiences around him. This was the time of crisis, the occasion of God's reprieve—act now before it is too late!

Jesus taught not like the scribes—the *scandal* is revealed not by any commentary on the Law (as the Scribes), nor by any interpretation into practical outworking (as the Pharisees) but by an audacity to change it. *Jesus claimed authority to subordinate the religious sanctity of the Law for the well-being of man* (as in the laws of divorce). For Jesus, God's will was man's well-being. There can be no clearer evidence of why the establishment was outraged—sufficiently to put him to death—than by his authority and daring to change what had been given to Moses on Sinai by God Himself. Yahweh had given precepts: "You have learned that they were told . . .", which Jesus interpreted in a highly provocative manner: "But what I tell you is this . . ." These, together with his deliberate and public flouting of the Sabbath observance, was not a creation of the early Christian community. The *scandal* was not an attempt to authorise the community's standing with Judaism regarding the place of the Torah, but was what set Jesus at odds with the Jewish rulers of the time. The *scandal* that compelled them to put up such a righteous man for execution was centred on his disregard for the Law (Acts 6:13, a feature notably absent in both the Synoptic and Johannine trials). Historical criticism has established that Jesus flouted the Sabbath and changed parts of the Torah, and it cost him his life!

The new and radical teaching in Matthew's Sermon on the Mount (or Luke's Sermon on the Plain) was hardly likely to have been given in the lecture form in which Matthew presents it (a literary style of this evangelist, Jesus, thereby, being the new Moses) but is no less historical if given in fragmented form (as Luke). Speculating on how it was given leads one to miss the point, for this authentic corpus of teaching marks true originality, and, here again, the *scandal* is evident. The new teaching probes at the baser motivations of human behaviour, which were unaffected by Judaism. Only authoritarian esoteric religion can ignore such compelling imperatives—imperatives, such as: taking no revenge, suffering loss, bearing the cost, controlling imaginative lust, refusing to find fault with others, and loving one's enemies. The imperatives of the Sermon ring true for us. We sense their truth, but religious prejudice and fanatical sectarianism can sometimes blind us, causing us to miss the essentials. This is God's Law, after all, and who are we to question the unfathomable mind of God? If Jesus never uttered such pronouncements, then a person as great as he must be invented to speak them. The *scandal* is brought out in the teaching of Jesus on love, not particularly the Golden Rule because this was not original to Jesus;[7] but in the sense of a love which is illustrated in the tangible form of a Jewish child's relationship with his father! The *scandal* lies in the fact that our pious sensibilities are disturbed and discomforted. The sinner is brought into fellowship with God in an undeserving sense, just as children are loved, wanted and made to feel of worth in the best of families, though at times they do little to warrant such love and acceptance. They are loved unreservedly because they are what they are, without merit, without being deserving.

Journey to Jerusalem

At some point in his ministry, Jesus came to the polis to pronounce his message of the kingdom. At Jerusalem he would confront Judaism! There is little reason to doubt that it would have been at the Passover, and the evidence is sound that he was executed in Jerusalem during the festival. It is historically inconceivable that such an outspoken rabbi from Galilee could quietly have passed off the scene as a misguided heretic in a submissive fashion. Neither is it conceivable that Jesus could have celebrated the Passover after the custom of his people merely as a passive pilgrim. A *scandalous* saying, such as "I have come to set fire to the earth, and how I wish it were already kindled!" (Luke 12:49–53), or a *scandalous* declaration like "My son, your sins are forgiven" (Mark 2:5), or the *scandal* of a blatant disrespect for the Sabbath customs, or a *scandalous* act of permissiveness in allowing a prostitute of the town to weep and fuss over him, was not likely to go unnoticed (Luke 7:36f.). We cannot be sure whether Jesus' mission lasted part of a year (Mark), or up to three years (John), neither can we be sure of any precise routes of travel and topography, but we can be certain that when he entered the buzzing and thronging city, his reputation had gone before him.

The 'Son of Man' predictive sayings found in the Synoptic Gospels are loaded with Messianic connotations. So too are the call of 'Son of David' by blind Bartimaeus and the jubilant shouts of 'Hosanna' from the crowds who scattered palms in the way. The entry into Jerusalem may have a core of historicity behind the final narrative, but the titles of the 'Son of David' and the 'Son of Man' sayings cannot be historical in the form in which they have been preserved. The 'Son of Man' sayings particularly cannot be historical. They are prophecies *ex eventu,* which served to illustrate the predictive insight of Jesus regarding his decease—they are post-paschal titles of faith. This is not to say that Jesus may not have used the Messianic title of the 'Son of Man', but it is likely that if he did so he would have used it in the third person to describe one who might come after him; it is not likely therefore to be a self-reference.

The Scheme of the Final Episode

I find little reason for not accepting the general account of Jesus' arrest, trial and crucifixion as being historical. The scheme—the Supper, the Arrest and Trial, the Crucifixion and Resurrection—is written up as a divine pre-planned course of events (Luke 18:31–34), but this is clearly post-paschal retrospection, and is therefore unhistorical. This shortest period of his life is given a disproportional coverage by each of the four evangelists. Though there has been modification in places, the narrative in the main is not Messianic, but couched in prosaic and matter-of-fact language. Although we know of no eye-witness who would have been present throughout the whole sequence of events, we cannot be uncritical and argue from silence that the tradition is not historical (the comment in John 18:15 only gives 'the beloved disciple' access to the courtyard, not to the Sanhedrin or Pilate's court). There are surprisingly few Messianic proof-texts over the arrest and trial, as over his execution and resurrection; we have therefore no *a priori* reason for rejecting the traditional accounts.

The Supper

The final supper—whatever, whenever, it was—has been influenced to a certain extent by the sequel of the passion, in that the Messianic content would have been read into what originally was a typical fellowship meal (as the Fourth Gospel suggests). Nevertheless, *it is conceivable that Jesus may have drawn a highly significant and altered meaning from the loaf and cup, different from that which was customarily given at the Passover.* With the meal, there was no 'institution'. For Mark it was a Passover, for John clearly not so.[8] There was no discrimination or preferred company for Jesus when eating and drinking throughout the ministry. The participants in the common meal were celebrating their entry into God's fellowship: "For the Baptist the baptism of penance was a typical sign in action; for Jesus and his message, the sign took the form of feasts held in an atmosphere of joy, in which people celebrated their common membership of the future kingdom." [9]

It is consistent and logical that Jesus, a highly perceptive prophet, would have sensed and predicted his own personal demise by reading reflectively his current situation. He was likely to have had an uncanny insight that he would not return to Galilee after the festival, to have sensed the probability of his execution, and to have predicted his downfall through the broken bread and poured out wine. The pattern was set by the prophets, in that their tombs surrounded the city, and the fate of the Baptist was well-known. According to Bornkamm, Jesus may have understood that suffering was a necessary part of the 'will of God' (the view is not entirely speculative but based on the authentic saying of Luke 13:31–33, which describes Herod being after his blood, together with the stereotyped programme of martyrdom prescribed for all the prophets of Israel).[10]

A saying widely acclaimed as not being a creation of the church's liturgical tradition, has the pledge that he would never drink wine again "until that day when I drink it new in the kingdom of God" (Mark 14:25). The earliest form of the saying was finally dropped from the liturgical formula, and in I Cor. 11:23–33 survives only in tenuous form: "until he comes". The eucharistic significance of the supper, whilst there in the words of the institution, is surprisingly slight considering the importance of the meal for the early community.

The Arrest and Trial

The arrest has been a notorious historical problem. The divinely planned programme has Judas as the main actor. We know who he betrayed, but what he betrayed and how he betrayed him is uncertain. One tradition describes the disciples being completely ignorant of the part Judas played, in spite of the fact that Jesus had clearly pointed him out at the table (John 13:24–30). The Gospels describe Jesus' preaching in the temple as being sufficiently public to have allowed the temple police to follow him in secret. It is equally uncertain how Judas died—both traditions are in conflict and are written as a fulfilment of scripture (Matt. 27:3–10; Acts 1:16–20). Regarding the trial, tradition has suggested that John, son of Zebedee, had some connections with the priests, to such an extent that he might have had access to information of the Sanhedrin proceedings (other traditions suggest Joseph of Arimathaea or Nicodemus), but this is questionable and does not explain who would have known what took place before Pilate. Is this part of the tradition speculation then? Possibly not! *Annas, Caiaphas and Pilate were indeed historical figures, of that there is valid extra-biblical source documentation,* but for precise information of the trials we have to rely exclusively on the Gospel narratives. The charges could have been post-paschal creations, deduced from logic in the light of the issues of the early community's trials with Judaism, but they could equally be historical. For the historian, it is significant that no charges are brought against Jesus regarding his open disregard of the Sabbath or his changing of the Law, but the post-paschal faith was attempting to reach Jews steeped in the Torah, for whom these things were still important (historically, the Jewish Christians believed that their new faith did not require them to relinquish every aspect of their old religion—hence the polemic in Galatians & Romans).

We cannot assume with any dogmatism that Jesus may not have attracted some members of the priestly guilds, as also members of the Imperial Roman court who later entered the Church and provided the first believers with accurate eye-witness information, even though their names may have become lost to us (see the story of the healing of the Centurion's servant and Acts 10). Insignificant details of the trials, which earlier formed the Oral Tradition and which later were incorporated into pre-Gospel narratives, then, have good grounds for historical authenticity, simply because they have no post-paschal references. The story of Pilate's agreement to release a chosen prisoner to the people at Passover time has no corroborative objective evidence outside the Gospel narratives, but we have no *a priori* reason to discount the arrangement on such grounds. The detail of Pilate's character has non-polemic source evidence outside the Gospels (Josephus) which stands in sharp contrast to the Christian version (particularly, the Fourth Gospel), and we have good reason, therefore, to question the Gospel narrative, not so much over what he did as over the description of his character. Detail like the dream of Pilate's wife is probably legendary, serving as a literary device to lift the status of Jesus before Rome, and must be discounted as being unhistorical.

The Crucifixion

The crucifixion would obviously have been witnessed by many, both of the supporters (though at a distance) and the enemies of Jesus. Although the method of Jesus' crucifixion can be verified in part by anatomical studies and sparse archaeological testimony (skeletons of crucified victims have been unearthed in the precincts of Jerusalem), we are again dependent on the post-paschal sources. Clearly, the records have been heavily overlaid with Messianic quotations—the sufferer of Psalm 22, Isaiah's Suffering Servant Song (Ch. 53) and others. These isolated Old Testament citations serve to amplify the 'fulfilment' aspect of the Passion narrative, but, again, we cannot be dogmatic in concluding that these details are all invented. They obviously serve to authenticate the events as being divinely ordained and planned beforehand (according to the Messianic programme), but they may also have claim to be genuine history.

Jesus was so absorbed in his own personal closeness to God that he could address him as 'Father', and he was also very well versed in the Old Testament scriptures. It is not unreasonable, therefore, to presuppose that such a prophet might recall the sentiments of Psalm 22 during his torture and apply the words to himself as being applicable to his suffering (22:2, 6, 12, 14, 15). This is particularly the case with those sentiments not cited by the evangelists: "I am a worm, not a man, abused by all men!" (22:6); "My strength drains away like water and all my bones are loose!" (22:14).

The incidental account of the soldiers dividing the spoils of the prisoner's possessions is a credible routine, yet the citation from scripture (Ps. 22:18), though fitting superficially, is hardly a significant Messianic event that proves anything other than an identity of Jesus' suffering with that of the psalmist. Clearly, an arbitrary searching in the volume of Old Testament scriptures will inevitably find some correlation for any random event with a matching (if stretched) 'proof-text'. Such an argument, however, is for the event to be historical, not invented, with the 'proof-text' being secondary and artificial.

Should we search for a pre-paschal meaning that Jesus may have had for his own execution, there are a number of historical anomalies that must be faced. At his end, there were no friendly witnesses to document his dying words; therefore, conjecture over the meaning of his death would have been inevitable. The cry of desolation was an appeal to God. In his life he had proclaimed the God of the sufferer, the God of the godless, yet at the point of highest dereliction, he suffered alone—the disciples had fled, there were none at the foot of the cross and women stood by only at a distance—*and the God he had proclaimed as being close to all men, he now felt to be absent too!* There was no peaceful departure such as by hemlock poisoning at the ripe old age of seventy (Socrates), no slipping away at one hundred and twenty after seeing the promised land (Moses), no comforting departure at eighty with friends around him (the Buddha), no returning to his home place to serve as tutor (Confucius), and no comforting end of political rule amongst a harem of favourite wives (Mohammed). There was just the terse description of a bleak and apparently meaningless execution—"and they crucified him!"

There is no embroidery here: the victim would bleed or choke to death after many hours of excruciating agony, often lasting into the next day (no Roman criminal suffered the ignominy of crucifixion—they were swiftly beheaded). His achievements from the secular perspective were unclear: he was a heretical teacher in that he challenged the Law and the religious system; a false prophet in predicting that the temple would fall, when before his very eyes it stood as surely as it had throughout his lifetime; a blasphemer in that he degraded God as a God of the godless; a seducer of the people by challenging the social system. Religiously, he died a curse to the Law, but he was no political agitator, in spite of the charge written on the cross. His influence on the world stage was hardly significant until the time that the Church became empire-centred. Should we seek meaning by highlighting who was to blame for his death, then only a tiny handful of people can be identified. (As an aside, it is a point of bitterest irony that the Jewish nation who in the Holocaust were charged with the responsibility of his death, resembled more closely the crucified Jew than the judges of his trials.)

The Resurrection

Whatever we may argue about the resurrection from the sequel of the historical reality of the Church, or from the psychology of a changed outlook of a large body of people, the narratives are considerably contradictory in accounting for the event of the resurrection. The 'empty tomb' records, particularly, are beyond reasonable harmonisation. The 'appearance' narratives are generally dubious and beyond psychological verification for us today, for "there is no way of telling the difference between a veridical vision and one that isn't veridical. Visions are visions, people have them", says Don Cupitt.[11] The crucifixion, resurrection, and ascension narratives, have legendary accretions to them, which in the modern age we have difficulty in accepting—even those Christians having an unshakeable conviction that 'Christ is risen'. The narratives, in this respect, cannot establish the faith in the resurrection but serve only as an obstacle to such a conviction. *Although the resurrection may not be regarded as a 'historical event', in the sense that the historian knows 'events', it does not necessarily follow that the resurrection was any less an 'event' outside history.* "Christ lives on", professes the Christian, 'but so too do Plato and Shakespeare, Rembrandt and Leonardo, Bach and Handel, Darwin and Marx', replies the cynic. The dilemma lies in reconciling the fact that the new life of Christ—which is more than a memory, more than the continuation of an art, more than a fulfilment of a new teaching, and more than the perpetuation of an ideology—remains somehow beyond verification in psychological or scientific terms.

It is Luke who first separates the resurrection from his being 'lifted up to heaven', thus emphasising the corporeality of Jesus' resurrection. He presents a period of human interaction before the ascension—portrayed after the manner of Elijah being received into heaven. In emphasising the corporality of Jesus' new life, Luke has paved the way for a bodily return. However, a range of problematical questions emerges: where did he go in space, at what speed, and how was it observed? The resurrection will inevitably defy historical reality, since it was not a historic event—understood as an event in space and time—but it was no less an event. If asked how we might imagine it, "we cannot", says Küng. It must defy our imagination because if our concepts and metaphors were able to explain it, the event would cease to be a non-historical event. We are left, therefore, with an article of faith; not a faith in the product of a revived spirit of the members of the early community, but a faith in the power of a 'divine act', for Jesus did not live through the faith of the community but through a new life in God.

NOTES

1. Strong's Concordance; C. K. Barrett, *The First Epistle to the Corinthians*, London, 1971, pages 54–56. The word is also preserved in Mark 6:3 RSV with reference to the rejection of the kinsfolk of Jesus: "And they took offence at him!" The malice of Jesus' brothers may lie behind John 7:1–3 RSV: "Now the Jews sought to kill him . . . . So his brothers said to him, 'Leave here and go to Judea.'"
2. H. Küng, *On Being a Christian*, London, 1977, page 123. The term 'Archetype' is borrowed from the psychoanalyst, Carl Jung, in which he describes archetypes as "the contents of the collective unconscious", which are "empty and purely formal", (C. G. Jung, *The Archetypes and the Collective Unconscious*, London, 1968, pages 5 & 79).

Küng qualifies his view that the Christian faith, through the figure of the historical Jesus, stands as definitive and archetypal for man's relations to God, with two fundamental points:

1) A distinction between religion which is 'advanced' and one which is 'primitive'.

2) An assessment of what beliefs conform with the modern world-view.

1) Firstly, we may take it as read that an 'advanced religion' is one which moves away from any dread of demons, magic or unnatural forces, from all forms of cruelty, some irrationality. Secondly, it is one which does not foster impersonal, unsociable or unhistorical attitudes.

In short, a religion is advanced which moves away from superstition towards liberation and enlightenment through the process of demythologising and the pondering of higher ethical ideals within the frame of 'God's Will'. This is a humanisation of religion to become a Faith, which is not determined by code or oracle, but which is a living expression and commitment. An advanced religion must include tolerance whilst claiming absolute validity. It must be ready to revise its own standpoint wherever it turns out to be in need of revision. Taoism and Hinduism fit few of these criteria, Islam fits some, and Christianity fits all. (page 114)

2) a) The various approaches to the 'scriptures' bear marked differences. Only in Islam with the Koran, or Sikhism with the Granth Sahib, does the devotee feel the need to wash his hands before handling the Holy Scripture, or pay the utmost reverence to the 'Book' itself, as opposed to the teaching it reveals. With the Koran, there has been no systematic literary criticism, and, in consequence, its civil and penal code and its subjugation of women makes it hopelessly out of place in the modern world.

b) The Koran, like the Bhagavad-gita, is completely unhistorical, the 'inspired divine utterances' (inerrant and infallible) have been dictated to the prophet by an angel.

c) The world-view of Hinduism, Buddhism and Indian Jainism is cyclical, not lateral. This does not fit in with modern thinking either communally or personally.

d) The conception of return and rebirth—linked inextricably with Hinduism—is alien to human consciousness, which pursues the rights of all irrespective of class and caste. Neither, too, is the four-divisional caste system (regulated by occupation and marriage) tenable according to modern theories of equality, nor the Christian Medieval programmes of Heaven and Hell, nor the fundamentalist pictures of a millennial reign of Christ.

e) The anthropomorphisms of God, as presented in the Bible (even the metaphor of 'Heavenly Father'), whilst attractive to our emotional and aesthetic needs and interests, are less credible than the transcendental distancing and detached presentation of him in Islam.

3. R. Bultmann, *Jesus and the Word*, pages 12–14, cited by H. K. McArthur in *In Search of the Historical Jesus*, pages 209–210.
4. J. Jeremias, *The Parables of Jesus*, London, 1972, page 191.
5. Ibid., page 15.
6. H. Küng, op. cit., page 547.
7. Moral and ethical codes and virtues are not original or peculiar to Christianity. The pre-history of the Ten Commandments is given by Küng, op., cit., page 542. The Golden rule is not specifically of Christian origin, and the virtues in Paul have been taken from Jewish and Hellenistic sources—Küng, op. cit., page 543. A recently discovered and popular quotation of a North American Indian chief underlies the universal ethic of the Royal Law: "Everyone likes to give as well as receive. No one wishes to receive all the time. We have taken much from your culture . . . I wish you had taken something from our culture . . . , for there were some good and beautiful things in it."
8. The evidence is well presented by J. Jeremias in, *The Eucharistic Words of Jesus*, London, 1973.
9. H. Küng op. cit., page 323.
10. R. H. Fuller, 'The New Testament in Current Study', in H. K. McArthur's, *In Search of the Historical Jesus*, page 182.
11. D. Cupitt recently discussed the nature of faith from the first-century community to modern times in a programme recorded by Radio 4, on Sunday 19/4/92:

> I don't think Christianity ought any longer to rely on objective historically occurrent miracles to certify its doctrines and, in the case of the resurrection, the faith is older than the stories; the faith came first. Originally, perhaps it meant that the general resurrection of the dead was beginning, the end of the world was on the way. Obviously we don't believe that now. For me, the resurrection is a symbol of hope and renewal . . . If the first generation had been uniquely privileged you couldn't have said they had faith, rather it was certified to them in a way that it isn't to any subsequent generation. But, of course, in fact, it was as possible to disbelieve in Christ if you had been his contemporary as it is today. The first generation weren't specially privileged; they didn't have guarantees that we lack. So, it seems to me a mistake to suppose that at the beginning of things there were great supernatural events that set the faith beyond question for those who saw it; on the contrary, it is reported that you could even see the resurrection and still doubt. The documents we've got, to my mind, are not historical sources, but I guess there may have been visions at the beginning, visions of the risen Lord. But, for me, those visions were created by the faith and the commitment and loyalty to Jesus of the people who had the visions . . . . There is no way of telling the difference between a veridical vision and one that isn't veridical. Visions are visions, people have them.

Although Cupitt sees God as a spiritual ideal rather than an ontological Being, his point on faith through time seems reasonable.

A further programme on BBC television called 'Heart of the Matter' disclosed the following: substantial numbers of Christian ministers, Anglicans and others, do not believe in the bodily resurrection. Some of them belong to the 'Sea of Faith' network in Leicestershire—a non-denominational group of some 200 clerics and laity who hold annual conferences and publish newsletters to share the belief that God is a creation of the human mind; the Christian story is a myth. It is difficult to be sure that the crucifixion was actually a real event, contend some priests. This, quite naturally, puts them at odds with their congregations, who hold to the Creed unquestioningly. Many members of the congregations of such priests are in fact leaving.

14

THE 'PERSONALITY' OF JESUS

For ours is not a high priest unable to sympathise with our weaknesses, but one who, because of his likeness to us, has been tested every way . . .

Heb. 4.15

THE HUMANITY AND SELF-CONSCIOUSNESS OF JESUS

The task of establishing the personality of Jesus has been found to be virtually impossible by scholars studying the historical Jesus. We cannot see Jesus otherwise than through the eyes of the evangelists, who are so influenced by the 'post-paschal faith' that it is impossible to segregate objective fact from interpretation. We are interested generally in psychology and have a desire to know how the mind of Jesus worked, and we understand more of mental functioning than our forebears could ever have done. Nevertheless, our wishes cannot and must not cloud our judgement or influence our research in this minefield of speculation. At the conclusion of *The Quest*, says Jeremias, Schweitzer, believing that he could bring Jesus into our home by freeing him from "the stony rocks of ecclesiastical doctrine", found only that he could not stay with us, for he was the 'one unknown': he was the prophet of Nazareth, the rabbi of his time; his proclamation of the kingdom utilised the imagery of contemporary apocalyptic and, in this guise, he remains a stranger to us![1]

I cannot share, however, the uncertainty and negative conclusions reached by some biblical critics who suggest that the task is a hopeless one! There is no doubt that the student has to be hesitant in claiming too much in this field of research, for it is so easy to read into the Gospel narratives ideas which are not in the text. It is possible to be too undisciplined and to infer notions from incidental details which would have been entirely foreign to the evangelists; ideas which amount to little more than subjective presupposition on the part of the exegete. The enterprise of investigating the psyche of Jesus, then, which is admittedly speculative, must be done with great caution. We must carry out our exegesis in a most objective and self-critical manner. We must begin from what we can know and avoid speculating with hypothesis upon hypothesis.

We may safely assume as a starting point, that *the Jesus of history was in every way human just as we know humanity*. He was no phantom, as portrayed in Docetic Christology, neither was he a mirage, a sham of humanity, a veiled form of divinity, as taught by Gnosticism, but was in every respect a human being. Because he was human, "He knew men so well, all of them . . . , for he himself could tell what was in a man" (John 2:24–25).

The next point to make is that *his adolescence cannot be known to us*. A natural starting point for studying the psyche of any person is to look at their human development and personality through adolescence. By examining the influences of the person's nurturing environment, we may understand the person, yet studies in sociology have revealed how 'adolescence' is a peculiarly Western phenomenon that does not necessarily occur with young people in all societies—in fact 'adolescence' is not an appropriate term to use in describing the latter years of Jewish boyhood during the first century. Secondly, the data for such an enquiry into Jesus' youth simply does not exist; the study of personality—the ego, consciousness, and the subconscious—came much too late for the evangelists, and thus they had no intelligible concepts and terms for such an analysis, added to which, the evangelists were not the slightest bit interested in such questions. The infancy narratives[2] and the visit of the twelve-year old boy Jesus to the temple are of no use for such an examination. While we now have a considerable knowledge of Palestinian village life during the times of Jesus, we cannot be certain how the environment affected his upbringing as compared with that of any other devout Jewish boy of the time.

All the New Testament sources describe the intimacy and closeness of Jesus to God, and we may be sure that such a relationship was cultivated throughout his youth. His unique way of addressing God was *'Abba'*. According to Jeremias:

> We can learn from the Targum, Jews deliberately avoided applying the Abba to God even outside prayers . . . We do not have a single example of God being addressed as Abba in Judaism, but Jesus always addressed God in this way in his prayers . . . , it will be clear why Palestinian Judaism does not use Abba as a form of address to God. Abba was a children's word, used in everyday talk, an expression of courtesy . . . Jesus dared to use Abba as a form of address of God; in this Jesus was unique.[3]

A central question occupying the minds of theologians over the last century was regarding the self-identity of Jesus and his 'Messianic consciousness'. Did Jesus perceive a special role and identity for himself in the divine programme, as opposed to seeing himself as yet another prophet in a line of predecessors? When he spoke of 'My Father', did he mean something different from 'Your Father', or 'Our Father'? This debate largely centres on the Messianic titles and whether or not Jesus applied them to himself. If he spoke of himself as the 'Son of Man', it appears difficult to avoid the conclusion that he saw himself as the Messianic figure of Daniel 7.[4] Although the mysterious figure of Daniel was a corporate figure, there can be little doubt that the Church saw in this prophecy a link with the corporate body of the Church as a body 'in Christ'. The debate over the Messianic consciousness can reach no satisfactory conclusion in order for us to construct a firm psychology of Jesus' self-identity, so we have little choice but to dismiss it as an uncertain datum.

Other data, however, can be of use to us. We can make deductions from the facts as we know them of the ministry of Jesus that historical criticism has secured beyond much reasonable doubt. I think there are some leads from incidental comments in the Gospel narratives that may help us gain further insight into how his mind worked, so long as we proceed with cautious optimism.

1. Jesus Facing Death

We can be sure that Jesus believed that his destiny was less than optimistic, as he trudged his way towards Jerusalem for his final Passover.

Like all of us having to rely on faith, he could not have known what lay on the other side of death. It requires little imagination to conjure up the gruelling butchery of the Phoenician crucifixion that the Roman administration had mastered to a fine art, not to mention the *scandal* of being condemned and executed as a criminal against the good of humanity (Roman perspective), or a 'curse of God' to the sacred Law (Jewish perspective). Jesus in no way avoids the confrontation; he activates it, believing all the time (but not knowing) that his Father would see him through—he would not see the details, quite naturally. In some way or other, he believed that his Father knew best, and in this certainty he trusted. It was not that Jesus suffered above all other men in the history of the world, and it was not because he was the only one to have been slaughtered innocently. Jesus is aligned with all those who similarly meet their end in travesties of justice, yet Jesus trusted. He, like all of us at moments of crisis, required the faith to carry him through, for no interpretation of the Jesus of history makes sense if it has no requirement for him to have had faith. The only way the story makes sense is if we understand Jesus to have received no divine guarantees that his end was secure.

In his disillusionment over all that was lost then, this sensitive soul weeps in bitter despair over a city beyond hope:

> How often have I longed to gather your children, as a hen gathers her brood under her wings, but you would not let me . . .
>
> Mat. 23:37

The saying describes no success but portrays a depressing sense of failure—everything had come to nothing! In the light of this uncertainty, he pleads agonisingly with his Father in Gethsemene—here is the fear, here the humanity, for the trauma is not so much the wrestling with pain but the bearing of uncertainty, uncertainty of what might lie beyond. *There were no guarantees of resurrection then, and, in the prospect of such doubt, Jesus walks voluntarily into the darkness!*[5] A sensitive imagination can capture the pathos of the historical Jesus as he handed himself over, not in the light of any surety of what he knew but in the confidence of what he believed.

2. Jesus Got Angry

Anyone witnessing a modern-day exorcism will see a great deal of aggression being vented. We have every good reason to suppose that when Jesus exorcised the demons he became aggressive and angry! *Jesus was a man who could get angry then, and get angry he did, particularly against religious hypocrisy!* He denounced the Pharisees in a resolute and derisive manner: "Whited sepulchres!", he called them, *outwardly looking spectacular, inwardly occupied with decaying skeletons!* "Hypocrites!", he called them, *play-actors at religion*: "You strain off a midge, yet gulp down a camel!" (Matt. 23).

With fierce conviction he pronounces judgement upon the villages skirting the shores of Galilee: "Alas for you, Chorazin! Alas for you, Bethsaida! If the miracles that were performed in you had been performed in Tyre and Sidon, they would have repented long ago" (Luke 10:13).[6] There is almost spite underlying his pronounced judgement on his own villagers for spurning the message: "A prophet will always be held in honour except in his home town, and amongst his kinsmen and family (Mark 6:4)." How was it possible to refuse the opportunity to take hold of the kingdom? But refuse it even his closest relatives did.

Some sayings illustrate an anger of single-minded authority. Here, the *scandal* of the kingdom divides even families: "I have come to set fire to the earth, and how I wish it were already kindled! . . . Do you suppose I came to establish peace on earth? No indeed, I have come to bring division!" (Luke 12:49–53). Such a saying, no doubt, would have been given in a most uncompromising fashion. Similarly, some sayings, not found in the canonical Gospels, have good grounds for authenticity by virtue of their linguistic similarities to Gospel sayings, such as one recalled by Origen:

> He that is near me
> is near the fire; [eschatological fire]
> He that is far from me
> is far from the kingdom![7]

The incident of the Cleansing the Temple in its earliest undeveloped form cannot be toned down to minimise the extreme anger that Jesus vented on the merchants. We may imagine a scene of relentless indignation, in which the fury of Jesus reached a pitch of almost no control. Like a raging tyrant he storms through the courts, vandalising the trestles, tables, pigeon cages and sheep fences, in the most graphic of scenes that would have been frightening to watch—just as the early *nabi* would have done under the influence of God's *ruach.*

In the end, however, we do not see an anger displayed at his trial, as many would to profess their innocence; we see only meekness and submission.

3. The Imaginative Wit of Jesus

His wit and vivid imagination were utilised to the full in the parables designed to change people's directions. *In the parables of Jesus there are frequent comments and ideas that illustrate his joyful and gay spirit, his pleasure in the sublime and ridiculous, and his lively sense of humour.*

When fencing in dialogue with a foreigner of Syria for the cure of her daughter, he could not fail to enjoy her humour in warding off his nationalistic contempt: "Let the children be satisfied first; it is not fair to take the children's bread and throw it to the dogs", he said. Her cynical rejoinder achieved its intention: "Sir, even the dogs under the table eat the children's scraps" (Mark 7:24–30). The insensitive stamp of his word was anything but flat and dead, but illustrates a humorous eye for pictorial details. In graphic exaggeration he makes his point: he speaks of "planks of wood!" obscuring vision to judge appropriately; of such absurdities as putting oil lamps under meal-tub covers; and of such ridiculous country-life pictures as camels being tugged through "eyes of needles!". There is a recognition of the most pathetic forms of human behaviour, such as the all too human spectacle of squabbling workers, mean enemies putting weeds in neighbour's crops, and children playing games of weddings and funerals in market places. All these were designed to humour the audience and call from them a response in real life situations.[8]

4. The Generosity of Jesus

We have good reason to suppose that Jesus was a generous man, not that he was sufficiently wealthy to donate his goods to the poor—historical criticism presents him as one who received from the wealthy more than one who gave to the poor. He was no philanthropist, then. He had "nowhere to lay his head". He could not afford the most meagre of life's necessities that foxes and birds have by right, such was the character of his mission. We must take care not to push a Victorian piety into any narrative which will not support it, but the early community was not materialistic during the time that the *Parousia* was believed to be imminent. We may well suppose that such an ethic emanated from Jesus himself.

He *noticed* a poor widow putting two meagre coins into the temple treasury, and, in giving her all, said Jesus, she had in principle given more than the rest—certainly far more than her ostentatious counterparts (Luke 21:1–4). He became *affectionately fond* of a rich young man who, though morally upright, became disheartened by the challenge to release his burdensome wealth—Jesus' "heart warmed to him" (Mark 10:21). In the artistic parable of the Good Employer of the Vineyard, he would ask, "Do you begrudge my generosity?" (Mat. 20:1–15 RSV). He recommends the hosts of parties to invite not their friends, who would repay their hospitality, but the "poor, crippled, the lame and the blind; and so find happiness. For they have no means of repaying you" (Luke 14:12–14). He is *sensitive to the hunger of people*. Before the Feeding miracle, Matthew records: "I feel sorry for all these people; they have been with me now for three days and have nothing to eat" (15:32). Even the most inconvenient of requests, such as an appeal for bread in the middle on the night, when a man has gone to bed with his family, must be met by the follower of Jesus, so as to avoid putting his friend in an embarrassing situation (Luke 11:5–10). *We see thereby the virtue of the practical ethic of generosity as being part of the nature of Jesus, even though the character of his mission did not necessitate that he personally should put the same into practice.*

Jesus could never have commanded a following if he was a 'hypocrite', as he claimed the Pharisees were! He was aware of the generosity of his Father—who "gives good things to those who ask him" —and he recommended his followers to "put away anxious thoughts about food and drink . . . [since] your Heavenly Father knows that you need them all" (Matt. 6:19–34). Similarly, he instructed his disciples to practise generosity: "Do not turn your back on a man who wants to borrow." This is not merely a teaching about a generous Father, but a revelation from a trusting and self-giving son that understood God to be excessively generous in his dealings with people.

5. Jesus Conversed with the 'Immoral' and 'Outcasts'

It is not difficult to imagine a highly principled person mixing freely with prostitutes, outcasts, lawbreakers and the irreligious, for many social reformers of the modern period have emulated Jesus' example in this way. However, it is difficult to imagine such a scholarly rabbi amiably dining, conversing and socialising with the reprobates as with the learned. Conversing with the two classes is an art rarely mastered, but Jesus mastered it.

There have been many attempts at a crude psychological interpretation of the story of the stoning of the prostitute in the Fourth Gospel (John 8:2–11), at speculating over why Jesus drew with his finger in the sand, and why he ignored the advances of the persistent elders or the ploys of the pious with stones in hands, etc., but they could all be wrong (the story is omitted in most of the early manuscripts). What was beyond dispute, was whose side Jesus was on. The character of Jesus was clearly evident in the whole body of tradition. He was an intellectual, in that he could outwit the cunning of his educated opponents, and he was a man of deepest compassion and warmth, in that he understood more than any of his contemporaries how men and women could change for the better. Children also warmed to him.

The surprise of Simon over the prostitute's insulting behaviour amongst his guests, when she had the audacity rudely to disrupt his hospitality, was one not of condescension but of bewilderment. He does not patronise Jesus as a misguided fool, but learns a new lesson of profound truth from one who was untutored in academic circles. How could Jesus mix these two seemingly irreconcilable classes? His principles were not undermined by his unprejudiced course of action, and the shrewd amongst the priestly clerics knew it. We cannot be present at every Gospel story, be flies on the wall, or make deductions from information not given, neither can we observe gesture, grimace, tension and atmosphere, but our imagination can fill in the gaps; our imagination fills in the gaps as the sensual hand of a prostitute strokes his skin; our imagination fills in the gaps as we consider what self-control of sexual instincts was put under test that day when the creature of beauty caressed him; our imagination fills in the gaps as we visualise him being adorned with the scent of the degrading profession, and as her liberal kisses begin to take him over; our imagination fills in the gaps as he gently checks her actions and brings her to the point of seeing the *true meaning of love* that even one like her can learn to live by; our imagination fills in the gaps!

We know by experience the tension that arises for the man of principle at dinner parties, as the wine begins to flow, as the language becomes choice, and as inhibitions are let go. So easy is it to retreat and express to our smug self-righteous friends our contempt over the debauchery that such occasions bring out, but to see Jesus there, in the midst of the group, indulging in the frivolity and light-hearted merry-making, and to have it further intimated that God might be there too—in the very person of Jesus—defies our sensibilities and moral judgements over what is good and what is proper! The charge of being a "glutton and drunkard" carries with it an insult of considerable *scandal*, for among Palestinian Jews of the time such slander was applied to the person born illegitimate. Here was one who could identify with the outcasts, since to be a 'glutton and drunkard' meant: *he is a bastard!*[9]

A preacher once stirred my imagination with a powerful lesson drawn from the story of the healing of the leper in Mark 1:40–45. Think, he said, of the encounter of Jesus with the leper. Jesus, whose face and long flowing hair was aglow with the early morning dew after a night spent in communion with his Father, reaches out to touch the decrepit leper—a man whose condition was clearly evident, whose dishevelled face was covered with rag, whose scabs marred a ruddy skin, whose ugly condition held little hope, whose cloud of stench hovered over his head, and whose ailment rendered him estranged, unwanted, unloved and unlovely! So, the dramatic scene was set at that poignant moment as they drew together: Jesus, the epitome of the fresh *spirit* of God; the leper, the epitome of death! The risk of contagion was high, but so too was the opportunity for cure and new life.

There is every good reason to accept many of the exorcisms and healings of Jesus as being historical, even though the evangelists have used some of them to solve Messianic mysteries. There can be no serious doubt that Jesus actually did more than invite the 'untouchables' and the sick into his fellowship, *he felt for them.* The choice of company for Jesus was in no way reserved for the prestigious classes, the healthy or the 'perfect' then, but was also extended to the unwanted and the unlovable. It is a fact of history that they were his greatest preference—here was *scandal* indeed.

In summarising the psychological make-up of the man, Jesus of Nazareth, I am inclined to see him as a dynamic teacher-prophet of his time, a genuine charismatic who called men and women into a fellowship with God, which he uniquely experienced in a spiritual sense. He was not God, for such a construct is meaningless! My understanding of him is not too far removed from what John Hick has described:

> He was a man marvellously open to God, living consciously in the divine presence and responsively to the divine purpose. Out of his intense God-consciousness he was able to speak with certainty about the heavenly Father, to convey the challenge of God's will, and to declare God's judgement and forgiveness; and the divine power of life flowed through his hands in physical healing. The intense sense of God's reality expressed in Jesus' life and words was infectious, so that in his presence men and women either joined him in a gloriously liberating surrender to God, or reacted violently against the man who made God real to them. Undoubtedly, in the world which he knew Jesus lived in a closer awareness of God and a more total obedience to God than anyone else, so that it was natural for him to call men to become his disciples.[10]

NOTES

1. J. Jeremias, 'The Problem of the Historical Jesus', in H. K. McArthur, *In Search of the Historical Jesus*, page 128.
2. E. Stauffer, *Jesus and his Story*, Ch. 23: G. Bornkamm, *Jesus of Nazareth*, pages 53–63.
3. J. Jeremias, *New Testament Theology*, Vol. I, London, 1972, pages 65–67.
4. H. E. Todt, *The Son of Man Sayings in the Gospel Tradition*, and R. H. Fuller, 'The New Testament in Current Study', in H. K. McArthur's, *In Search of the Historical Jesus*, pages 176–180.
5. D. Cupitt—see Ch. 13, note 11.
6. For a discussion on these judgement pronouncements, see J. Jeremias, *Jesus' Promise to the Nations*, London, 1958, particularly pages 46–51.
7. J. Jeremias, *Unknown Sayings of Jesus*, London, 1957, pages 54–55. This useful little book discusses the authenticity of twenty-one sayings in circulation during the early Christian period that have not found their way into the Gospels: sayings that are found in other books of the New Testament (Rom. 14:14; I Cor. 7:10; 9:14; 11:24; I Thess. 4:16; Acts 20:35); the Patristic writings; the Talmud; and the Gnostic Oxyrhynchus Papyrus—Gospel of Thomas, Gospel of Truth, Gospel of Philip. See also R. M. Grant, *The Secret Sayings of Jesus*, London, 1960.
8. C. H. Dodd, *Parables of the Kingdom*, London, 1961, pages 16–17.
9. E. Stauffer, 'Jesus and His Story', in H. K. McArthur, *In Search of the Historical Jesus*, page 200.
10. J. Hick, *The Centre of Christianity*, London, 1977, page 27.

15

THE NATURE OF FORGIVENESS

THE POWER OF THE 'WRITTEN' TEXT OF SCRIPTURE

What is the true essence of Christianity, and what *scriptures* make it plain? Like most fundamentalists, I was brought up spiritually to regard *all scripture* as the sacrosanct authority on life, and there was no reason for me then to doubt it. However, the social and spiritual conditioning of being in a fundamentalist sect has an effect upon the way certain New Testament *scriptures* are interpreted that is not seen until one leaves such a community. It is arguable whether one's ideas of *truth* are formed from the reading of pre-selected passages of the Bible or whether the ideas are given first from one's community environment, with the texts serving to reinforce those ideas. Whichever is the case, such *truths* soon become 'internalised' as part of one's own belief-system. I am not sure, therefore, whether any person's unconscious selection of biblical passages is completely arbitrary. The significant 'magic' text stands out from the printed page and speaks to the individual's condition because that person is, in part, looking for it! Conversely, the reader's mental selective processes will unconsciously reject extraneous material not in support of the belief that is held. In either case, the subject is exercising some unconscious control of what is believed; beliefs are not arrived at *intuitively* but are culturally determined. That is why fundamentalists are generally convinced they are right even when irrefutable evidence contrary to their viewpoint is put to them.

The sayings of Jesus that *stood out for me* were those which challenged the Church's middle-class morality and value-system, particularly since the Church has traditionally (albeit unwittingly) closed its doors to the wayward—how often are the social misfits called into the services on Sunday evenings? In studying the life of Augustine, I was struck by the access-for-all character of his church—it seemed to be open to all and sundry:

> The man who enters is bound to see drunkards, misers, tricksters, gamblers, adulterers, fornicators . . . ; he must be warned that the same crowds that press into the churches on Christian festivals, also fill pagan theatres on holidays.[1]

The passage that has been the core of my own religious insight would probably be the saying in Matthew's parable of the Final Judgement (Matt. 25:31–46). The definition of the sheep called into the kingdom intrigues me—they are those who anonymously follow the Master's teaching of caring for the ill-fortuned:

> I tell you this: anything you did for one of my brothers here, however humble, you did for me. [i.e., fed the hungry, clothed the naked, visited the sick and imprisoned, etc.] . . . And they too will reply, "Lord, when was it that we saw you hungry or thirsty or a stranger . . .
>
> Matt. 25:40–45

It is interesting how modern psychologists and psychotherapists have arrived at the very same conclusions that Jesus preached and practised two thousand years ago. *The employment of overtly-critical and punitive approaches serves only to disempower and deflate human potential, to de-motivate, to store guilt and to bare grudges, whereas to accept the 'unworthy' and encourage the 'wayward' builds self-esteem and motivates individuals to improve their behaviour to change for the better.*

There is one picture that runs consistently throughout the Gospel narratives and which provides a unifying strand of irrefutable tradition—Jesus going out to the sinners, accepting them into his fellowship, and authorising their entry into the fellowship of God.

In Mark, there is the paralysed man, who is not only healed by Jesus but is forgiven by him (Mark 2:1–12); the healing follows the benediction:

> My son, your sins are forgiven.
>
> Mark 2:5

There is the choice of Jesus' company at dinner in Levi's home, and the criticism that results:

> He eats with tax-gatherers and sinners?
>
> Mark 2:16

This saying characterises his social preference, and earned for him the title of being greedy and indiscriminate. This deliberate action is highly significant in a nation whose religious culture had marked the meal as more than a participation in a necessary and conventional activity; it was a sign of social and religious acceptance *per se*. Matthew preserves the same tradition:

> Look at him! a glutton and a drinker, a friend of tax-gatherers and sinners!
>
> Matt. 11:18–19

Matthew also records an alarming statement that insulted the cantankerous chief priests and elders:

> I tell you this: the tax-gatherers and prostitutes are entering the kingdom of God ahead of you.
>
> Matt. 21:31

Such an address epitomised what Jesus was able to achieve in his own ministry, as compared with his contemporaries. The great new commandment outlines the purpose of the love-ethic:

> Love your enemies and pray for your persecutors; only so can you be children of your heavenly Father.
>
> Matt. 5:44–45

This ethical pronouncement marks a depth of love which Jesus practised daily. The ploughman's saying of rest describes a touch of country warmth and social acceptance:

> "Come to me, all whose work is hard, whose load is heavy; and I will give you relief. Bend your necks to my yoke, and learn from me, for I am gentle and humble-hearted; and your souls will find relief. For my yoke is good to bear, my load is light."
>
> Matt. 11:28–29

Luke has touching stories of human affection: there is the woman's deed of gratitude for her sins forgiven (Luke 7:36–50); the conversion story of the tax-collector, Zacchaeus—the little man with the big heart (Luke 19:1–10); there are the parables of the Lost Son (Luke 15:11–32), the Widow's Vindicator (Luke 18:1–5), and the Humble Tax-collector (Luke 18:9–14) who was justified more than the pious Pharisee.

The Fourth Gospel preserves a narrative of a prostitute who was forgiven by Jesus. Though not found in the oldest manuscripts, the story represents a genuine recollection of the type of stance Jesus took (John 7:53–8:11); it closes with a homily: "You may go; do not sin again" (John 8:11). There is also a narrative of a lame man (John 5:2–15) with a similar closing homily: "Now that you are well again, leave your sinful ways, or you may suffer something worse" (John 5:14).

C. H. Dodd in his final book says:

> The Author of the parables must have been genuinely interested in people . . . Our informants draw special attention to his association with people who were neither socially accepted nor morally approved. He was censured as a friend of tax-gatherers and sinners . . . Obviously these dubious characters must have liked his company a good deal better than they would have liked that of his critics, even if these had not held them at arm's length.[2]

PRACTISING LIMITLESS FORGIVENESS

> Love wholeheartedly, and then do what you will.
>
> Whoever thinks that he is able to nibble at the life of absent friends, must know that he is unworthy of this table.
>
> St Augustine

There have been many attempts at constructing Atonement theories, both from a biblical point of view (V. Taylor, *The Atonement in New Testament Teaching*[3]) and a historical one (L. W. Grensted, *The Atonement in History and in Life*[4]), but the work I have found to be the most compelling read on this subject is a chapter in William Temple's, book, *Christus Veritas*.[5] It is not novel to expound Jesus as one who had taught and practised the supreme moral virtue of forgiveness, not merely of one's closest friends but of one's enemies too, but Temple asks of the implications inherent in such a teaching on God's forgiveness:

a) What of the question of unconditional forgiveness and the place of the majestic Law of Justice?

b) What of the question of the wrong-doer who remains impenitent?

c) What is the role of the Church as compared with that of the individual in respect to the offending member of the community?

d) Does forgiveness necessarily mean a cancellation of the penalty?

All these are very pertinent ethical questions indeed and ones requiring answers. Temple makes the point that the Atonement is not a teaching on the justification of God's dealings with men (as it might be for the philosopher), but rather that it is principally a theory of relationship—at least for the religious person. It is not the misdeed of the person that is offensive to God, but its damaging effect upon intimate relationships, whether in the human sphere or the divine.

In the Lord's prayer, the plea for God's forgiveness is conditional upon the petitioners themselves being able to forgive their fellows:

> Forgive us the wrong we have done,
> as we have forgiven those who have wronged us.
>
> Matt. 6:12

This is qualified both positively:

> For if you forgive others the wrong they have done, your heavenly Father will also forgive you.
>
> Matt. 6:14

And negatively:

> But if you do not forgive others, then the wrongs you have done will not be forgiven by your Father.
>
> Matt. 6:15

God's forgiveness is bound up within man's forgiving. In this, the Christian can be assured that he is saved, that he is forgiven because he forgives his brother. In this sense, God can be restricted by our own will and intransigence: *God can only forgive us as we forgive others. Should we not forgive others, what is God able to do for us?*

The Christian is qualified as being 'perfect', not in moral excellence but in his or her own inexhaustible practice of forgiveness:

> You, therefore, must be perfect,
> as your heavenly Father is perfect.
>
> Matt. 5:48 RSV

This is a degree of love which many in the world do not know. Many pragmatists see little option but to deal with misdeeds by the meting out of punishment and penalties, to ostracise the offender for the protection of society, and to ridicule the person displaying a forgiving spirit as being weak and of pathetic character! Against such attitudes, Christ teaches a limitless forgiveness:

> If your brother wrongs you, reprove him; and if he repents, forgive him. Even if he wrongs you seven times in a day and comes back to you seven times saying, "I am sorry", you are to forgive him.
>
> Luke 17:3–4

And should the point still be missed:

Jesus replied, "I do not say seven times; I say seventy times seven."

Matt. 18:22

This is the test of truly being a Christian and it is no simple matter. *God's forgiveness of us cannot be separated from our forgiveness of one another*, but what of the condition? What if the sinner does not repent? What is the role of the Church in cultivating the ethos of forgiveness and reforming the 'secular' spirit of intolerance? In answering such questions, the emphasis is still on that of relationships:

> If your brother commits a sin, go and take the matter up with him, strictly between yourselves, and if he listens to you, you have won your brother over. But if he will not listen, take one or two others, so that all facts may be duly established on the evidence of two of three witnesses. If he refuses to listen to them, report the matter to the congregation [Church RSV]; and if he will not listen to even the congregation, you must then treat him as you would a pagan [Gentile RSV] or a tax-gatherer.

Matt. 18:15–17

The point here is not to set the boundary of a reasonable limit to forgiveness, but to spell out that *Christian forgiveness must have no limit*:

> If your enemy is hungry, feed him; if he is thirsty, give him a drink; by doing this you will heap live coals on his head." Do not let evil conquer you, but use good to defeat evil.

Rom. 12:20–21

The 'heaping coals of fire on your enemy's head' has one of two possible interpretations, but the point in both is the same. For Temple the saying means: "So we shall soften his hard heart as the smith softens the iron by heaping upon it coals of fire."[6] Alternatively, it has been pointed out that it was an eastern custom of charity for the wealthy to lower glowing coals upon the tray of the peasant as he passed by under his flat roof in the evening. The coals would have been graciously received so as to keep him and his family warm throughout the long chilly night. The point for both is:

> Do not let evil conquer you, but use good to defeat evil.

Rom. 12:21

> Do not set yourselves against the man who wrongs you.

Matt. 5:39

Should everything fail to bring about a turn of mind in the offender, then "you must then treat him as you would a pagan or a tax-gatherer" (Matt. 18:17). How, might we ask, did Jesus deal with the pagan and the tax-gatherer? To answer that question, a further glance at the Gospel narratives is called for.

* * *

After reading a moving story of the death of a girl from the Remembrance Day bombing at Enniskillen, I came across the equally moving prayer of an unknown

Jewish woman which was found on a piece of wrapping paper in the concentration camp of Ravensbruck. It read:

> O Lord, remember not only the men and women of goodwill but also those of illwill. But do not remember the suffering they have inflicted upon us; remember the fruits we bore, thanks to this suffering: our comradeship, our loyalty, our humility, the courage, the generosity, the greatness of heart which has grown out of this; and when they come to judgement, let all the fruits that we have borne be their forgiveness.[7]

NOTES

1. Augustine's church: P. Brown, *Augustine of Hippo*, Glasgow, 1967, page 213.
2. C. H. Dodd, *The Founder of Christianity*, London, 1971, pages 55–56.
3. V. Taylor, *The Atonement in New Testament Teaching*, London, 1940.
4. L. W. Grensted, *The Atonement in History and in Life*, London, 1929.

Various theories of the Atonement have occupied the minds of theologians from the first century onwards. They represent a need to systematise the means of salvation in logical terms from leads, inferences and deductions of scripture.

Any genuine Christology must begin from the 'nature of Jesus' on the human level, not from the 'nature of God' on the divine. *The Satisfaction theory* is such a case. It was a deductive way of interpreting the death of Jesus that was affected by medieval theology. Studying the Genesis stories, Augustine postulated a theory of 'inherited sin' from Adam to all men. It was a legalistic logic beginning from God rather than man. It asked the wrong questions: how is God offended?; How do we right things?; What must be done to propitiate him? These new and extra-biblical ways of interpreting the death of Jesus were confusing, misleading and wrong. Christ was conceived of as a new 'Law Giver', no doubt under Roman influence; it was a rejudaizing of the Gospel! This was a reading into Genesis, not a reading out of it. These early accounts are not descriptions of what happened at the beginning—how did the first man fall to sin from grace, etc.—but are descriptions of what is the nature of man, what is the effect of sin in terms of man's relations and relationships with God and his fellows. The 'Satisfaction theory' was a blind alley, travelled along when asking the wrong questions, from the wrong premises, deduced from the wrong application of scripture; it should be regarded as a distortion of the Christian message.

The Ransom theory, similarly, has evolved from an isolated text in Mark 10:45; it represents a wrong conclusion deduced from the wrong premise: how is the sinner's soul bought back from the Devil? What price must be paid by Christ in ransom? Again, the logic (immoral logic) follows not from the human question of Jesus but from formulae of the divine.

The Expiation theory represents a need to preserve a sacrificial cult (in modernised form). It arises from the question of relevance: cultic sacrifices no longer form the religious obligations in modern man's environment, and there is no longer the need to point to a Christian 'sacrifice' in defending the Faith against pagans. The concept of expiatory sacrifice, therefore, becomes unintelligible. The letter to the Hebrews was written by an unknown Hellenistic author who was not unaccustomed to Pauline motifs. The letter utilises Old Testament sacrificial analogies to point to the novel and distinctive nature of Christ's sacrifice, but these images serve only as links. The meaning lies outside the reference: the death of Christ epitomised the whole life of Jesus offered up, and his intercessory priesthood was to plead the case of his brethren—a further metaphor. God's love does not protect us against all suffering, but the point is that *through all suffering God can be found*. For some, suffering is the rock of atheism, for others it is the occasion of trust—Job found no rational explanation to account for his hardships, only trust. Jesus, unlike Job, dies from his suffering, alone and deserted, but still he trusts.

Incarnation theories, similar to the beliefs of the Pre-existence of Christ, are inferences drawn from the post-paschal faith in the Resurrection. Such thoughts were directed not from the beginning to the end, but from the end to the beginning. The difference between a real and an ideal pre-existence was of limited interest at a time when ideas—under Plato's influence—were regarded as real. The miraculous birth of the religious founder was not novel—Buddha, Confucius, Zarathustra, and Mohammed, all had miraculous births. Under Hellenistic influence, the proclamation of *scandal* becomes one of mystery, questions of function—as the New Testament asks—become questions of essence. The status of the Son becomes of greater importance than his function as advocate, spokesman, deputy and representative. New categories for meaning are utilised to describe the Son's ontological generation and unity (essence, nature, hypostasis, person, substance and union). This represented a significant move from biblical 'sin-grace dualism' to a dangerous 'matter-spirit dualism', and the life and crucifixion of Jesus give way to cosmic speculations concerning the Son. Redemption has become absorbed in the Incarnation of the *Logos*, and the resurrection serves primarily to confirm the Incarnation. Greek theology depicts the whole history of mankind as a continuous, upward-leading, educational process, and this world-view no doubt influenced this unbiblical teaching. These ideas are artificial and unintelligible to the modern outlook. Irenaeus may say, "God became man so that man might become God", but does a reasonable man today want to become God? Our problem is not the deification of man, says Küng (*On Being a Christian*), but the humanisation of man.

5. W. Temple, *Christus Veritas*, Ch. XIV, 'The Atonement', London, 1924.
6. Ibid., page 267.
7. Gordon Wilson, *Marie*, 1990, page 116.

16

CONCLUSION

Where does this leave the fundamentalist if it is conceded that the various books of the Bible are to be seen as the product of their age? Where does it leave the various sects and denominations of the divided Church if it can be demonstrated that the basis of their standing is unsound? What 'authority' can remain if the Bible is not in itself the 'Word of God'? The presence of Islam in the modern world illustrates all too clearly the pitfalls of a closed-minded fanaticism, particularly amongst the uneducated, yet there is no sign that Islam will die, and, I suspect, neither will Christian fundamentalism pass away in the foreseeable future. As long as people want dogmatism and a simple solution to the complexities of life, Christian fundamentalism will not die. In such persuasions there is little demand to think, and certainly no requirement to step out in the dark—the imperative of true faith. There is just the decree to obey!

If Christianity is larger than fundamentalism, can it be practised without allegiance to a church, denomination or sect? This question brings up for discussion the importance of *the religious community* for cultivating the spiritual life. Although this study has not attended to the authority of the Church as such, it is an inevitable corollary that the place of the institutional Church should be considered when examining the authority of the Bible as the guide for Christian living.

I went to church one Easter morning, and it struck me how far removed the exercise was from what Jesus had prescribed for his immediate followers. It is questionable whether Jesus was a religious founder in the ordinary sense of the word, for it is doubtful from the Gospel sources whether he had any intention of founding the Church as we know it today. The Christian Church, fundamentalist or otherwise, purports to follow in Jesus' name and, in consequence, sees its own spiritual authorisation to be of God; now, here is the crux of the problem: *is the Church the continuation of what Jesus came to do, or is it of human construction designed to meet particular social needs?*

We cannot know for certain how Jesus viewed his mission at the close of his life, yet the Church believed itself to be the natural extension of the Gospel and the 'material' representation of the Lord on earth. The fact remains, however, that there is no statement that is unambiguously an instruction of Jesus that his followers should found a religious order, a sect, or a denomination, in continuation of his message.* He clearly did not think of forming a large religious 'institution' or see the sacred 'organisation' as the natural outcome of his teaching. Jesus regarded himself from the very first as the herald sent out *only* to the children of Israel—the universal command

---

* See Appendix

found in Matthew (28:19–20) to proselytise and make disciples of all nations is evidently a post-paschal invention. Whatever the Church was in the first century, and however we see its authority and function today, it certainly was not the creation of Jesus.

It is credible that the emergence of the Church can be seen as a historical accident, an inevitable outcome of social and political pressures, but for the 'biblicist' its emergence was foreordained by God and was fully in accordance with his will, just as it is so understood today. Historically, the counterparts of modern-day assemblies and brotherhoods were around during the times of Jesus, yet he gave them no allegiance so far as we know. For Jesus, there was to be no special élitist group or 'school' (Pharisees), no monastic settlement (the Buddha, the Essenes and the monks of Qumran), no training college (Confucius), no expanding religious state (Mohammed), and no 'holy remnant' ('Teacher of Righteousness'—Dead Sea Scrolls), but the modern-day Church is many of these things.

Being a Christian in the early period was contentious and highly dangerous. There was *scandal*, even if the *scandal* was not identical to the challenge of the kingdom. The *scandal* of the historical Jesus was that of a man wanted for sedition, one who was a criminal anarchist, one under suspicion of overthrowing the established order! He was judged as a conspirator and was dressed poorly, having no rank or office. He was believed to be a mere carpenter by trade, a visionary idealist, unemployed, yet a friend of commoners and vagrants. The chasm separating the mission of the historical Jesus and the witness of the Gospel in every type of church, sect or denomination, is enormous. The gulf dividing Jesus from the liturgy of a church or cathedral, or the sober meditation of the Quaker meeting house, or the spiritual exuberance of an Evangelical house-fellowship, or even the peaceful solitude of a monastic brotherhood, appears un-bridgeable. The Christ of piety, the 'Sacred Heart', the gentle Jesus, or the 'Holy infant tender and mild', is a million miles from the historical figure behind the post-paschal faith. The young, beardless, kind-hearted, shepherd of the early Christian catacombs, the domesticated Jesus plaster cast of the high church—who, in the words of Hans Küng "neither feels nor can feel pain"—are inventions of religion not the semblance of history. From the first century onwards, the sharp focus of the Christ-image became blurred; the 'Father of Jesus' became the 'God of the philosophers'. In modern times the image has again become blurred, as Nietzsche has said: "People have now got used to the cross, borne not as a burden on the back, but as a decoration on the chest." The *scandal* for the modern-day Church is not nearly so contentious as it was either for Jesus or for the earliest community (in fact, it is barely a 'scandal' at all), but what about the fundamentalist sects and denominations? Can they make claim to have preserved the *scandal* of the original message of Jesus?

The fundamentalist sects and denominations of the divided Christian Church will have their place and their self-justifying purpose for existence, and I am not decrying any of that, but can any community as an 'institution' justifiably claim to emulate the one who is said to be its founder? I think not! We have presented the evidence as we understand it to be; readers must judge for themselves. Each church community will have its own set of priorities, of course, but the object for many in being a member of a sect or denomination centres on the maintenance of the 'institution' as an end in itself, or as a means within which to bring up the young in having the right moral and spiritual outlook, for good or for bad. Such a community has only the merest trace of the ideology and the spirituality of the historical Jesus.

There is a broadly acknowledged dilemma for those needing communal relationships. Small exclusive sects create a better quality of community than *movements* endorsing open-ended enquiry. The authority of an exclusive community is preserved and reinforced by the outlawing and censoring of radical discussion. Consequently, numbers will increase with the inflexible dogma of the Jehovah's Witnesses, or the charismatic appeal of the Evangelicals, so long as the message can be carried with conviction. The increasing number of converts is not the sole criterion of truth, however, even though swelling numbers and large brotherhoods are indicators of life and spirit for a community. Hence, those Christian sects that stress with unwavering conviction the *authority* model of faith are likely to expand, I suspect, since this model engenders a culture of religious dependence, a dependence which is attractive for those unsure of their way. We are not speaking about truth here, but about feelings and emotions, and, as I have previously said, fundamentalists make a considerable emotional investment in a belief in biblical inspiration and inerrancy, because uncompromising doctrine undoubtedly serves to keep the unthinking members of the community more firmly held together. We do not 'trade in' our investments too readily unless there is some profitable return in the process, particularly those of us who are old.

We have dismantled the fundamentalist's Bible, and we have seen that many sects are founded upon a falsehood, but fundamentalism is not dead, nor is it even dying; on the contrary, it is alive and kicking, and going to be with us for some time yet. It is to be hoped that the young are able to see the return of a nobler form of spirituality from the 'trade in' of an inerrant Bible, and, perhaps, lead some of the old along the way.

I think there is likely to be an ongoing polarisation amongst the more rigidly fundamentalist sects and denominations if some radical thinkers begin 'rocking the boat', by pushing for church-unity in deference to doctrinal distinctions, or by questioning those presuppositions that form the boundaries of particularism and denominational identity. The reaction of polarisation is an unconscious drive for self-preservation; it occurs because such radical criticism, however virtuous and sincerely intended, does not address the more pressing issues of a sociological nature that make a community a *community*. If open enquiry is too probing, the 'middle of the road' members begin to make their majority voice heard, in order to secure the conservative identity of the group. The evangelising of fundamentalist preaching will not be daunted by scepticism or by the doubting ethos of the post-modern age, and new converts will be won over to their respective communities just as before, perhaps in even greater numbers as sects become more marginalised in the modern world.

In spite of the critical outlook of the modern age, we have to concede that it appears that some people respond more readily to dogmatic expressions of belief than to technical and philosophical theories to guide them through life's troubles. Those sects and denominations that embrace a passionate 'bibliolatry'—from the American Bible belt to the less-spectacular fundamentalist groups making up the divided Protestant Church—will no doubt carry on in ignorance of every piece of empirical evidence contrary to an inerrant Bible that research presents as being plausible to modern ways of thinking. Expositors and theologians of fundamentalist sects have a work to do then, since that which authorises their separateness and distinctive character is founded upon a myth. I am not advocating a complete swing into the objective camp of empiricism, however, since those empiricists making claims beyond that which their evidence supports—who unwittingly promote the idea that we can understand all there is by a form of reductional analysis of total human experience—rarely give any credence to those areas of experience that I have described as 'non-rational' and *numinous*.

For committed fundamentalists, and I think most are, the time is ripe for a *new vision of Christ*, one which supersedes the doctrinaire mould and one which empowers spiritual people to think afresh and meet with enthusiasm the challenge of the kingdom. If the fundamentalist discounts criticism and the evaluation of personal belief, then there will have been a failure to build a Christian faith upon a footing that is credible and reasonable for a world in search of salvation from self-centredness. It is psychological suicide for the leaders of sects to direct converts blindly into the adoption of uncritically founded belief-systems that will need correcting in the light of further knowledge and experience; the end result of a seeker's delusion and uncertainty in having to alter course again is more unsettling than their state prior to finding salvation. Evangelists beware! Christian fundamentalists must at some point critically evaluate the biblical scriptures if they are to discover the *essence* of the message from the garb of ecclesiastical words with which it has been surrounded. To question the belief in biblical inerrancy and infallibility is not a case of throwing out the baby with the bath water, but it is a case of helping the baby to *grow up*. I have tried to show that the teaching of an 'inspired' Bible is a blind alley in establishing criteria for genuine *revelations* of God. Christianity cannot be reduced to fundamentalism; it existed before the fundamentalist sects came into existence, and it will survive the many misgivings of sectarian bigotry. Christians of the fundamentalists, more than those of the larger Church, hold to the view that the New Testament canon of the first century was the *final revelation* of God, but they appear to have overlooked the fact that this is precisely what the Muslims say took place with the Koran in 610, and Sikhs with the Adi Granth in 1732, and even Joseph Smith with the Book of Mormon in 1830; they are unable to recognise that this is the greatest unverified presupposition that they *choose* not to question, and for quite obvious reasons!

We have demonstrated that Jesus was quite unique, and yet every Christian community, as a social sub-culture, is anything but unique. The distinction between being a Christian and being a *modernised moral being* is not so clearly obvious as it once was, and some theologians of the modern period (such as Michael Goulder) are prescribing the teaching of morality as being the only valid form of Religious Education in our schools. Morality in the modern period can no longer be tied to Christianity. There are some who work out their own faith from an admixture of the best elements of Christianity and Buddhism (Don Cupitt), and there are many who work out their own morality from no basis of Christianity at all (Jonathan Porritt). After two thousand years, the Western Church of the modern age has assumed for itself a middle-class conventional character and an embodiment of the moral order of society. This was not the case, however, during those early days of persecution; at that time, the Church was radical and unconventional. Since the Industrial Revolution, the Church ceased to be radical by becoming modernised and by taking the lead in social reform, but in the current political situation it has shed its social responsibilities of education, hospitalisation of the sick, fighting for the rights of women and ethnic groups, countering exploitation around the world, and campaigning for the welfare of the poor. All these former concerns have now become absorbed within *secularisation*, and it is no longer clear what distinctive assignments remain for the Church to complete.

This book has not focused on the Church as such, but on the fundamentalist wing of the Church that is rooted in the Bible. My overall intention has not been to discount everything the Bible has to say, and certainly not to disqualify the effect of the Bible in drawing men and women to become more God-like and caring human beings. I am committed to making the Bible more accessible for those *secular* spiritual people whose yearnings make it clear that man is more than a non-reflective species within time and space. It is regrettable that some, who are engaged in the quest for meaning, might have rejected the Bible as an outmoded product of the past simply on the grounds of ignorance, an ignorance of what biblical writings really have to teach. I have never read a book quite so compelling as the Bible, and I have a personal passion and intellectual interest in studying the scriptures at a scholarly level. I hope that the reader may thereby be encouraged to look again at what the biblical scriptures show us of God, but from a critical point of view, if for no other reason than that of discounting my analysis of the fundamentalist's position.

As I understand it, the Bible is neither a manual of correct belief nor a code of prescriptive conduct; rather it is the product of *intuitive spiritual insights* that have been shaped within the minds of men and women living in quite specific, but very different, historical contexts. The 'Word of God' came not to those who were merely spectators of such dramas of religious tension, but to those who were participants. The hearts of the children of God were touched as they bravely faced predicaments in the staunch belief that *the divine was truly there*. These were theophanies of the richest kind, experiences that prompted new ways of looking at things. Although the 'record' we have is couched in the printed word, the words can no less speak to our condition, excite us to move, and compel us to be moved. There is a lesson we can take for the challenges of our day therefore: *the message of the Bible is a message of engagement in attempting to build a better world by the process of individual spiritual advancement of all people.* It is not one of withdrawal from the world to preserve one's own piety and personal holiness in a detached sense; it calls for a single-minded life aimed at transforming all that is evil. For the searcher for truth, whose ideology and orientation may not be too far out of step with the historical Jesus, the imperatives are not necessarily carried out by becoming a member of a church, denomination or sect, but they will call for an engagement.

All hope of a new dawn of spirituality is not lost. I detect a departing trend from an unquestioning propositional faith amongst some of the friends of my former Christian community, and also a spiritual growing up, and I wonder how widespread this is. I notice a different form of spirituality coming to birth from the childhood dependence on the benevolent 'Heavenly Father' image of juvenile faith. The need for an *autonomous, self-regulated and internalised faith* (as evidenced by the recent SCM *Trust* circular) has drawn out some disenchanted believers from the communities of their formative years. Such are the magnetic pulls of the modern cynical outlook that many reflective Christians have felt their new inclinations and leanings to be disheartening evidence of personal apathy and a drifting apart from the life of faith, rather than a yearning for a new form of spirituality. I detect also a thirst for that spiritual dimension to life for those having no formal religious allegiances or affiliations to a community, particularly amongst the young—in spite of their large-scale disinterest in the Church. It would be tempting at this point to move off in our need for greater precision and carry out an extensive analysis of the very 'substance' of the spiritual experience, particularly in respect of what we know about psychology, but this is a task requiring a book in itself. In this conclusion, however, I offer as a pointer for further enquiry a possibility from a few personal observations. We suggested earlier that it might suit the propaganda of fundamentalist organisations to argue that the condition of being open and receptive to religious experience requires the pre-condition that in itself involves some persuasion and suggestion. We recall, also, Cupitt's line of reasoning in connection with mystical experience, where he said that the phenomenon was presented by its devotees as though some were in possession of a special sense organ to act as a receptor which others clearly lacked. Against both propositions, I offer the following.

May it not be considered as all that unreasonable to suppose that the *numinous* may have its 'secular' or 'natural' manifestation through which its substance is communicated within the experience, a medium which might not be distinguishable from its non-tangible source? While returning from holiday on one occasion, I stopped at a beach that ran alongside the road. I stopped for no other good reason than to grant a request of my travelling companion, Dwain (a school pupil and fellow helper). He wanted to explore the shoreline before his return to the bustle and hubbub of his impoverished street back home. Given that he was a gregarious character by nature, one who loved fun and activity more than reflective, thoughtful pursuits, and one not usually content with his own company, I was surprised by his level of engagement and playful exploration. For over an hour, his solitary figure could be seen in the distance silhouetted against the rolling waves, engrossed and captivated in apparently futile endeavour. Often he turned up stones, frequently they were skimmed, at other times he just stared at the sea in an almost trance-like state of 'drinking in' the rich experience never before enjoyed. As I sat in the car waiting for him to return in his own time, I mused over what he might have been thinking. It seemed as though the very asking of the question would have been in itself a violation of the privacy of his soul and its 'contact' with the spirit of the sea, a brutal intrusion to make the 'spiritual' something 'material' by *having to put into words and rational constructs* something that had all the hallmarks of 'natural-ness' and spontaneity. I let the experience remain with him and be his. Just in front of the car there were seagulls and starlings feeding on what passers-by had strewn on the beach. My eye had preferred the seagulls (they being the most unfamiliar) to the starlings, owing to their drab appearance and general commonality in the place where I live. But then, I began to study more attentively one starling that had ventured from the group and stalked his way towards my car. I 'noticed' the comical way it jostled for its food. I 'noticed' its pretty head and beak prodding at the crust. I 'noticed' its startling winter plumage of glossy black-purple-ish feathers, lavishly splashed with gold and cream specks. As I mused over what consciousness the little creature might have, I 'noticed'. I 'noticed' aspects of its being that my prejudice had hitherto prevented me from seeing. My concentration was broken as Dwain returned. His face and demeanour were serene and tranquil. He was at peace with himself and his world (and, dare I say, his God, even though he had made no formal profession!), and he showed me his stones and shells. Is this 'noticing' or 'attending to' those things which were formerly hidden or were considered profane, a religious experience, or is it merely a 'natural' one? What of those captured moments of intense closeness and comradeship that most human beings experience, albeit fleetingly, at least once in their lives? Are those 'contacts' of intimacy and one-ness spiritual contacts, or must the spiritual always be reserved for those experiences which occur within a conventional religious context? A matter of opinion more than a question of fact, surely, for the similarities are striking. The 'substance' of the experience evokes the same emotional excitation, energy, warmth, euphoria and identity of being in relatedness, with all the various but similar physiological conditions that accompany such feeling states, whether we speak of the experience as being 'natural', 'filial', 'communal', 'psychological' or 'spiritual'. The results of the experience are not entirely dissimilar either—often there is a 'purging' of the soul, a 'good' feeling and inner peace for having had the experience, and an avowed obligation to become more committed to something or someone. Indeed, there are many psychologists and psychotherapists who are quite at a loss to separate into water-tight categories ('spiritual', 'aesthetic', 'natural', 'mystical', 'psychological', 'paranormal' and the like) those aspects and feelings that occur during peoples' peak experiences through life, as John Rowan observes: "A peak experience is one of those times, experienced by many millions of people, when pretence and fear seem to drop away, and we seem to be in touch with the whole universe. It is a timeless and ecstatic moment of intense feeling, which comes to some people when they see a sunrise on a mountain, or hear great music, or look at a child, or make love, or experience a religious ceremony."* The intention of drawing this parallel is not to reduce the spiritual to the order of the profane, but to see the spiritual in what is encountered in the natural, and in the here and now—the point of any incarnational faith, I believe.

In promoting the mystical alternative to that of slavish bibliolatry, I am not consciously resorting to a God-of-the-gaps option of holding on to that dimension that can never be falsified by empirical evidence, I am recognising what I believe to be the case: that the depth of spiritual consciousness lies in cultivating for oneself this *numinous* aspect, and leaving oneself open and responsive to a *continuous call* of God which draws the seeker ever closer to the needs of people and thereby closer to the being of God. The *continual call* of God may become apparent through the voice of a person, a glimpse of pressing need, a significant event, the thoughts of a theologian, the exhortation of the preacher, or it may speak through the 'printed word' of scripture, but its power to effect change is still the same whatever its medium. The decision of the individual to become open and receptive to the *numinous* is *intensely spiritual* but culturally neutral. I have not suggested that culture may not have given rise to, and helped to form to a person's private spirituality, but I have argued that it is not contingent upon it. This form of personal spirituality is not conceived of as an escapism or a resort to conventional moral living of a given culture, for all through this book I have presented the *numinous* 'non-rational' life-orientation as being anchored to a commitment to the world, as against any notion of world denial. The

---

* J. Rowan (1992), 'What is Humanistic Psychotherapy?'. In *British Journal of Psychotherapy*, Vol. 9 (1), p. 77

Jesus that struck an existentialist chord within my own personal experience was the historical figure that empowered the weak and beggarly to climb above their impoverished stations to become members of God's fellowship. It is in the face of the helpless and destitute that I personally see more clearly the face of Christ.* I cannot, of course, say that my spirituality should be that of others, or that what I commend as the *essence* of the religious life should be a universal experience, irrespective of everything else. I can only speak for myself when inviting the reader to look through this particular religious lens.

Propositional beliefs give structure to religious growth till a form of spirituality fully emerges that is no longer dependent on belief-systems. They serve, therefore, as a type of springboard to project us upward or launch us outward. Propositional beliefs cannot and must not become fixed or eternally binding upon us—as though the absolute had been reached—because they will impede our growth in a world of perpetual change.

Being brought up within a fundamentalist brotherhood gave me two propositional beliefs that served as my springboard. One I have discarded, the other has become a very insignificant part of my life. I was indoctrinated with the teaching that the Bible was the inspired Word of God—infallible and inerrant, with all its contradictions of empiricism and historical and literary criticism. Secondly, I was directed to anticipate an imminent *Parousia* of Christ. The first propositional belief in an inerrant Bible has been totally discarded for reasons outlined in this book. The second belief, in the return of Christ, I barely retain, even though it may be stored in some rear closet of my unconsciousness as a legacy from earlier sectarian days. My belief in a literal *Parousia* has developed, then, towards an agnostic position, just as had taken place for believers in the first century; it was not owing to conflicting empirical reasoning but to a contradiction of logic regarding time and history. From the first time the teaching attracted me and made me curious over things happening in the world at large, to a present position of an inability to imagine the scale of such an event that would see the winding up of history, I have changed, as we should expect in any growth. The literal *Parousia* belief now seems inconceivable in the way it was first presented to me. In studying the Fourth Gospel however, the argument was finally clinched. This early writer had already begun to demythologise the cruder aspect of a physical descent of Jesus from the heavens, by presenting the alternative *Parousia* of the coming of the Spirit to the believer. There was a shift from an **imminent** *Parousia* towards an **immanent** *Parousia*—the idea of a God 'who is' to replace a divine figure 'who would come'. Already, for this writer and his community, then, a new form of spirituality was growing out of the traditions of his formative religious background. Can we not imagine that the same process should not continue for some time to come? I certainly hope so.

* See my autobiographical comment on Christian 'spirituality' in *Coming through the Tunnel*, Birmingham 1994, 1 Holywell Lane, Rubery, B45 9EJ, England

APPENDIX

DID JESUS AUTHORIZE THE RITE OF BAPTISM?

AN EXPOSITION OF JOHN 3:22–4:3

Ian McHaffie has suggested that the statement found in John 3:22 (4:1–2) describing a ministry of baptism might be an indication that Jesus had every intention of establishing a following, and founding a community in his name, that might be described as the embryo of the Church. The text appears to be an authentic record of history, since it looks as though it has not been thoroughly worked over by themes of Johannine theology. The observation demands some consideration, therefore. The passage reads:

> After this, Jesus went into Judaea with his disciples, stayed there with them, and baptized. John too was baptizing at Aenon, near to Salim, because water was plentiful in that region; and the people were constantly coming for baptism. This was before John's imprisonment.

The passage introduces a section (3:22–36) which some exegetes have argued is out of place, principally upon the grounds that it alters the theme and breaks the continuity of the whole passage. There are a series of four doublet ideas that run parallel to each other in this early part of the Fourth Gospel—Jesus' ministry of baptism and the Baptist's mission that follows the Prologue of chapter one (3:22–36 and 1:19–39):

• John the Baptist is not the Messiah	1–19–21	3:28
• John is sent before him	1:30	3:28
• John's rank is lower than Jesus'	1:30	3:30
• John's mission is to reveal the Messiah	1:31	3:29

R. E. Brown* presents an analysis of the research findings that account for this parallelism, and concludes, on linguistic grounds, that an early source document of the activity of John the Baptist has been edited and utilised by the author. C. H. Dodd has demonstrated† that the form and position of 3:22–36 suggests a number of probabilities:

a) The sections of 3:22–23 and 4:1–3 were part of a genuine source handed down to the author that he has seen fit to adapt only marginally. The first text has no phraseology peculiar to the Fourth Gospel, neither is the whole section of 3:22–36

* *The Gospel According to John*, 1978, page 154.

† *Historical Tradition in the Fourth Gospel*, 1976, pages 236; 249-50; 279; 292.

particularly Johannine in character (symbolic acts followed by revelatory discourse), apart from a few phrases (3:31–36). The section has clearly been utilised from a fragment to suit the author's purpose (particularly, 3:33–36).

b) The section 3:22–23 reads as a connecting "itinerary fragment", which relates to no specific incident but to a whole period of ministry,* similar to that found in Mark. Further, it may well have been used to correct an assumption from the Synoptics that Jesus's ministry only began publicly in Galilee after John was arrested.†

c) There are clearly chronological difficulties when comparing John 3:22–36 with Mark 1:14, the latter suggesting that Jesus calls his disciples only after John's arrest, while the former suggests quite an established following and ministry conducted contemporaneously with that of the Baptist—to the extent of a public baptism of the populace.

d) There are hints that the author has used the text to serve as a polemical denouncement of the Baptist to his sectarian following—known to be around at the time: "as he grows greater, I must grow less", says the Baptist (3:30), together with the aphorism given in 3:29.

e) It is likely that a redactor has altered the latter part of the awkward introduction to chapter four. There is an observation in 4:1— "A report now reached the Pharisees: 'Jesus is winning and baptizing more disciples than John'" —which is followed by a qualification in 4:2: "although, in fact, it was only the disciples who were baptizing and not Jesus himself." After having recorded Jesus' popularity compared with that of the Baptist, the author (or redactor) was eager to refute any claim that Jesus personally baptised anybody.‡ Most commentaries I have consulted see 4:2 as the work of a redactor who realised how dangerously close this received tradition was in presenting Jesus as another prophet like unto the Baptist. After having expressly stated that the baptism of Jesus was of the Spirit, far superior to that of water (1:32–34; 3:5–8), he cannot leave a source intact which describes Jesus authorising, if not administering, a water-baptism without amending it slightly. "It is difficult to believe that any writer would have made a statement and contradicted it in the same breath, to the hopeless ruin of his sentence. It seems that here at least we must allow for the work of a subsequent editor, who took exception to the idea that Jesus was a second Baptist", says Dodd.** The phrase, "because water was plentiful in that region" (3:23), appears to have escaped the redactor's eye (a baptism of the Spirit requires no water), which again points to the source being historical, even if it was embarrassing to the beliefs of a Church set in rivalry to the Baptist sectarians.

In view of the above, it is quite feasible that the section 3:22–24, and particularly 4:1–3 (without the embellishment of 4:2), is authentic; it is an early source document

---

* C. H. Dodd, op. cit. page 236.
† Ibid., page 280.
‡ R. E. Brown, op. cit. page 164.
** C. H. Dodd, op. cit. page 285.

of genuine history. The places of Aenon and Salim cannot be identified with certainty.* So we have a testimony of an early witness to the fact that Jesus' disciples—though not Jesus himself—conducted a baptism. Being in Judaea (3:22—wherever Aenon may have been), Jesus was in the region of Qumran country and influence, where baptismal rites were practised by the eschatological community of God. The setting was appropriate, for not only were the Essene lustrations in evidence, but the Pharisees of Judaea had elaborate washing purification rites too. However, these two references in the Fourth Gospel (3:22–23; 4:1–2) are the only places in the Gospels where it is alleged that Jesus baptised or authorised a baptism. To argue from these two passages in the Fourth Gospel that Jesus had every intention of founding a community has, in my opinion, no solid evidence to back it up. The point is unfounded for the following reasons:

i) If the refutation in 4:2 is historical and not polemical, then Jesus clearly did not baptise, even if the disciples did.

ii) This parallel ministry of baptism is supplied with no meaning in 3:22–24 or 4:1–2. There is no emphasis on eschatology (Qumran), repentance (John the Baptist), purification (Pharisees), pre-paschal foreshadowing of the resurrection (Paul—Rom. 6) or didaction for *catechumens* (put into the mouth of Jesus by the early Church: "baptise, 'in the Name of the Father and of the Son and of the Holy Spirit,' in running water" [*The Didache* VII]).

iii) Even if the records of 3:22–24 and 4:1–3 are regarded as historical, the ministry of baptism takes place in the earliest possible part of Jesus' ministry—i.e., before John's arrest and before his retiring to Galilee, 4:4—and can in no way be accepted as the uniform programme of discipleship.

iv) No other saying or action in the Fourth Gospel, or the Synoptics, gives any suggestion that Jesus baptised his followers in order to form a community: "This is a statement [3:22] for which nothing else in the New Testament prepares us", says Dodd.† It may well serve as evidence for an impulsive and instinctive activity for Jesus being in league with the religious conventions around him at the time before he had fully conceived the true nature of his mission, i.e., before John's arrest!

No saying or action of Jesus suggests the requirement that his disciples should administer baptism, either at the missionary tour in Mark 6:7–13 (and parallels, Mat. 10 and Luke 9)—even though the disciples were to require repentance from the villagers (Mark 6:12), or during his last days in Judaea—when his interests might have focused more attentively upon the formation of a group to continue the cause, say, during the Last Supper. The reply of Jesus in Mark 10:38–40 to the request of the sons of Zebedee is not dependent on any liturgical baptismal rite, but rather points

---

* See C. K. Barrett, *The Gospel According to St John*, 1976, page 183. R. Bultmann considers them to be real enough places, but to have symbolic significance for the evangelist [Aenon = "spring" ; Salim = "peace"], but this seems pressed.

† C. H. Dodd, op. cit. page 285.

to the baptism of his sufferings. The reply given in Mark 2:18, "Why is it that John's disciples and the disciples of the Pharisees are fasting, but yours are not?", brings an aphorism in reply (similar to that in John 3:29) which clearly differentiates Jesus' mission from that of the Baptist, and suggests that Jesus wished to make a break with external seals of forming brotherhoods. Barrett quotes a counter viewpoint put forward by W. F. Flemington: "If . . . baptism were practised with approval of Jesus, it becomes easier to explain why, immediately after Pentecost, baptism took its place as the normal rite of entry into the Christian community",* but then, follows on to criticise him: "It should however be added that baptism practised during the ministry (even if historical) cannot be regarded as a sufficient explanation of the later rite."† Whatever reason the early Church had in adopting water-baptism as the means of entrance to the brotherhood, it cannot be supported by the texts of John 3:22 and 4:1, for there are no specific instructions or inferences in these passages which authorise or condone the practice.

v) Should Jesus have seen baptism as the rite of entrance to *his community*, it would have been necessary for him to have baptised his own disciples, not for his disciples to baptise the populace. It is also significant how the traditional baptism scene—presenting Jesus as role-model for discipleship—is omitted from John Chapter One (in fact, the proclamation, ". . . you will know that this is he who is to baptise in Holy Spirit [rather than water]", implies, that, for this author, it didn't take place). The text of 4:2, on linguistic grounds, does not say that Jesus only baptised his disciples, but says, "It was only the disciples who were baptizing and not Jesus himself". Although the Baptist baptised his own disciples, I would not say that the Baptist himself had any intention of forming a brotherhood in his name, even though one resulted and continued well into the second century.

The fact remains, then, that there is no act by which we may infer that Jesus wished to form a community of faithful brethren. There is no saying that categorically states, or implies, that Jesus expected, or taught, the requirement of a water-baptism of repentance for his followers as a precondition of their entrance to the kingdom of God. Consequently, we have no *a priori* grounds for arguing that a ministry of water-baptism implies that Jesus intended to set up a Church of followers by baptism, or by any other form of initiation for that matter.

---

* W. F. flemington, *The New Testament Doctrine of Baptism* (1948), page 30f.

† C. K. Barrett, op. cit. page 192.

BIBLIOGRAPHY

Ackroyd P. R. *Exile and Restoration,* ET., SCM Press, London, 1976

Augustine *Confessions,* ET. by R.S. Pine-coffin, Penguin Books Ltd., Middlesex, 1973

Barr J. *Fundamentalism,* SCM Press, London, 1977

Barrett C. K. *The first Epistle to the Corinthians,* Black's New Testament Commentaries, Adam & Charles Black, London, 1971

Barrett C. K. *The Second Epistle to the Corinthians,* Black's New Testament Commentaries, Adam & Charles Black, London, 1973

Bonhoeffer D. *Letters and Papers from Prison,* SCM Press, London, 1970

Bornkamm G. *Jesus of Nazareth,* ET., Hodder and Stoughton, London, 1973

Bornkamm G. *Paul,* ET., Hodder and Stoughton, London, 1975

Borsch F. H. *The Son of Man in Myth and History,* SCM Press Ltd., London, 1967

Borsch F. H. *The Christian and Gnostic Son of Man,* SCM Press Ltd., London, 1967

Bronowski J. *The Ascent of Man,* BBC Publications, London, 1973

Brown P. *Augustine of Hippo,* Faber and Faber, Glasgow, 1967

Brown R. E. *The Gospel According to John,* Geofrey Chapman, London, 1971

Buber M. *The Prophetic Faith,* ET. by C. Witton Davies, New York, 1949

Bultmann R. *The History of the Synoptic Tradition,* ET., London, 1931

Bultmann R. *Theology of the New Testament,* Volume I, ET., SCM Press Ltd., London, 1952

Bultmann R. *The Gospel of John,* ET., Basil Blackwell, Oxford, 1971

Caird G. B. *Principalities and Powers,* Oxford, 1956

Caird G. B. *The Language and Imagery of the Bible,* Duckworth & Co Ltd., London, 1980

Caird G. B. *The Revelation of St John the Divine,* Adam & Charles Black, London, 1966

Carr E. H. *What is History?,* Penguin Books, Middlesex, 1987

Cullmann O. *Christ and Time,* ET., SCM Press Ltd., London, 1950

Cullmann O. *The Christology of the New Testament,* ET., SCM Press Ltd., London, 1959

Cupitt D. *Taking Leave of God,* SCM Press Ltd., London, 1980

Darwin C. *The Origin of Species by Means of Natural Selection,* Ed. J. W. Burrow, Penguin Books, Middlesex, 1968

de Chardin P. T. *The Phenomenon of Man,* Collins, London, 1959

de Chardin P. T. *The Future of Man,* Collins, Fontana, 1969

Dibelius M. *From Tradition to Gospel,* ET. by B. L. Woolf, James Clarke & Co. Ltd., London, 1971

Dibelius M. *Studies in the Acts of the Apostles,* ET., SCM Press Ltd., London, 1973

Dodd C. H. *New Testament Studies,* Manchester University Press, Manchester, 1953

Dodd C. H. *Historical Tradition in the Fourth Gospel,* Cambridge University Press, London, 1963

Dodd C. H. *The Apostolic Preaching,* Hodder and Stoughton Ltd., London, 1944

Dodd C. H. *The Bible To-Day,* Cambridge University Press, London, 1968

Dodd C. H. *The Founder of Christianity,* Collins Clear-Type Press, London, 1971

Dodd C. H. *The Interpretation of the Fourth Gospel,* Cambridge University Press, London, 1953

Dodd C. H. *The Parables of the Kingdom,* Collins Fontana, London, 1961

Driver G. R. *Canaanite Myths and Legends*, T & T Clark Ltd., Edinburgh, 1976
Dunn J. D. G. *Unity and Diversity in the New Testament*, SCM Press Ltd., London, 1977
Dryden W. Ed. *Individual Therapy in Britain*, Harper and Row, London, 1984
Eusebius *Ecclesiastical History*, Volume I, Loeb Classical Library, ET. by Kirsopp Lake, London, 1949
Fromm E. *The Art of Loving*, Unwin Books, George Allen & Unwin Ltd., London, 1962
Fuller R. H. *Interpreting the Miracles*, SCM Press Ltd., London, 1963
Goulder M. & Hick J. *Why Believe in God*, SCM Press Ltd., London, 1983
Grensted L. W. *The Atonement in History and in Life*, SPCK, Ltd., London, 1929
Hayes E. H. *Yarns on Social Pioneers*, The Religious Education Press, Surrey, 1960
Heidel A. *The Babylonian Genesis*, The University of Chicago Press, London, 1942
Hick J. *Death and Eternal Life*, William Collins Sons & Co Ltd., London, 1976
Hick J. Ed. *The Myth of God Incarnate*, SCM Press, London, 1977
Hick J. *The Centre of Christianity*, SCM Press Ltd., London, 1977
Hume D. *Humes' Enquiries*, ET. by L. A. Selby-Bigge, Oxford University Press, London, 1966
James M. R. *The Apocryphal New Testament*, Oxford University Press, London, 1955
Jaspers K. *The Origin and Goal of History*, Routledge & Kegan Paul, London, 1949
Jaynes J. *The Origin of Consciousness in the Breakdown of the Bicameral Mind*, Allen Lane, London, 1979
Jeremias J. *Jesus' Promise to the Nations*, ET., SCM Press Ltd., London, 1958
Jeremias J. *New Testament Theology*, Volume one, ET., SCM Press Ltd., London, 1972
Jeremias J. *The Eucharistic Words of Jesus*, ET., SCM Press Ltd., London, 1973
Jeremias J. *The Parables of Jesus*, ET., SCM Press Ltd., London, 1972
Jeremias J. *Unknown Sayings of Jesus*, ET., S.P.C.K., London, 1957
Johnston F. *Fatima: the Great Sign*, Augustine Publishing, Devon, 1980
Jung C. G. *Contributions to Analytical Psychology*, ET. by H. G. and C. F. Baynes, 1945
Jung C. G. *The Archetypes and the Collective Unconsciousness*, ET., Routlege, London, 1969
Käsemann E. *New Testament Questions Today*, ET., SCM Press Ltd., London, 1967
Kelly J. N. D. *Early Christian Doctrines*, Adam and Charles Black, London, 1959
Kümmel W. G. *Theology of The New Testament*, ET., SCM Press Ltd., London, 1976
Küng H. *On Being a Christian*, Collins, London, 1977
Lambert W. *Inspiration and Revelation*, reprinted 1990, and available from I. McHaffie, 176 Granton Road, Edinburgh EH5 1AH
Lines D. *Coming Through the Tunnel*, Lines, 1994, and available from the author, 1 Holywell Lane, Rubery, B45 9EJ, England
Manson T. W. *The Sayings of Jesus*, SCM Press Ltd., London, 1975
McArthur H. K. *In Search of the Historical Jesus*, SPCK, London, 1969
McLeod J. *An Introduction to Counselling*, Open University Press, Buckingham, 1993
McNeil A. H. *An Introduction to the Study of the New Testament*, Oxford Press, London, 1953
Moule C. F. D. *The Birth of the New Testament*, Adam & Charles Black, London, 1971
Morison F. *Who Moved the Stone?*, Faber & Faber, London, 1930
Noth M. *The History of Israel*, Adam & Charles Black, London, 1965
Otto R. *The Idea of the Holy*, ET. by J. W. Harvey, Oxford University Press, New York, 1958
Packer J. I. *"Fundamentalism" and the Word of God*, Inter-Varsity Fellowship, London, 1958
Pannenberg W. *Jesus, God and Man*, ET., SCM Press Ltd., London, 1968
Perrin N. *The Kingdom of God in the Teaching of Jesus*, SCM Press Ltd., London, 1963
Plato *Phaedo*, ET. by D. Gallop, Claredon Plato Series, Oxford, 1975
Rahner K. *Visions and Prophecies*, Burns & Oates, London, 1963

Rees R. *Simone Weil A Sketch for a Portrait*, Oxford University Press, London, 1966
Renan E. *Life of Jesus*, Walter Scott, Ltd., London, 1835
Ringgren H. *Israelite Religion*, trans. by D. Green, SPCK, London, 1974
Robinson J. A. T. *Redating the New Testament*, SCM Press Ltd., London, 1976
Robinson J. A. T. *Twelve New Testament Studies*, SCM Press Ltd., London, 1962
Robertson R. *Sociology of Religion*, Penguin, Middlesex, 1971
Rogers A. K. *A Students Hstory of Philosophy*, Macmillan, New York, 1932
Rowley H. H. *The Faith of Israel*, SCM Press Ltd., London, 1956
Russell B. *Mysticism and Logic*, Penguin Books, London, 1918
Russell D. S. *The Method and Message of Jewish Apocalyptic*, The Westminster Press, Philadelphia, USA, 1964
Seaver G. *Albert Schweitzer The Man and His Mind*, Adam & Charles Black, London, 1955
Shaeffer F. A. *How Should We Then Live: The Rise and Decline of Western Culture*, Fleming H. Revell, New Jersey, 1976
Schweitzer A. *On The Edge of the Primaeval Forest*, Adam & Charles Black, London, 1922
Schweitzer A. *The Quest of the Historical Jesus*, Adam & Charles Black Ltd., London, 1936
Sparks H. F. D. *A Synopsis of the Gospels*, Adam & Charles Black, London, 1970
Streeter B. H. *The Four Gospels: a Study of Origins*, Macmillan & Co Ltd., London, 1936
Tart C. T. *Transpersonal Psychologies*, Routledge & Kegan Paul, London, 1975
Taylor E. B. *Primitive Culture*, John Murray, London, 1973
Taylor V. *The Atonement in New Testament Teaching*, Epworth Press, London, 1940
Taylor V. *The Life and Ministry of Jesus*, Macmillan, London, 1955
Temple W. *Christus Veritas*, Macmillan & Co Ltd., London, 1924
The Gospel of Thomas ET. by A. Guillaumont et. al, London, 1959
Tillich P. *Perspectives on 19th and 20th Century Protestant Theology*, SCM Press Ltd., London, 1967
Todd J. M. *Martin Luther*, Burns and Oats, London, 1964
Todt H. E. *The Son of Man in the Synoptic Tradition*, SCM Press Ltd., London, 1965
von Rad G.
Old Testament Theology, ET., Volume I, SCM Press, London, 1975
Vermes G.
The Dead Sea Scrolls in English, Penguin Books, Middlesex, 1973
Weber M.
The Sociology of Religion, ET., Methuen & Co Ltd., London, 1971
Wegener G. S.
6000 Years of the Bible, Hodder & Stoughton, London, 1958
Whiteley D. E. H. *The Theology of St. Paul*, Basil Blackwell, Oxford, 1974
Wilson B. *Sects and Society*, Hodder & Stoughton, London, 1961
Wilson B. *Patterns of Sectarianism*, Hodder & Stoughton, London, 1967
Williams C. S. *The Acts of the Apostles*, Adam & Charles Black, London, 1964